Sarah Anderson was born in London. She has a degree in Chinese from the School of Oriental and African Studies. A keen traveller, she founded and ran for many years the Travel Bookshop in Notting Hill, London. Sarah Anderson is the author of *Anderson's Travel Companion* and is currently writing, researching and painting. She lives in London and continues to travel widely.

The
Virago Book
of Spirituality

Of Women
and Angels

Edited by Sarah Anderson

A *Virago* Book

Published by Virago Press 1997

First published by Virago Press 1996, reprinted 1997

This collection and Introduction copyright © Sarah Anderson 1996

Acknowledgements on pp. 331–6 constitute an extension of this
copyright page.

The moral right of the author has been asserted

A CIP catalogue record for this book is available
from the British Library

ISBN 1 86049 367 X

Typeset in Horley Old Style by M Rules
Printed and bound in Great Britain by
Clays Ltd, St Ives plc

Virago
A Division of
Little, Brown and Company (UK)
Brettenham House
Lancaster Place
London WC2E 7EN

CONTENTS

INTRODUCTION

If the world be shut without, I'll sail the hidden seas within.

MARGARET PRESCOTT MONTAGUE

THE EXPLORATION OF 'the hidden seas within' is a journey on which we can all embark. This anthology brings together writings that illustrate some of the many ways in which women over the ages have approached and experienced their inner lives. I like to envisage spirituality as playing an intrinsic role in our daily lives unbound by the strictures of an organised religion. Inner peace and compassion – threatened by today's materialistic culture – are sustained by spirituality. In turn, an awareness of our 'hidden seas' can lead to personal transformation and growth; to grow spiritually can allow one to become less concerned with superficial matters and develop a simpler personal vision. Rather than a retreat from the world this signifies an entry into the fullness of life, to which other people's writings can act as a guide.

We live in an age of instant gratification. Spirituality represents the opposite to this in giving no immediate feedback but requiring, instead, a disciplined approach leading to long and silent growth. Its aim is to get beyond the self, to transcend it and thereby perceive the boundless possibilities and grandeur of what spirituality has to offer.

There are several profound differences between men's and women's spirituality. Firstly, there is the obvious difference of neglect; women through the ages and in different cultures did not, on the whole, hold public office and found it difficult to publish their work and thoughts. In the Western tradition the Church has always been patriarchal and in the Middle Ages woman was perceived as having links with the powers of evil, a tradition inherited from Pythagoras: 'There is a good principle which created order, light and man and an evil principle which created chaos, darkness and women.' Hildegard of Bingen, Julian of Norwich and Mechtild of Magdeburg were all strong independent thinkers, who had to cut themselves off from the world to fulfil themselves. *Because* women had little or no opportunity for outward activities, these very limitations forced them to look inward, an activity which led to the acquisition of an inner strength, a self-reliance and increased spirituality. 'Woman must be the pioneer in this turning inward for strength' (Anne Morrow Lindbergh). It is perhaps easier for women to identify with Kathleen Raine's 'inner living universe'; the solitude needed to find the true essence of ourselves was often forced upon women. 'My peace, O my brothers, is in solitude' (Rabi'a the Mystic). Women were left alone in the home, allowing them time to reflect on both their own lives and those of their children. Mothers, historically, have had more opportunity than men to observe their children and more time to ponder their sensitivities and emotions.

I have looked at spirituality in the broadest sense of the word as witnessed by the many writers quoted and have included pieces from as wide a range of cultures and religions as possible. Although this is certainly not a religious book there is a strong religious element to many of the pieces, as many of the women included belonged to organised religions. The pieces show a bias towards the West and towards Christianity due to my western Christian upbringing and partly due to the material available. Although there have been great Christian mystics who were intensely spiritual – for example, St Teresa of Avila and Gemma Galgani – Christianity, with its emphasis on dogma and morality, has tended to neglect spirituality in the sense in which I have taken it.

Barriers of time and geography fade into the background in the face of the many common themes running through the pieces gathered here. For instance, the belief that one is awarded a 'great gain' once one has accepted the death of a close friend is contained in the writings of Ann Griffiths, an eighteenth-century farmer's wife; the letters of Louisa May Alcott; and the contemporary poetry of Ruth Pitter. There are also surprising similarities between musings on secular emotions and on religious experiences. For example, the passion evident in St Teresa of Lisieux's writings on her love for Jesus is echoed quite clearly in Anne Bradstreet's poem 'To My Dear and Loving Husband'. More often than not, I found that poetry describing nature could be read on a deeper level, as Simone Weil describes: 'A poem is beautiful to the precise degree in which the attention whilst it was being composed has been turned towards the inexpressible.'

Communication of feelings is essentially bound by language, but there is a special quality to those words managing to convey deep feelings successfully. It is this kind of writing that I have looked to include in this anthology. Immanence – finding God or the centre within – and transcendence – seeing God as an outside Being – are equally represented. Jane Hamilton's recent novel, *A Map of the World*, describes this distinction well: 'For Theresa, God was something that was outside of her, some unfathomable being who made the highway radiant. I thought in the harsh December wind that for me God was something within that allowed me, occasionally, to see.' Some people 'see the world in a grain of sand' (Blake), whereas others have the need for a broader spectrum. Evelyn Underhill's poem 'Immanence' begins 'I come in the little things/ Saith the Lord' whereas Henriette d'Angeville, standing on the summit of Mont Blanc, was so awed by the grandeur and majesty around her that she felt as if she was witnessing the birth of creation. All have a place in this anthology.

The book is divided into seven sections, each of which has, as its title, a quotation from the works included: most of these sentiments touch people at some time during their lives. Because I want each piece of writing to have as much possible relevance to everybody I have left out certain themes such as motherhood. I have included fiction as it often clarifies the way we see and feel. Because fiction is about people, we draw from it a concrete rather than an abstract humanity; a diversity of ideas and thoughts can be articulated through characters we have grown to know and with whom we can identify. Hetty's confession to Dinah in George Eliot's *Adam Bede* is a touching and poignant example.

There is much pain and torment in many of these writings – a reminder, should one need it, that life was never going to be easy. But I have not intended to create an undemanding read or book of consolations. Reading about women who have had to deal with the same kind of pain through the centuries can be helpful. And there is a lot of joy – in nature, in creativity, in beauty, in love – in the following pages.

Although my definition of spirituality encompasses far more than mysticism, many of the extracts I include are mystical. Mystical prose writing can approach poetry in its intensity; for example, Julian of Norwich's prose descriptions are as vivid as paintings. There are three specific kinds of mysticism: a sense of union with the created world; a belief in the self as the Absolute Reality; and a direct supra-rational union with a personal God by means of love. Each of these contains an element of awe. There is as much pain as there is happiness in the writing of the mystics. Julian of Norwich understood pain as inseparable from mystical union with God and could see in a hazelnut the eternal act of creation. Again, the similarities through the ages are striking; in the twentieth century, Alice Walker, in *The Color Purple* writes of 'feeling of being part of everything' which echoes the sixteenth-century St Teresa of Avila when she wrote of 'spiritual marriage' as the highest degree of union with God. 'To be a mystic is simply to participate here and now in that real and eternal life; in the fullest, deepest sense which is possible to man' (Evelyn Underhill, *An Introduction to Mysticism*).

Many of my discoveries were due to serendipity. I was thrilled to discover the earliest example in the book in the London Library. Dating from 1500 BC, this is the only instance in

Egyptian annals of the personal description of a woman given by herself: words written in her own praise by the Egyptian Queen Hatshepsut. Another exciting discovery was the work of the American Mary Austin, a prolific writer, mystic and artist who understood and wrote about the Native Americans of the American south-west.

This is naturally a very personal choice; I'm sure that I will have left out some people's favourite authors, but I hope everyone will find something that pleases them, both old favourites and new discoveries. And I wish the book could have been twice as long. Research led me down unexplored avenues and I hope that my readers get as much pleasure from reading it as I did from working on it.

Sarah Anderson, London 1996

ACKNOWLEDGEMENTS

I would like to give special thanks to Anthony Aris who gave me the idea for the book, to Giles Swayne for his translations and to Elisabeth Anderson for her proof-reading. Also thanks to all the many friends and acquaintances who introduced me to women previously unknown to me and to the helpful staff at the London Library and the British Library.

1

THE WHOLE WORLD IS A WORK OF ART

Of all the arts the living of a life is perhaps the greatest

KATHLEEN RAINE

from Gift from the Sea

QUIET time alone, contemplation, prayer, music, a centering line of thought or reading, of study or work. It can be physical or intellectual or artistic, any creative life proceeding from oneself. It need not be an enormous project or a great work. But it should be something of one's own. Arranging a bowl of flowers in the morning can give a sense of quiet in a crowded day – like writing a poem, or saying a prayer. What matters is that one be for a time inwardly attentive.

Solitude, says the moon shell. Center-down, say the Quaker saints. To the possession of the self the way is inward, says Plotinus. The cell of self-knowledge is the stall in which the pilgrim must be reborn, says St. Catherine of Siena. Voices from the past. In fact, these are pursuits and virtues of the past. But done in another way today because done consciously, aware, with eyes open. Not done as before, as part of the pattern of the time. Not done because everyone else is doing them; almost no one is doing them. Revolutionary, in fact, because almost every trend and pressure, every voice from the outside is against this new way of inward living.

Woman must be the pioneer in this turning inward for strength. In a sense she has always been the pioneer. Less able, until the last generation, to escape into outward activities, the very limitations of her life forced her to look inward. And from looking inward she gained an inner strength which man in his outward active life did not as often find. But in our recent efforts to emancipate ourselves, to prove ourselves the equal of man, we have, naturally enough perhaps, been drawn into competing with him in his outward activities, to the neglect of our own inner springs. Why have we been seduced into abandoning this timeless inner strength of woman for the temporal outer strength of man? This outer strength of man is essential to the pattern, but even here the reign of purely outer strength and purely outward solutions seems to be waning today. Men, too, are being forced to look inward – to find inner solutions as well as outer ones. Perhaps this change marks a new stage of maturity for modern extrovert, activist, materialistic Western man. Can it be that he is beginning to realize that the kingdom of heaven is within?

Moon shell, who named you? Some intuitive woman I like to think. I shall give you another name – Island shell. I cannot live forever on my island. But I can take you back to my desk in Connecticut. You will sit there and fasten your single eye upon me. You will make me think, with your smooth circles winding inward to the tiny core, of the island I lived on for a few weeks. You will say to me 'solitude.' You will remind me that I must try to be alone for part of each year, even a week or a few days; and for part of each day, even for an hour or a few minutes in order to keep my core, my center, my island-quality. You will remind me that unless I keep the island-quality intact somewhere within me, I will have little to give my husband, my children, my friends or the world at large. You will remind me that woman must be still as the axis of a wheel in the midst of her activities; that she must be the pioneer in achieving this stillness, not only for her own salvation, but for the salvation of family life, of society, perhaps even of our civilization.

ANNE MORROW LINDBERGH

from My Life

I SPENT long days and nights in the studio seeking that dance which might be the divine expression of the human spirit through the medium of the body's movement. For hours I would stand quite still, my two hands folded between my breasts, covering the solar plexus. My mother often became alarmed to see me remain for such long intervals quite motionless as if in a trance – but I was seeking and finally discovered the central spring of all movement, the crater of motor power, the unity from which all diversities of movements are born, the mirror of vision for the creation of the dance – it was from this discovery that was born the theory on which I founded my school. The ballet school taught the pupils that this spring was found in the centre of the back at the base of the spine. From this axis, says the ballet master, arms, legs and trunk must move freely, giving the result of an articulated puppet. This method produces an artificial mechanical movement not worthy of the soul. I on the contrary sought the source of the spiritual expression to flow into the channels of the body filling it with vibrating light – the centrifugal force reflecting the spirit's vision. After many months, when I had learned to concentrate all my force to this one Centre I found that thereafter when I listened to music the rays and vibrations of the music streamed to this one fount of light within me – there they reflected themselves in Spiritual Vision not the brain's mirror, but the soul's, and from this vision I could express them in Dance – I have often tried to explain to artists this first basic theory of my Art. Stanislavski mentions my telling him of this in his book: 'My Life in Art.'

It would seem as if it were a very difficult thing to explain in words, but when I stood before my class of even the smallest and poorest children and said: 'Listen to the music with your soul. Now, while listening, do you not feel an inner self awakening deep within you – that it is by its strength that your head is lifted, that your arms are raised, that you are walking slowly toward the light?' they understood. This awakening is the first step in the dance, as I conceive it.

Even the youngest child understands; from then on, even in walking, and in all their movements, they possess a spiritual power and grace which do not exist in any movement born from the physical frame, or created from the brain. This is the reason why quite small children in my school appearing in the Trocadero or the Metropolitan Opera House before vast audiences have been enabled to hold those audiences with a magnetism generally possessed only by very great artists. But when these children

grew older the counteracting influences of our materialistic civil-
isation took this force from them – and they lost their inspiration.

The peculiar environment of my childhood and youth had
developed this power in me to a very great degree, and in different epochs of my life I have been enabled to shut out all outside
influences and to live in this force alone. So, after my rather
pathetic efforts to gain earthly love, I had a sudden revulsion and
return to this force.

Hereafter when André presented himself somewhat timidly
and apologetically I deluged him for hours with my discourses on
the Art of the Dance and a new school of human movement, and
I must say that he never seemed bored or tired but would listen
with the sweetest patience and sympathy while I explained to
him each movement I had discovered. I also then dreamed of
finding a first movement from which would be born a series of
movements without my volition, but as the unconscious reaction
of the primary movement. I had developed this movement in a
series of different variations on several themes, – such as the first
movement of fear followed by the natural reactions born of the
primary emotion or Sorrow from which would flow a dance of
lamentation or a love movement from the unfolding of which
like the petals of a flower the dancer would stream as a perfume.

These dances were without actual music, but seemed to create
themselves from the rhythm of some invisible music. From these
studies I first attempted to express the preludes of Chopin. I was
also initiated to the music of Gluck. My mother was never wearied of playing for me, and would repeat the entire score of
'Orpheus' over and over until dawn appeared in the studio window.

ISADORA DUNCAN

Passion and Peace

Poetry, like all passion, seeks for peace.
Wild creature, look into the pool and learn.
There in the level water shines the face,
The summer eyes that can both weep and burn,
Mirrored so calmly in the quiet place;
Fire in sweet water lulled, questions that turn
At long last to the simple need for rest.
Have I not still the peace of the unborn,
Have I not learned of death to be possessed?
O put off passion, and with passion scorn,
And think that this quiet water is my breast,
Calm, yet without that image, most forlorn.
O let the fervour of the princely sun,
Which makes the desert solitary, sleep
Here in the water his dominions weep.
Binding all peace and passion into one.

RUTH PITTER

from The Chasm of Fire

13 December

AND so it came . . . it slipped itself into my heart, silently, imperceptibly, and I looked at it with wonder. It was still, small; a light-blue flame trembling softly, and it had the infinite sweetness of first love, like an offering of fragrant flowers made with gentle hands, the heart full of stillness and wonder and peace.

'Love will be produced,' you had said. And since then I kept wondering how it will come to me. Will it be like the Voice from the Burning Bush, the Voice of God as Moses heard it? Will it be like a flash of lightning out of a blue sky making the world about me a blaze of glory? Or will it be, as L. suggested, that you will produce Love in general, Love for everything, and the Teacher will be included in it? But I told her that it could not be so for me;

to be able to surrender completely, to sweep away all resistance, it must be big, tremendous, complete; without reserve; without limit; the conditionless, absolute, forgetting oneself.

But what I felt was not so. It was just a tender longing, so gentle, so full of infinite sweetness.

Like all laws governing this universe, love will follow the way of least resistance. In all my life I never knew the feeling of love flashing suddenly into my heart. It always came softly, timidly, like a small flower at the side of the road, so easily crushed by the boots of those who may pass by; growing slowly, steadily, increasing until it became vast, sweeping like a tidal wave, engulfing everything that stood in its way and at last filling all my life. So it was in the past and this time too; it is coming to me in the same way. I suppose because our hearts are made in a certain way we cannot help being what we are.

16 December

Adyar was as lovely as ever, and so fragrant with many flowering shrubs and trees. Looking up to the deep blue sky, as was my habit, I saw your face, my Guruji, clearly outlined against the azure of the sky. Perhaps not exactly your face – but the expression of it. As I have seen it when you smile; first with your eyes and then it deepens to vanish into the beard; or the faraway look and the blank expression, when, still and composed, you slide the beads of the mala through your fingers; or the face as if cut out of stone, hard, severe, as old as the hills, as ancient as humanity.

When I came to you a little more than two months ago, I knew nothing about Sufism. Nothing of its glory, its tradition, its boundless freedom, its never-ending love! It was like a revelation and I realized how much I had missed by not knowing it before. Even the little I have learned about it fills me with enthusiasm. Once more I thanked my good star (or my destiny) for guiding me to you.

IRINA TWEEDIE

Poppy

1

Shuttered petals
concealing alertness
as the flowers
stay awake, keeping
watch
patiently in Christ's
favourite garden.

Scarlet, they bleed
vivid patches
of blood – such life
from the parched earth
bleeding for their Lord.
Keeping watch

Over the centuries
of soldiers who have died
in Christ's name,
when he taught us
never to kill
another. When he laid

Down his life, body racked
broken naked,
to enable us to live
our lives to the full,
if only we'd listen
to the cry coming

From the cross.
At the blackest hour
when the skin

> of the earth is being torn
> apart, pierced through;
> and blood and water
>
> Poured out for parched
> lips as the poppies
> (pretending to sleep)
> stay awake
> while we, our eyes blind
> sleep on, in his garden.

HEATHER LAWTON

from Letter XII

I LEFT East Rusoer the day before yesterday. The weather was very fine; but so calm that we loitered on the water near fourteen hours, only to make about six and twenty miles.

It seemed to me a sort of emancipation when we landed at Helgeraac. The confinement which every where struck me whilst sojourning amongst the rocks, made me hail the earth as a land of promise; and the situation shone with fresh lustre from the contrast – from appearing to be a free abode. Here it was possible to travel by land – I never thought this a comfort before, and my eyes, fatigued by the sparkling of the sun on the water, now contentedly reposed on the green expanse, half persuaded that such verdant meads had never till then regaled them.

I rose early to pursue my journey to Tonsberg. The country still wore a face of joy – and my soul was alive to its charms. Leaving the most lofty, and romantic of the cliffs behind us, we were almost continually descending to Tonsberg, through elysian scenes; for not only the sea, but mountains, rivers, lakes, and groves, gave an almost endless variety to the prospect. The cottagers were still leading home the hay; and the cottages, on this road, looked very comfortable. Peace and plenty – I mean not abundance, seemed to reign around – still I grew sad as I drew near my old abode. I was sorry to see the sun so high; it was broad noon. Tonsberg was something like a home – yet I was to enter without lighting-up pleasure in any eye – I dreaded the solitariness of my apartment, and wished for night to hide the starting tears, or to shed them on my pillow, and close my eyes on a world where I was destined to wander alone. Why has nature so many charms for me – calling forth and cherishing refined sentiments, only to wound the breast that fosters them? How illusive, perhaps the most so, are the plans of happiness founded on virtue and principle; what inlets of misery do they not open in a half civilized society? The satisfaction arising from conscious rectitude, will not calm an injured heart, when tenderness is ever finding excuses; and self-applause is a cold solitary feeling, that cannot supply the place of disappointed affection, without throwing a gloom over every prospect, which, banishing pleasure, does not exclude pain. I reasoned and reasoned; but my heart was too full to allow me to remain in the house, and I walked, till I was wearied out, to purchase rest – or rather forgetfulness.

Employment has beguiled this day, and tomorrow I set out for Moss, in my way to Stromstad. At Gothenburg I shall embrace my *Fannikin*; probably she will not know me again – and I shall be hurt if she do not. How childish is this! still it is a natural feeling. I would not permit myself to indulge the 'thick coming fears' of fondness, whilst I was detained by business. – Yet I never saw a calf bounding in a meadow, that did not remind me of my little frolicker. A calf, you say. Yes; but a *capital* one, I own.

I cannot write composedly – I am every instant sinking into reveries – my heart flutters, I know not why. Fool! It is time thou wert at rest.

Friendship and domestic happiness are continually praised; yet how little is there of either in the world, because it requires more cultivation of mind to keep awake affection, even in our own hearts, than the common run of people suppose. Besides, few like to be seen as they really are; and a degree of simplicity, and of undisguised confidence, which, to uninterested observers, would almost border on weakness, is the charm, nay the essence of love or friendship: all the bewitching graces of childhood again appearing. As objects merely to exercise my taste, I therefore like to see people together who have an affection for each other; every turn of their features touches me, and remains pictured on my imagination in indelible characters. The zest of novelty is, however, necessary to rouse the languid sympathies which have been hacknied in the world; as is the factitious behaviour, falsely termed good-breeding, to amuse those, who defective in taste, continually rely for pleasure on their animal spirits, which not being maintained by the imagination, are unavoidably sooner exhausted than the sentiments of the heart. Friendship is in general sincere at the commencement, and lasts whilst there is any thing to support it; but as a mixture of novelty and vanity is the usual prop, no wonder if it fall with the slender stay. The fop in the play, payed a greater compliment than he was aware of, when he said to a person, whom he meant to flatter, 'I like you almost as well as a *new acquaintance.*' Why am I talking of friendship, after which I have had such a wild-goose chace. [sic] – I thought only of telling you that the crows, as well as wild geese, are here birds of passage.

MARY WOLLSTONECRAFT, from *Letters Written during a Short Residence in Sweden, Norway and Denmark 1796*

October Love

Was nothing there? No resin smelling pine,
no mushrooms, moss, or fingers touching mine,
no empty cottage, no one there to play
the broken old piano in the shed?
 – and did I dream I turned to walk away
but hands caressed me, lips on my lips said
no one was watching, why then should I go?
Was I alone when suddenly I found

the soft mimosa gold where none should grow,
and was there no one wrapped their arms around
me crying 'celebrate?' Was there no kiss?
Ah love, there is no truth in this.
It was all there, kisses, mimosa tree,
but things as these are not for all to see.

ANNE LEWIS-SMITH

from Pottery, Form and Expression

It is not a soul, 't is not a body that we are training up,
but a man and we ought not to divide him.

MONTAIGNE

THIS is more than a technical book. I shall touch technical points only insofar as I think that they are important in the education and the development of a young craftsman into a complete man. To escape the danger of generalization and empty abstraction I have used technical examples of the depth of basic knowledge and of the intensity of human effort that are required if we want to educate craftsmen to be more than one-sided technicians.

The aim of this book is to make clear that it is not enough to teach techniques. We want to develop young people for a wholesome and hopeful generation, – for a generation which believes in the value of the humanities, which will face the problems of our time honestly and without fear, with the deep will to understand other men and to learn to build a better future.

Technique alone, without any moral and ethical point of departure or aim, has brought us to the very edge of a universal catastrophe that we have in no way overcome. To achieve this necessary future victory over ourselves and the terrifying world that we have created, we will need to find again a synthesis between technical knowledge and spiritual content. It is not a question of the crafts only, the problem is as wide as the whole of human civilization. Unsolved, it will be fatal to all mankind. It is thus for every one of us – craftsman, artist, teacher, scholar or scientist – to help build towards a more human way of life, one that can lead man in the coming generations to personal dignity, integrity and peace.

But generations are made of many single individuals, each with his special abilities. We can either develop these to maturity or we can let them go to waste. We can lead a student towards a sound, human and creatively intelligent point of view or we can corrupt him totally. If we want the life of man as a whole to have a deeper content, with a cultural basis, we must educate every single human being to find a deeper spiritual content for his own life. Neither peace of mind nor 'happiness' can be bought by machine, money, success or a high standard of living. Man must make the effort himself and develop his way of life from the very depth of his own being. The real revolutions, truth and lies, originate in the minds of men. There it is that we must start to clarify, to educate, to build up.

The technical problems of education are necessarily different in the various fields, but human problems are basically the same for all fields of the mind. We must develop, cultivate, inspire and discipline the creative and spiritual abilities of man. We must not waste, corrupt or slant for material purposes those qualities that make him more than an animal: his sense of beauty, his idea of truth, his ability to think, his creative intuition and his vision of God.

We know that there are many men and women – artists, scholars, teachers, scientists – lost in the wide world, in big cities or the backwoods, in schools and colleges, in factories and on farms, people deeply disturbed by the current materialistic trend, people who are searching for more than they are finding. It is essential to give them affirmation and hope, to coordinate all their efforts into a more conscious group of honest workers towards an aim that has human dignity and personal integrity.

Craftsmen of all times have battled with the materials they have used, with the difficulties of the technique, with the problems of form and expression. While in the more primitive times the main difficulties lay in the technique, in our times of technical advancement the real problems lie almost wholly in form and expression. We have solved many technical difficulties and most of the restrictions of materials and machines; but we have lost in the process of an increasingly materialistic education, the essential relation to nature, to man and to God.

Those problems that loom so large before us cannot be solved from the top down, in vague general lines, in conferences and educational meetings. We will have to start at the very basis of human occupation and of thought. As one of the oldest basic occupations of man, pottery, I feel, may well be chosen as a representative example for similar issues in parallel fields.

What are the problems in teaching the crafts in our times? Why is it apparently so difficult to develop creative craftsmen who are able to convey their own ideas with excellent craftsmanship, honest conviction and complete integrity? How is it that with all our perfected techniques we have failed to rear those craftsmen in our generation?

To be a craftsman apparently requires a definite attitude towards work and life, something evidently few schools are able to convey, something that cannot easily be taught in courses on techniques and theories. Mass school education quite naturally consists of more or less abstract and impersonal ideas, facts and techniques. To a large percentage of students all this is being conveyed en masse and with a conformity that is apt to restrict the thinking process and the personal struggle of a student towards maturity. Instead they impose certain rules and theories that will bring him quick results and a degree. This will limit the scope of his feelings, of his thoughts, his ideas, his likes and dislikes, his personal conception of art and his total growth as a man and as an artist. There is something that a young student must learn, something formative and essential that he cannot easily get in our school system. It is something that he gets in the daily contact with a man who has worked and has concentrated all his energies in that one special field he has chosen as his life-work. The daily interchange of ideas, of experience, of thought, the common interest of student and teacher in the solving of the recurring difficulties of their profession – not in a classroom but in an actual life situation – will necessarily bring the student close to the way of life of that master. An intuitive understanding of that man, his attitude, his standards, will help the student to a certain assimilation of all that the master represents and this assimilation becomes obviously a part of his education and his personal development. This is the all-important issue.

Thus, if I manage to convey something of this essence, of this spirit to the reader in the following pages, so that the subject matter becomes for him a creative experience, I shall have achieved what I somehow foolhardily set out to do.

MARGUERITE WILDENHAIN

Consecrating the Chase

In name of the Holy Three-fold as one,
In word, in deed, and in thought,
I am bathing mine own hands,
In the light and in the elements of the sky.

Vowing that I shall never return in my life
Without fishing, without fowling either,
Without game, without venison down from the hill,
Without fat, without blubber from out the copse.

O Mary tender-fair, gentle-fair, loving-fair,
Avoid thou to me the silvery salmon dead on the salt sea,
A duck with her brood an it please thee to show me,
A nest by the edge of the water where it does not dry.

The grey-hen on the crown of the knoll,
The black-cock of the hoarse croon,

After the strength of the sun has gone down,
Avoid, oh, avoid thou to me the hearing of them.

O Mary, fragrant mother of my King.
Crown thou me with the crown of thy peace,
Place thine own regal robe of gold around me,
And save me with the saving of Christ,
      Save me with the saving of Christ.

MARY GILLIES

from The 27th Kingdom

AUNT Irene really inclined to that simplest of all views: the one expressed so cogently in Genesis, which explained everything with appealing clarity. This was the only view that explained, for instance, mayonnaise. It was patently absurd to suppose that mayonnaise had come about through random chance, that anyone could ever have been silly or brilliant enough to predict what would happen if he slowly trickled oil on to egg yolks and then gone ahead and tried it. An angel must have divulged that recipe and then explained what to do with the left-over egg whites. Meringues – that was another instance of the exercise of super-human intelligence. To Aunt Irene the Ten Commandments seemed almost insignificant compared with the astonishing miracle of what you could do with an egg. As the angel had left in his fiery chariot he must have added, 'And don't forget omelettes, and cake and custard and soufflés and poaching and frying and boiling and baking. Oh, and they're frightfully good with anchovies. And you can use the shells to clarify soup – and don't forget to dig them in round the roots of your roses', the angelic tones fading into the ethereal distance.

ALICE THOMAS ELLIS

from Katherine Anne Porter: Conversations

[with Barbara Thompson]

P: [. . .] So I got a newspaper job.

I: I remember that you once warned me to avoid that at all costs – to get a job 'hashing' in a restaurant in preference.

P: Anything, anything at all. I did it for a year and that is what confirmed me that it wasn't doing me any good. After that I always took little dull jobs that didn't take my mind and wouldn't take all of my time, and that, on the other hand, paid me just enough to subsist. I think I've only spent about ten percent of my energies on writing. The other ninety per cent went to keeping my head above water.

And I think that's all wrong. Even Saint Teresa said, 'I can pray better when I'm comfortable,' and she refused to wear her haircloth shirt or starve herself. I don't think living in cellars and starving is any better for an artist than it is for anybody else; the only thing is that sometimes the artist has to take it, because it is the only possible way of salvation, if you'll forgive that old-fashioned word. So I took it rather instinctively. I was inexperienced in the world, and likewise I hadn't been trained to do anything, you know, so I took all kinds of laborious jobs. But, you know, I think I could probably have written better if I'd been a little more comfortable.

I: Then you were writing all this time?

P: All this time I was writing, writing no matter what else I was doing; no matter what I *thought* I was doing, in fact. I was living almost as instinctively as little animal, but I realize now that all that time a part of me was getting ready to be an artist. That my mind was working even when I didn't know it, and didn't care if it was working or not. It is my firm belief that all our lives we are preparing to be somebody or something, even if we don't do it consciously. And the time comes one morning when you wake up and find that you have become irrevocably what you were preparing all this time to be. Lord, that could be a sticky moment, if you had been doing the wrong things, something against your grain. And, mind you, I know that can happen. I have no patience with this dreadful idea that whatever you have in you has to come out, that you can't suppress true talent. People *can* be destroyed; they can be bent, distorted, and completely crippled. To say that you can't destroy yourself is just as foolish as to say of a young man killed in war at twenty-one or twenty-two that that was his fate, that he wasn't going to have anything anyhow.

I have a very firm belief that the life of no man can be explained in terms of his experiences, of what has happened to him, because in spite of all the poetry, all the philosophy to the contrary, we are not really masters of our fate. We don't really direct our lives unaided and unobstructed. Our being is subject to all the chances of life. There are so many things we are capable of, that we could be or do. The potentialities are so great that we never, any of us, are more than one-fourth fulfilled. Except that there may be one powerful motivating force that simply carries you along, and I think that was true of me. . . .When I was a very little girl I wrote a letter to my sister saying I wanted glory. I don't know quite what I meant by that now, but it was something different from fame or success or wealth. I know that I wanted to be a good writer, a good artist.

I: But weren't there certain specific events that crystallized that desire for you – something comparable to the experience of Miranda in 'Pale Horse, Pale Rider'?

P: Yes, that was the plague of influenza, at the end of the First World War, in which I almost died. It just simply divided my life, cut across it like that. So that everything before that was just getting ready, and after that I was in some strange way altered, ready. It took me a long time to go out and live in the world again. I was really 'alienated,' in the pure sense. It was, I think, the fact that I really had participated in death, that I knew what death was, and had almost experienced it. I had what the Christians call the 'beatific vision,' and the Greeks called the 'happy day,' the happy vision just before death. Now if you have had that, and survived it, come back from it, you are no longer like other people, and there's no use deceiving yourself that you are. But you see, I did: I made the mistake of thinking I was quite like anybody else, of trying to live like other people. It took me a long time to realize that that simply wasn't true, that I had my own needs and that I had to live like me.

I: And that freed you?

P: I just got up and bolted. I went running off on that wild escapade to Mexico, where I attended, you might say, and assisted at, in my own modest way, a revolution.

Spell of the Elements

Fire and water, air and earth
Contend, unite. A magic birth
Is taking place somewhere not far
Celebrated by a star.

Take the music of the wind,
Take the fingers of a mind
Making, breaking, letting go.
Take the blanket of the snow

And a necklace of the stars,
Take the footsteps of the hours.
All can spell-bind, all can build,
All will come if you have called.

We are subject to a spell.
It is married to free-will.
Come the spring, the earth will lie
Lucky under lucky sky.

No determinism has
Power to hold us long. We pass
Into every element,
Come and gone but never spent.

ELIZABETH JENNINGS

from My Life

I WENT to the Lido, and sitting there, with little Deirdre playing on the sands, I spent some days in meditation. What I had dreamed in the Cathedral of St. Marco filled me at the same time with joy and disquietude. I loved, but I now knew something of the fickleness and selfish caprice of what men call love, and this sacrifice coming for my Art – perhaps fatal for my Art – my work – and suddenly I began to suffer an intense nostalgia for my Art – my work – my School. This human life seemed so heavy beside my dreams of Art.

I believe that in each life there is a spiritual line, an upward curve, and all that adheres to and strengthens this line is our real life – the rest is but as chaff falling from us as our souls progress. Such a spiritual line is my Art. My life has known but two motives – Love and Art – and often Love destroyed Art, and often the imperious call of Art put a tragic end to Love. For these two have no accord, but only constant battle.

ISADORA DUNCAN

from A Writer's Diary

THEN, for a moment, we saw the sun, sweeping – it seemed to be sailing at a great pace and clear in a gap; we had out our smoked glasses; we saw it crescent, burning red; next moment it had sailed fast into the cloud again; only the red streamers came from it; then only a golden haze, such as one has often seen. The moments were passing. We thought we were cheated; we looked at the sheep; they showed no fear; the setters were racing round; everyone was standing in long lines, rather dignified, looking out. I thought how we were like very old people, in the birth of the world – druids on Stonehenge; (this idea came more vividly in the first pale light though). At the back of us were great blue spaces in the cloud. These were still blue. But now the colour was going out. The clouds were turning pale; a reddish black colour. Down in the valley it was an extraordinary scrumble of red and black; there was the one light burning; all was cloud down there, and very beautiful, so delicately tinted. Nothing could be seen through the cloud. The 24 seconds were passing. Then one looked back again at the blue; and rapidly, very very quickly, all the colours faded; it became darker and darker as at the beginning of a violent storm; the light sank and sank; we kept saying this is the shadow; and we thought now it is over – this is the shadow; when suddenly the light went out. We had fallen. It was extinct. There was no colour. The earth was dead. That was the aston-ishing moment; and the next when as if a ball had rebounded the cloud took colour on itself again, only a sparky ethereal colour and so the light came back. I had very strongly the feeling as the light went out of some vast obeisance; something kneeling down and suddenly raised up when the colours came. They came back astonishingly lightly and quickly and beautifully in the valley and over the hills – at first with a miraculous glittering and ethe-reality, later normally almost, but with a great sense of relief. It was like recovery. We had been much worse than we had expected. We had seen the world dead. This was within the power of nature. Our greatness had been apparent too. Now we became Ray in a blanket, Saxon in a cap etc. We were bitterly cold. I should say that the cold had increased as the light went down. One felt very livid. Then – it was over till 1999. What remained was the sense of the comfort which we get used to, of plenty of light, and colour. This for some time seemed a defi-nitely welcome thing. Yet when it became established all over the country, one rather missed the sense of its being a relief and a

respite, which one had had when it came back after the darkness.
How can I express the darkness? It was a sudden plunge, when
one did not expect it; being at the mercy of the sky; our own
nobility; the druids; Stonehenge; and the racing red dogs; all that
was in one's mind. Also, to be picked out of one's London drawing room and set down on the wildest moors in England, was
impressive. For the rest, I remember trying to keep awake in the
gardens at York while Eddy talked and falling asleep. Asleep
again in the train. It was hot and we were messy. The carriage was
full of things. Harold was very kind and attentive. Eddy was
peevish. Roast beef and pineapple chunks, he said. We got home
at 8.30 perhaps.

VIRGINIA WOOLF

The Bird in the Tree

That tree, and its haunting bird,
            Are the loves of my heart;
But where is the word, the word,
            O where is the art,

To say, or even to see,
            For a moment of time,
What the tree and the Bird must be
            In the true sublime?

They shine, they sing to the soul,
            And the soul replies;
But the inner love is not whole,
            And the moment dies.

O give me before I die
            The grace to see
With eternal, ultimate eye,
            The Bird and the Tree.

> The song in the living green,
>   The Tree and the Bird –
> O have they ever been seen,
>   Ever been heard?

RUTH PITTER

from The Journey

ART, as is true of all of man's profound experiences, is not for art's sake, nor for religion's sake, nor for the sake of beauty nor for any 'cause.' Art is for man's sake. It may be for one man's sake, or two billion. It may be for man today or man a hundred years from now. No matter. Man, the artist, creates what he creates *for himself as a living part of mankind* – not because of external compulsion but because of a passionate need to bring forth the inviolate part of his deepest experience and fuse it with elements of both earth and human past until it suddenly has a life of its own. And when he does this, other men call it theirs, also. The dialogue may rise and fall in cadence, now becoming a mighty chorus in which the whole world seems to be participating, now only a whisper. But it never ceases. A time will come when it seems to rise again from the dead: that piece of sculpture or an entire age of painting, or a book or poem – and once more, millions of men are talking with it, sharing their unborn dream with this ancient thing and taking from it what their dream needs to bring it alive.

And by the listening and the sharing we not only are enriched but we bestow wealth on our world. For we are 'in dialogue,' we are forming a new quality of human relationship. In doing so, we are, as Henry Miller has said, 'underwriting' our age 'with our lives,' because we believe utterly in its power to transmute its terror and grief and sorrow and mistakes into a music which the future can claim as its own.

And yet, how lone the artist feels in his ordeal. As alone as

Guillaumet when his plane came down in the Andes; as Saint Exupéry on that flight to Arras when he came to terms with the word *responsibility*; or the young Lindbergh as he opened up a new path in the sky. As alone as little Bill on those nights when his heroes somehow were not there to sustain him and it was too dark to read the letters his father had written him in Korea; or Marty, as she struggled to find her way to the love in her nature which was so long blocked off by her fears; or Mrs. Timberlake, arranging shells and starfish on small windswept graves to speak her faith; or two Negro women, on a stormy night, driving along a dark highway – who must have felt that the whole world had a white face and there was no acceptance written on it.

But the artist is never alone. He has an intimate relationship with the wood he is carving, the paint and canvas, the words, the stone: these are making their demands and their plea and offering their gifts and he is answering and the dialogue sustains him – as do another man's beliefs and memories and the knowledge that there are those who care. The artist knows something else, wordless, oftentimes, but he knows it deep within him: that were it not for the struggle and the loneliness he undergoes in his search for integrity there would be no strength or beauty in his work. (And though art is not for the sake of beauty, beauty must be there or the profound revelation the artist makes would be unbearable.)

The artist in us knows, the poet in us knows: it is the mark not of ordeal but of mastered ordeal that gives a face, a life, a great event, or a great work of art its style. The wound is there but the triumph also, the death and the birth, the pain and the deep satisfactions: it is all there in delicate equilibrium, speaking to us.

LILLIAN SMITH

from A Selection from the Letters of Geraldine Jewsbury to Jane Welsh Carlyle

I HAD an advent the other night. I went to hear the 'Creation', the very grandest thing in the shape of music I can conceive. It seemed to take one into a new world of sound, it broke one up altogether, and called one out of oneself, possessed one like a new spirit. It was music that had nothing to do with passion or emotion, but when it was over one felt as if one had been banished to a realm of common things, without sunshine, and nothing but an east wind. I have been miserable ever since, as I used to be, when a child, after a great pleasure. Jenny Lind sang very wonderfully, but the music itself swallowed up all she did. One never thought of her, at least I did not. She seemed to do what she was wanted to do, nothing more. The music was too grand to let anything else be thought of. There was a prayer, an old Catholic one, which I wish you could have heard. It was Pergolesi's 'Lord, have mercy upon me, for I am in trouble.' It went down to one's inmost soul. Jenny sang a very wonderful song, a sort of 'Cheval de Bataille,' about the 'Bright Seraphin,' but it did not touch anything but my organ of wonder. Here I am interrupted, so good-bye, and write me a good letter, and not a perverse one!

Yours,
G.E.J.

from The Bloodaxe Book of Contemporary Women Poets

THE roots of my poetry go back for more generations than I can trace them. I have written of my childhood in the first volume of my autobiography, *Farewell Happy Fields* – of the rich world of a country childhood in Northumberland during the First World War, and of the very different inheritances I received from each of my parents. On my mother's side I inherited Scotland's songs and ballads – lowland Scotland, not the Gaelic Highlands, which has another culture altogether – sung or recited by my mother, aunts and grandmothers, who had learned them from *their* mothers and grandmothers before universal literacy destroyed an oral tradition and culture that scarcely any longer exists. The number of songs and ballads my mother and my aunts knew seemed endless, for memory, uncluttered by the daily chatter of radio and television, retained whole unwritten volumes of songs and stories. My mother's memory for poetry was remarkable, and besides her Scottish songs and ballads she could, even in her old age, repeat long passages from Milton and many other English poets whom she loved. The Bible was daily reading in my childhood, and I learned, both at home and at school, many psalms and passages from the New Testament by heart, words perhaps barely understood at the time, to be recalled in later years when their full meaning could bring consolation or wisdom in time of need. It is the words we have by heart that are ours, are part of us in a way that words we merely read, enjoy and forget, never can be. I am glad that I grew up in a world in which the memorising of the great literature – Shakespeare and the Bible especially – was an essential part of education.

My father was the English master at the County High School, Ilford. His native county however was Durham, and for Durham University he had written his M.Litt. thesis on Wordsworth, a fellow north-countryman; but his real love was Shakespeare, and he never missed an opportunity of taking me and my mother to see Shakespeare acted. I first saw Hamlet played by a repertory company not at Stratford-on-Avon but at Stratford-atte-Bow. From my father I learned to love the English language and its Latin and Old English roots, to see words as the embodiment of centuries of human thought and experience. From my father also I learned to regard the words of the great poets as expressions of the same order of truth (though in a lesser degree) as we found in the Bible. Both were 'inspired' from beyond the everyday human mind, and were expressions of a knowledge different in kind from the natural knowledge we gather from everyday experience or scientific experiment. This 'inspired' character was indeed the mark of what we called poetry; not something invented but something given; something that gave a kind of luminosity to even some quite slight poems by minor poets. There was of course also comic verse and satire, which were clever and ingenious, but not, in the true sense, 'poetry', which was rather a quality of experience – 'the poetry of life' as my father would have said – than a form of words. It was not the purpose of poetry to record anything and everything, to merely describe either the outer world or some subjective mood, but to speak from the imagination of the poet to the imagination of the reader.

Brought up as I was in a household in which the poets were so regarded it naturally became my ambition to become a poet. I confided this intention one day to my father as we bicycled to the school where he taught and I studied, and was much surprised at the cool and sceptical reception he gave to this proposal which I had thought would have pleased him, as a clergyman or a doctor might have been pleased to know that a son wished to follow his father's profession. But to my father the poets belonged to a higher world, to another plane; to say one wished to become a poet was to him something like saying one proposed to write a fifth Gospel.

But for my mother the world of poetry was close at hand; it was the world in which she herself actually lived her life. It was she who wrote down my baby-poems in a book before I could hold a pencil and write my own; and then she kept those as well. In retrospect it seems to me that she implanted in me the habit of making poems in imitation of those she sung or said to me. I have often thought that it is *her* desire I have fulfilled, for to her poetry was the very essence of life. I used then to think that everyone must want to be a poet, and that only by sacrificing that one desire, which all must have, did some become milkmen, or businessmen or follow some other joyless trade. And if Blake is right in declaring that every man and woman should practise one of the arts of Imagination – painting, music, poetry and architecture – perhaps I was right; by what straying away from our true identity do we become enslaved to the meaningless tasks created by a soulless technocracy?

Beyond that early formation I am grateful for an excellent education, for acquiring the discipline of work and a respect for exact knowledge. I left school with an Exhibition in Natural Sciences from Girton College, Cambridge, where I studied botany and zoology. Why not English literature? Because, for me, literature and poetry had nothing to do with 'school', they were part of life: why study as an academic subject the literature of one's own language, which one reads as a matter of course? I have since read most of English literature, much French, and in translation half the wisdom of the world. Reading, like travel, leads one on and on, yet it is impossible to have visited all the 'realms of gold' just as it is impossible to visit more than a few of the innumerable places of this beautiful earth. Both kinds of exploration are endlessly enriching. But at a certain point each of us has to discover what is our own and which among the gifts offered to us, tangible and intangible, we need and can make use of.

I have gone on all my life reading and studying and am, I suppose, comparatively learned, at least in my chosen field of study (William Blake and his sources and the Neoplatonic tradition in English literature). All this has enriched my own poetry, and, ultimately, simplified it too; for whereas, when I was young, I was impressed by complexity and a display of learning in verse (I think of the kind of poetry my Cambridge contemporary and friend William Empson was writing), I have come to understand that the profound themes can – and must – be expressed with great simplicity. Not that all simple verse is profound, or all verbally rich and complex verse superficial (I think of Dylan Thomas, Vernon Watkins and David Jones) but my own method has increasingly been to pack much meaning into few words. I hope to stir vibrations on several levels; and when a reader asks in certain of my poems 'does the world (or the sentence) mean this, that?' the answer is very often that both meanings (perhaps many meanings) are meant to vibrate together, like a chord of music. I therefore use much care in the arrangement of simple words.

Blake wrote 'Improvement makes strait roads; but the crooked roads without Improvement are roads of genius.' Improvement comes from without; genius summons from within. My teachers used to impress upon us that genius is an 'infinite capacity for taking pains'. True genius may demand that we do take infinite pains, but that is not in itself 'genius'. Rather it is 'inspiration', the summoning from within of an 'other' mind, beyond our trivial daily mind. And it is not poets and musicians only who know this 'crisis that unites for certain moments the sleeping and the waking mind' – so Yeats defines it – but mathematicians, physicists, imaginative thinkers of every kind. This 'other' mind poets once called the Muse; modern psychology has other and longer names for it; Yeats called it the 'age-old memoried self' whose memories go back far beyond ours and belong to 'the soul of the world'. That is why poets do not follow the beaten tracks; they serve another master.

Not that poets are by any means all rebels, drop-outs, ignoramuses, revolutionaries, or drinkers in pubs; merely that Imagination knows the way it must take and creates for each of us the appropriate situation. I have known poets of all stations of life. T.S. Eliot was a successful banker and then a publisher; Herbert Read a curator at the Victoria and Albert Museum; Yeats a theatre-manager and later a senator; Vernon Watkins escaped not from, but *to* a bank in Swansea. Comparing myself with these I feel some shame that, well qualified as I was to engage in many of the hard and useful tasks of the world, I could never persuade my *daimon* to let me settle down to a quiet and useful practical life, as in certain moods I think that perhaps I should have done or perhaps what I ought rather to regret is the meagreness of my contribution to poetry.

By the standards of the outer world it might seem that poetry comes from some invisible grain of sand in the sensitive organism, or a wound compensated by the growth of the pearl or ambergris of poetry. Yeats wrote that 'The intellect of man is forced to choose/Perfection of the life or of the work.' Like everyone else I would have liked to have my cake and eat it, but that hard choice has again and again been forced upon me – or rather

I have again and again been forced back to it much against my will – every gain of the poet being counterbalanced by some corresponding sacrifice of life. Or perhaps there never was any choice, and I took the only way I could ever have taken. The price, for myself and for others has been high – too high, perhaps, for a handful of verses.

But the poet is not allowed to serve two masters. We serve an inner living universe of far greater authority than the voices which tell us what we ought and ought not to be doing from a practical point of view. I have always found, in fact, that when we follow that inner guidance somehow or other practical solutions are always forthcoming; we live by miracle. My Inspirer has always been very real to me; not the feminine figure of the muse, but as it were the *puer eternus*, the Eternal Child, an unageing presence nearer and more intimate than friend or lover, and not to be denied, at the price of life itself – imaginative life that is, a life that, once tasted, the poet cannot endure to be parted from. A Greek legend tells how Bellerophon, who once rode Pegasus, the winged horse of inspiration, through some folly or betrayal was thrown to the ground and went limping through life thereafter.

There is something of the poet in all of us, of course, or of the painter or the musician or the dancer or the architect. But of all the arts the living of a life is perhaps the greatest; to live every moment of life with the same imaginative commitment as the poet brings to a special field. The fashion in a society whose values are material and which sets little store on any other asks not what we 'are' but what we 'do'; worse, the phrase 'what is he worth?' has come to mean, 'How much money has he?' How sad, how false, and what a betrayal! What we are 'worth' is not what we have, not even what we have made or done, but what we are. Poetry is not an end in itself but in the service of life; of what use are poems, or any other works of art, unless to enable human lives to be lived with insight of a deeper kind, with more sensitive feelings, more intense sense of the beautiful, with deeper understanding? According to Plato the soul knows everything, but in this world has forgotten; and the poem reminds us of what we

ourselves know, but did not know we knew; reminds us, above all,
of what we are.

KATHLEEN RAINE

Retreat

Silver-pale, solitary, hewn perhaps from
two giant breakwaters,
It stands, leaning backwards, powerful on
the crest
Of a parched hill. Beams bleached oak
binding back sea-flood
At Rhyl, now rooted in the dung-sweet
infested earth. The only skulls
Those of oatmeal sheep who crop crusts of
dry grass and scatter,
Heads held high in disdain, arched haun-
ches swaying, as I approach,
Talking aloud. Glad to hear the sound of a
voice outside my head.

Preparing my search for gifts to bring back
to you
I perch on a boulder, noting in my police-
man's notebook:
Snowdon still in mist, her foothills inked
gently grey-green on horizon.
Opalescent sea; ribbon of River Clwyd;
faint hum of motorway traffic.
Loneliness – even sheep won't answer my
call; nature is never spent.

I stare down through the beech leaves
which barely camouflage

The mock-gothic turret of the Jesuit house
    where Hopkins broke silence
With *The Wreck of the Deutschland*;
    fished; and was ordained priest.
Delivering his first sermon in a chapel,
    converted now to a dining room.
Where we, retreatants, pick pink linen
    napkins from a wooden rack,
And file up to the hot plate, suppering at
    circular tables.
Our eight-day silence broken only by the
    scraping of stainless steel on china;
And a scratched recording of *The Magic
    Flute* crackling from speakers,
Concealed in the darkly-carved pulpit from
    where poet once preached.

Behind me, the horizontal beam of the
    cross is dripping tears of solidified
Black tar, and the vertical beam is defaced,
    splashed white with paint.
At the intersection of the two beams are
    four rusty nails hammered
Into a square, holding an invisible or a lost
    sign. I crouch spiked by gorse
To find my presents for you who are
    leaving for upstate Seattle and a cabin
In a mountain where, you say, there are
    bears. Where you will be within earshot
Of a woman surnamed Knight who chan-
    nels the words of Ramtha
Reminding you 'of a heritage which you
    forgot long ago'.

In my purse-belt I stash away a feather, a
    stone, and a skein of ivory wool,

Which I inspect for nits much like a mother
    might her child's hair.
I want my feather to be a windhover's;
    probably it is a gull's.
I haven't a clue about birds, and need a
    guide to chart distinctness.
The stone too is ordinary: small, charcoal,
    neither jagged nor entirely smooth,
With two purple lines veining into one.
    This I hope shall represent for you

An end to dualism. I note: Extreme
    beauty. The sun rising behind the cross.
The crown of the wild hill might be a
    prairie; where – out of the blue –
A wagon may advance travelling west.
    And suddenly I remember The Who
    and Tommy;
And (out-thrilling all bird-song) I scream,
    high into the air, 'I'm free'.

HEATHER LAWTON

from Gift from the Sea

ACTUALLY these are among the most important times in one's life – when one is alone. Certain springs are tapped only when we are alone. The artist knows he must be alone to create; the writer, to work out his thoughts; the musician, to compose; the saint, to pray. But women need solitude in order to find again the true essence of themselves: that firm strand which will be the indispensable center of a whole web of human relationships. She must find that inner stillness which Charles Morgan describes as 'the stilling of the soul within the activities of the mind and body so that it might be still as the axis of a revolving wheel is still.'

This beautiful image is to my mind the one that women could

hold before their eyes. This is an end toward which we could strive – to be the still axis within the revolving wheel of relationships, obligations, and activities. Solitude alone is not the answer to this; it is only a step toward it, a mechanical aid, like the 'room of one's own' demanded for women, before they could make their place in the world. The problem is not entirely in finding the room of one's own, the time alone, difficult and necessary as this is. The problem is more how to still the soul in the midst of its activities. In fact, the problem is how to feed the soul.

ANNE MORROW LINDBERGH

from Pottery, Form and Expression

AND, if he has a meditative mind, he will also look at man and his occupation in the district where clay lies; he will see that the potters have always settled as near to their material as they could, especially in former times when transportation was a problem. He may also discover that the clay that they found and used has been responsible for certain techniques and practices that became the characteristic elements in the production of that part of the country. He will thus discover the potteries from Kentucky and Tennessee, the stoneware potters from the Rhine or the Faenza pottery from Italy and others. As he looks into the work of those men in their natural habitats, there is no end to the things that he will get involved and interested in: the ways those men lived and worked, what they thought and believed; how all this influenced the pots they made and what these looked like; what the techniques and the themes of their decorations were; what their religion and their art were. He will also see that there never is anything stagnant in life, how all forms varied through the ages as inventions, ideas and techniques moved through the lands, and how one country learned from another.

So the whole world is open for him to discover, for his investigation, for his research and for his education. He can learn from all nations and all times, from good and bad. No human expression is without value for whoever wants to learn, whoever aspires to a more complete vision, whoever is honestly inquisitive and wants to improve his total judgment.

Life is not a mechanical and technical process, so it is evident that abstract information and techniques cannot be an end in themselves of the education of man. All this knowledge must not remain something in the brain only, a bare accumulation of data and names, a cold registration of facts; those would be of no use as such to a creative man. No, everything that a man learns should change him in his innermost self, should clear his mind more and more of false assumptions, of a hodgepodge of unclear concepts and ideas; it should make him expand and long and search for truth over ever larger and deeper areas, areas that he formerly ignored and could never have imagined.

It is a known fact that the more one learns, the more remains to be learned and the more it seems that one will never reach that total view one is aspiring to. But, is that not the best of life? One never reaches an end (one only: death); but as one tries and searches his capacities seem to multiply and to grow. That all this cannot be arrived at consciously is evident, you cannot go out and be sure 'to grow wise.' I can only say that there is some chance of getting to the real depths of things, of thought, of art and truth, if you are open for learning and for the search towards the things of the mind – and none if you do not seek for that wisdom.

When work and life have a really deep relation, when the former is, so to say, the manifestation of what a man thinks, feels lives for, knows; when the spiritual content transcends the material knowledge, real form will then grow silently as the natural result of a man struggling with his materials, his techniques, his emotions, his ideas and his knowledge. Those forms then will have some of the growing qualities of the forms of nature, something that has surpassed the technical form and is alive. For, whether it is a Sung vase or a pot from Peru, a statue of a devil or of God, it is what man puts into his work of intangible values that ultimately decides form.

But, as in nature, where the sum of elements of different forms and functions (heart, lungs, blood, etc.) makes the total live man, so in the realm of form there are different fundamental constituents that are essential for the life of the whole, elements that are only held together by the spirit and the idea of a man. Form also requires a certain alphabet that, to a certain extent, has to be learned. There is a relation of volumes and planes to each other, but that is not enough. Since apparently the inner vision of the creative man expresses itself through the medium of those parts, those volumes, those different elements, it will be to our definite advantage to learn something about these.

MARGUERITE WILDENHAIN

Gloria

However she's personified
Or represented,
I won't forget
How space expands inside me,
Can easily contain
A million goddesses or concepts.

Sophia, Anima, or Kali,
Black or white, death or wisdom,
The central fire
Or all-engulfing water:

My muse is in myself;
And as all past and future
Exist between my own two eyes,
My living need
Is symbolised
By her resplendent figure.

She makes me dance,
She frightens me at night

With horrors,
Leads me to the burning-place.

She stands behind the mountains
Like the sun,
And lifts her arms to show
That they are only flesh,
That all this valley is alive
Because she wills it so.

RUTH FAINLIGHT

Hanford House

for Enid Canning

AS, LONG ago, the imagiers, forgotten now – unknown – hammered gold to a beauty so effectual and sufficient, so did you seek to dispose the heart: painstaking, beat for it a badge that action would not tarnish.

Now, as I read these letters, after your death, I arrive again in the radiant, ineffaceable landscape of the days of your life, identify you – the white rider – advancing, in a dream, alone. You turn your head and meet my eye, ride on, on beyond the frame, beyond recall, into a world of light unknown.

From inmost thought I write, dip a pen into this inkwell, your bequest. In an instant the pages are changed – into cupolas, white and gold, arcades of light and shadow, cruciform of some Isfahan, inviolate white city, built all of folded paper, immaculate as Flemish hats, by whose water-mirrors this correspondence was sustained.

Conversing mind to mind, quick and dead, we sip the elixir of memory, take the lyric leap into the yellow heart of light; dream with Saul in a Prussian-blue night, sleeping white-hatted under a rosy tent, troubled by perfection, desirous of number. There are sentinels outside. A stem of the mystic white rose lies on the table like a feather.

Or are our eyes now drawn to the hills folding quietly into themselves, another exquisite day slipping swiftly away over the golden stubble? To the thrush, with his mouthful of worms and apprehensive eye?

Obedient to the herald, a scarlet-legged child steps from the trees, affects the feather-capped lover with courteous, elaborate bow. The incidental music to the Dream issues unquenchable from the bluebell grass hatched under the dappled beech. The river Moldau, in spring flood, pours straight between the pilasters in the white drawing-room.

We are transported to blue Italy, to the set at Arezzo, to a blue-green noon at the turning-point of Time, witnesses to that high nativity; arms raised in salutation with the shepherds', feet singing with the angels'; chorus to their inextinguishable praise: there at the presentation of the Child, laid out on the broken earth's crust for adoration, for all men, by the mother.

Or are we standing in the shadow of the cloister at San Marco, where happening, heralded by the rush and beat of the angel's wing, perfectly established itself, after the earnest reckoning of centuries, in the perfected womb?

Mother of God, whose waiting made of space that liquid light into which the future might flow unadorned, unharmed: whose humility made of Time a peace to charm creation.

Mild lady, by whose restraint the serpent was undone; before whom throbbing life was made manifest in the wondrous tree,

growing only in that garden, heavy with fruit, before which even
she did not raise her eyes, and of whose death she has spoken not
a word.

Many then are the places where we might reverently stand, trow-
els fashioned in gold, smooth with use, hanging at our belts: a
knowledge of cornerstones, mortar, angles and gardens needed by
builders and makers to bring things into line.

Did you wait as well upon the Queen of Sheba, see her clasp the
hand of Solomon? Watch Mary Magdalene hurrying, ardent, to
the tomb? Were you, too, forever cleansed, ensouled by the *con-
trapposto* in the garden?

Did you stand ranked behind the Madonna, far-seeing, a diadem
on your brow and at your throat? Did you prostrate yourself
beside Giotto's rock, kiss the earth before the miracle of spring?

For you were the bearer of the news of these propitious times. Or
are they known by all who dare, by those who have seen the shining back of Time, 'moving their dwelling-places, the heavens
also moving'?

In your house there were no seasons: the shutters closed for no
heart's winter; no disconsolate padlock hung at unapproachable
wrought-iron gates to conceal illicit pleasures.

Weathered, wooden gates merely served to comfort colossal-
limbed horses compelled by night's embrace to thunder far, far
beyond the confines of their canvasses into the world of colours:

The only sentinels the dreaming, waving beeches, planted with
the bleeding hands of memory, growing again from the ground
up, signifying those fiercely loved and beyond Time,

Time that pleads 'O sleeping, sleeping man, rise up. Flare eyes.

Hurry, hurry. In vain passion. In vain vicious pursuit. Rise! Defy the cruel laws! There is glory here. O hearts, hearts, you may forever ascend!

'Do you not see that the sun returns, that the rain loves, the winds call and call, and the moon rides with desire? Can you not sense the hushed circle of the breathless stars? They were here above the lovely shadow of this house. Here, where storms and plagues, prepossessed, conformed to goodness; from whose chimneys plumed the celestial dome, righteously discharging space; just habitation, circumscribed by a sky full of angels, curious, astonished?'

This bowl is filled with petals, petals that fell in the rose-garden. They fall suddenly, all at once, a shower of thought in the mind of one who walks there. Settling, they lie one upon the other, boat-shaped, distilled in this transparent orb, this glass bowl, a weight to be held by two hands, which I pass now to you.

For we must climb the golden ladders, pressed against the air, erect the scaffolding against the odds: ant-builders. To be sure, angels slip by night into the porch of the chapel of the hill, sit in the shadows, shielded by their wings, to bend an ear.

And, for the work, we must remember. Remember, as the crickets thread up and down the fringe of noon, and tongues of tulips loll in a profundity of silence over the polished tables.

Collarless, loose-sleeved, co-heirs of huge, uninhabited cathedrals, we may still plunge our gilded fore-arms, cup our hands, even after many centuries, into the illumined bowl.

Into the tinctured gold too of the ribboning mouths of finches, the throat of the lily, and the back of the fast brown river; clasp the solid gold transported for the pillars of the temple built in another's heart.

And you will enter from the wings of Time, woman-king, seraphim, centre of the order, command the women to go back and forth carrying buckets spilling with light, easy burden.

Gladly did I labour then, for many times had I run my eye the length of an immense ribbed roof, heard the thirsty tongues of huge bells clamouring in their seismic chambers, hooded giants, forest of trees swaying in a stupendous, manmade storm of sound, calling upon God, discomposing fields and cities.

Had mounted with the leaping organ, shadow-boxing in the vaulted nave; had seen, at my feet, the work of string and rule, square, compass, proportional divider, the great laborious work of bishops, masons, master-builders.

Stay now. Accept duration. The Word walks abroad. God's armourer gives the sign without which the children building in the thicket, busy as birds, will be neither deft nor swift.

They stream, a long flight of swallows, through the black porch, into the great house, find the stout tables set, a crust of bread and an orange on every plate, blue hydrangeas to right and left, every pot and vessel in its place, not to disgrace this meal.

You sit at the table's end, behind you the high window, the light of evening water on your shoulders. You juggle the two golden balls, Alpha and Omega, in sure large hands, your rod a lodestar, your house a universe, expectant, on this body conferring emblems; love advancing to meet us: the sun overhead, at night the stars kind, conciliatory, signalling benediction.

Yours was no exclusive order, the world's work plain, wanting, but only careful hands make makers, and you would turn us to righteousness, have us make.

Here then were assembled the last traces of Breughel's busy

workaday mysterium: the gardener, the gardener's boy, the cook, the schoolmaster, matron and stablehand, maker of stained glass, arms full, their labours magnifying a dewdrop world in the amber, lustrous mid-morning of Time. It is late now, the labour Love, and you would drive us too, beyond expectation, into the uncommon light of the real.

Sleeping in the summerhouse, I return thirty years, lie in the garden, attentive to the day's ending. The western sky is pouring back into the world's heart brushed with lemon, straw and gold, crumpled turquoise, its last gift a necklace of pearls, undone. Spears of light rain onto the tall grass, flies dancing in attendance.

An opal moon, suspended on some invisible thread, floats in a violet sky over the house – still now – four walls quietly breathing at the end of day. Doves croon, low-voiced, in the stone gables. Arch-eyed greyhounds lie on the steps resting their pensive heads.

The trees merge into their shadows. Dogs bark far-off, and, from the house, Dowland's sad ceremonious lute steps across the garden. Later, the black-tongued arias of the Queen of the Night pierce the dark. There is silence. The lights go out in all the windows, one by one.

I turn to sleep, the last one left awake in the whole world. The tom-cats start up, and I am filled, wise with unknowing, wondering, helpless, summoned by futurity, and incomprehensible grief.

Gatherer of sorrows, you had on a great cream-coloured mantle falling in folds like a habit – did you sing on Irish shores with Celtic choirs? In your huge arms you carried me across the garden by night; pitying, saw within me coiling life unfurl: life, uncontrovertible, putting forth leaves.

We passed through the door, the door of your house the door into the yew wood, into the side of the hill, into the unending passage

of the world, guarded by collar doves that sing at the threshold
night and day. As large as the south wind we were.

You set me down in the sacred grove. We looked into the lit world,
looked on beauty's core and on the metal face of terror. You spoke,
free-tongued, and in your voice I heard the pentecostal song.

You created me your equal, anointed me my second self, greatly
loved, and strong. As the noble Enkidu was made, so you placed
me, a star at your feet.

I took to the road, your scion, high in hope, well-favoured.
Unheeding, I took the long road out of your country. And on the
royal road of white boulders, the road of the lonely Caledonian
pine, I was beggared by the heart's avarice, by senses' greed.
Inexactness drew a filmy shutter over my eye. For many years I
waited by the well.

Your hamstone house loomed unsteady in the mind, glowing,
enchanted, beyond reach, a ship calling from the heaving bed of
a fathomless sea. I saw black insane cities piling up, saw, close-up,
the pitiless palaces of commerce darkly gleaming, saw cities burning; focussing, saw my own apparition, alone, kneedeep in ruins.

Sometimes, disburdened by the golden calm of evening spreading
slowly inexorably before me, I saw you in a mirage across a wide
water, threw out a line. Snaking into the light, it would unloose
itself, useless, irretrievable.

I saw you again, in a dream, sternly appraising the cloth and pattern of my diamond sleeve, my pointed shoe. I shrank into the
shadows, heard you pray for my harlequin soul: 'O may the pack
fall quietly into place every time.'

You spoke from your eyes, slowly: 'The kingdom is not lost. See,
in your hand, you hold the covered cage. In it sits the blue falcon,

of fierce and active eye, of restive, folded wing, bird of hope and the empty shining hollow. Now place him on your wrist.'

I ran from the trees. Care fell away. I embraced your steadfast sovereign person, your faithful remembering, your cognizing's sheer accomplishment. I lay my razored, chiselled head, heavy as stone, in your lap; watched, it seemed for centuries, the seeds of your thoughts drift, wordless, across us, into eternity.

In the gathering dark I saw the great white bird of wide wingspan, strong and muscular, saw it arriving noiselessly over the black lake. And I felt my hands begin to fly, light, skilled and sure, spinning from true heart's desire: strict, circumspect, exact.

June 1993
FRANCES HOWARTH

from The Letters and Works of Lady Mary Wortley Montagu

WHOEVER will cultivate their own mind will find full employment. Every virtue does not only require great care in the planting, but as much daily solicitude in cherishing as exotic fruits and flowers; the vices and passions (which I am afraid are the natural product of the soil) demand perpetual weeding. Add to this the search after knowledge (every branch of which is entertaining), and the longest life is too short for the pursuit of it, which, though in some regards confined to very strait limits, leaves still a vast variety of amusements to those capable of tasting them, which is utterly impossible for those that are blinded by prejudices, which are the certain effect of an ignorant education. My own was one of the worst in the world, being exactly the same as Clarissa Harlowe's, her pious Mrs Norton so perfectly resembling my governess (who had been nurse to my mother) I could almost fancy the author was acquainted with her. She took so much pains from my infancy to fill my head with superstitious tales and false notions, it was none of her fault I am not at this day afraid of witches and hobgoblins, or turned Methodist.

The Sunflower

Till the slow daylight pale,
    A willing slave, fast bound to one above,
I wait; he seems to speed, and change, and fail;
    I know he will not move.

I lift my golden orb
    To his, unsmitten when the roses die,
And in my broad and burning disk absorb
    The splendours of his eye.

His eye is like a clear
    Keen flame that searches through me: I must droop
Upon my stalk, I cannot reach his sphere;
    To mine he cannot stoop.

I win not my desire,
    And yet I fail not of my guerdon; lo!
A thousand flickering darts and tongues of fire
    Around me spread and glow.

All rayed and crowned, I miss
    No queenly state until the summer wane,
The hours flit by; none knoweth of my bliss,
    And none has guessed my pain.

I follow one above,
    I track the shadow of his steps, I grow
Most like to him I love
    Of all that shines below.

DORA GREENWELL

from Experiences Facing Death

LATER I discovered a recurrent appetite for mathematical refresh-
ment, which was satisfied by reading anything in that line that
was just a trifle beyond my capacity to deal with intellectually. I
read anything that brought me up on the tiptoes of my mind, and
found all my creative processes augmented, raised to higher levels. I hadn't thought very much why this should be the case,
simply filed away the information for use in periods of dryness
and loss of creative power. When a story didn't 'go,' I took down
my geometry, as a last resort, and had a bout with it. Then, one
day I got into a Fifth Avenue bus and sat down in front of two
men who were avidly discussing a lecture they had just heard on
the mathematics of proportion as applied to art, to Greek vases in
particular. I drank it in; I knew my stuff when I heard it.
Fortunately the talkers went all the way to the Metropolitan
Museum – I forgot what I had started out to do – and I stuck to
them, eavesdropping shamelessly until they left the bus, and I
with them, demanding to know where I could hear more and
from whom. It was, the subject of their discussion, as you may
have guessed, Hambidge's *Dynamic Symmetry*. Afterward I
bought the book, took it to the woods with me and made it part
of my experience. For those who do not know the work in question, it may be described as a careful exposition of the
mathematics of growth, a knowledge of which – but whether felt
or apprehended no one really knows – underlies all Greek art;
recovered and made modernly intelligible by J. Hambidge. It is
not very abstruse, but I should not like, many times as I have
been through the book, to be called upon to demonstrate without
reviewing it. I couldn't, in fact, solve the equation which Sinclair
Lewis postulates as marking the turning point at which
Arrowsmith left off being a medical man, and began to be a scientist, though I might have when I left College. I can't read
Einstein, of course, but I do read Bertrand Russell and others
who interpret him, and this is what happens to me. I read on in a
sort of intellectual trance, similar to the trance of music, not

remembering what I read, possibly not apprehending it. . . . I should say that the meaning goes past me as great music goes, as the splendor of a sunset. And afterward, I find pictures and patterns in my mind that I recognize vaguely as being derived from my mathematical reading. I am aware of the underlying structure of my own work firming to principles felt to be universal rather than personal. I find my unpremeditated ideas of space and time becoming more fluent; my apprehension of reality more dynamic. Something in me knows more mathematics, makes better use of it, than I do.

I am acquainted with business men and engineers who say they get similar clarifications by listening to good music of which they know no more than I do of synthetic tensors. But music helps me not at all except pleasurably, the emotional overtones and inclusions soothe rather than excite subconscious activity. If I were to write under the influence of the sonata Eroica, I might get the composer's pattern but not an original, fundamental structure of human behavior, such as is primarily a behavior of consciousness. But I can get subjectively at such structures by reading mathematics beyond my capacity intellectually to understand.

And that is why I say that the challenge is from the artist and the mystic to the scientist. There is undoubtedly a mathematical structure that will explain the alteration in consciousness involved in the experience called death; but it is as experience that death changes must first be met and resolved. And I think the joke is on Mr. Einstein and Mr. Russell if, in saying that I meet death as an artist, I nevertheless can say that I meet it in better countenance for what I have been able to get out of a less – or more than – intellectual consciousness of mathematics. I get it as a poet gets a poem, or a painter a picture, out of knowledge pushed down below the threshold, refused until it has been lost completely and then recovered by the intelligence. Every creative artist knows exactly what I mean by the law that must be forgotten before it will work fruitfully.

If death is a gate, and not the dead end of the passage, I shall get through by means of what I have learned as folklorist, as mystic, as artist. But, except by a direct revelation from the other world, which, without expecting it, one admits as possible, I am convinced we shall not be able to rationalize immortality without the help of the highest type of scientific intelligence. All the activities of life, and not only human life but all those in which consciousness is evident or can by any manner of means be descried as playing a part; and all the departments of such activity, not only those called intellectual, but the creative, the mystical, the activities of genius, of protective mimicry, of the so-called artistic temperament as well as the religious temperament, all the activities within the shadow of which stands God, must be scrutinized, identified, set in order. Then perhaps we shall produce a satisfactory philosophy of the soul. And in the meantime the artist and the mystic will know what they know.

MARY AUSTIN

from Memoirs of Madame Vigée Lebrun

FINALLY we reached Dresden by a very narrow road skirting the Elbe at a great height, the river flowing through a broad valley. The very day after my arrival I visited the famous Dresden gallery, unexcelled in the world. Its masterpieces are so well known that I render no special account. I will only observe that here, as everywhere else, one recognises how far Raphael stands above all other painters. I had inspected several rooms of the gallery, when I found myself before a picture which filled me with an admiration greater than anything else in the art of painting could have evoked. It represents the Virgin, standing on some clouds and holding the infant Jesus in her arms. This figure is of a beauty and a nobility worthy of the divine brush that traced it; the face of the child bears an expression at once innocent and heavenly; the draperies are most accurately drawn, and their colouring is exquisite. At the right of the Virgin is a saint done with admirable fidelity to life, his two hands being especially to be noted. At the left is a young saint, with head inclined, looking at two angels at the bottom of the picture. Her face is all loveliness, truth and modesty. The two little angels are leaning on their hands, their eyes raised to the persons above them, and their heads are done with an ingenuity and a delicacy not to be conveyed in words.

The Visiting Sea

As the inhastening tide doth roll,
Home from the deep, along the whole
    Wide shining strand, and floods the caves,
     – Your love comes filling with happy waves
The open sea-shore of my soul.

But inland from the seaward spaces,
None knows, not even you, the places
    Brimmed, at your coming, out of sight,
     – The little solitudes of delight
This tide constrains in dim embraces.

You see the happy shore, wave-rimmed,
But know not of the quiet dimmed
    Rivers your coming floods and fills,
    The little pools 'mid happier hills,
My silent rivulets, over-brimmed.

What! I have secrets from you? Yes.
But, visiting Sea, your love doth press
    And reach in further than you know,
    And fills all these; and, when you go,
There's loneliness in loneliness.

ALICE MEYNELL

from Moments of Being

. . . I ONLY know that many of these exceptional moments brought with them a peculiar horror and a physical collapse; they seemed dominant; myself passive. This suggests that as one gets older one has a greater power through reason to provide an explanation; and that this explanation blunts the sledge-hammer force of the blow. I think this is true, because though I still have the peculiarity that I receive these sudden shocks, they are now always welcome; after the first surprise, I always feel instantly that they are particularly valuable.

And so I go on to suppose that the shock-receiving capacity is what makes me a writer. I hazard the explanation that a shock is at once in my case followed by the desire to explain it. I feel that I have had a blow; but it is not, as I thought as a child, simply a blow from an enemy hidden behind the cotton wool of daily life; it is or will become a revelation of some order; it is a token of some real thing behind appearances; and I make it real by putting it into words. It is only by putting it into words that I make it whole; this wholeness means that it has lost its power to hurt me; it gives me, perhaps because by doing so I take away the pain, a great delight to put the severed parts together. Perhaps this is the strongest pleasure known to me. It is the rapture I get when in writing I seem to be discovering what belongs to what; making a scene come right; making a character come together. From this I reach what I might call a philosophy; at any rate it is a constant idea of mine; that behind the cotton wool is hidden a pattern; that we – I mean all human beings – are connected with this; that the whole world is a work of art; that we are parts of the work of art. *Hamlet* or a Beethoven quartet is the truth about this vast mass that we call the world. But there is no Shakespeare, there is no Beethoven; certainly and emphatically there is no God; we are the words; we are the music; we are the thing itself. And I see this when I have a shock.

VIRGINIA WOOLF

Intelligent Prayer

A star by world-connivance seems part of the hill.
A tree not by mere folly stands up creature-like.
Such painstaking acts of intelligence widely accost.
It is a compliment to nature to perceive them.
The mind is already full, near overflowing.
It is no mean compliment to stop and smile
And verse such imperfections perfectwise.

Lyricism has had humane use in time:
To allow the bragging population to recover
From the exertion of behaving intelligently –
By commending the intelligence
Of nature's stupid also prone to think,
Though these have only leaves for minds, or less.

You are, however, no longer a population.
If you are tired – good. This is a charm against
The brisk philosophies that conjure wisdoms
Satisfying to the ambition of time
To hold up its head among other times, other wisdoms.

You are, however, no longer an unknown number.
The calculation is completed, there now remains but
The copying of the determined selves
Into a closed gazette of memories
Where in the chary happiness of the dead
You lay you down, to think no more again.

If you are tired – good. Tiredness is to pray to death,
That it shall think for you when speechlessness
Tells how you lie so full of understanding each,
Sorry of life in his own grave of mind each.

LAURA RIDING

from Creed or Chaos

THE unsacramental attitude of modern society to man and matter is probably closely connected with its unsacramental attitude to work. The Church is a good deal to blame for having connived at this. From the eighteenth century onwards, she has tended to acquiesce in what I may call the 'industrious apprentice' view of the matter: 'Work hard and be thrifty, and God will bless you with a contented mind and a competence.' This is nothing but enlightened self-interest in its vulgarest form, and plays directly into the hands of the monopolist and the financier. Nothing has so deeply discredited the Christian Church as her squalid submission to the economic theory of society. The burning question of the Christian attitude to money is being so eagerly debated nowadays that it is scarcely necessary to do more than remind ourselves that the present unrest, both in Russia and in Central Europe, is an immediate judgment upon a financial system that has subordinated man to economics, and that no *mere* adjustment of economic machinery will have any lasting effect if it keeps man a prisoner inside the machine.

This is the burning question; but I believe there is a still more important and fundamental question waiting to be dealt with, and that is, what men in a Christian Society ought to think and feel about work. Curiously enough, apart from the passage in *Genesis* which suggests that work is a hardship and a judgment on sin, Christian doctrine is not very explicit about work. I believe, however, that there *is* a Christian doctrine of work, very closely related to the doctrines of the creative energy of God and the divine image in man. The modern tendency seems to be to identify work with gainful employment; and this is, I maintain, the essential heresy at the back of the great economic fallacy which allows wheat and coffee to be burnt and fish to be used for manure while whole populations stand in need of food. The fallacy being that work is not the expression of man's creative energy in the service of Society, but only something he does in order to obtain money and leisure.

A very able surgeon put it to me like this: 'What is happening,' he said, 'is that nobody works for the sake of getting the thing done. The result of the work is a by-product; the *aim* of the work is to make money to do something else. Doctors practise medicine, not primarily to relieve suffering, but to make a living – the cure of the patient is something that happens on the way. Lawyers accept briefs, not because they have a passion for justice, but because the law is the profession which enables them to live. The reason,' he added, 'why men often find themselves happy and satisfied in the army is that for the first time in their lives they find themselves doing something, not for the sake of the pay, which is miserable, but for the sake of getting the thing done.'

I will only add to this one thing which seems to me very symptomatic. I was shown a 'scheme for a Christian Society' drawn up by a number of young and earnest Roman Catholics. It contained a number of clauses dealing with work and employment – minimum wages, hours of labour, treatment of employees, housing, and so on – all very proper and Christian. But it offered no machinery whatever for ensuring that the work itself should be properly done. In its lack of a sacramental attitude to work, that is, it was as empty as a set of trade union regulations. We may remember that a medieval guild did insist, not only on the employer's duty to his workmen, but also on the labourer's duty to his work.

If man's fulfilment of his nature is to be found in the full expression of his divine creativeness, then we urgently need a Christian doctrine of work, which shall provide, not only for proper conditions of employment, but also that the work shall be such as a man may do with his whole heart, and that he shall do it for the very work's sake. But we cannot expect a sacramental attitude to work, while many people are forced, by our evil standard of values, to do work which is a spiritual degradation – a long series of financial trickeries, for example, or the manufacture of vulgar and useless trivialities.

DOROTHY L. SAYERS

from My Ascent of Mont Blanc

THIS astonishing sky, the desolation of colossal mountains, the fretwork of clouds and grey peaks, the eternal snows, the solemn silence of the wastes, the absence of any sound, any living being, any vegetation, and above all of a great city that might recall the world of men: all combined to conjure up an image of a new world or to transport the spectator to primitive times. There was a moment when I could believe I was witnessing the birth of creation from the lap of chaos.

HENRIETTE D'ANGEVILLE

from Truth or Dare

The Last Story

And so the time comes when all the people of the earth
 can bring their gifts to the fire
 and look into each other's faces
 unafraid

Breathe deep
Feel the sacred well that is your own breath, and look
 look at that circle
See us come from every direction
 from the four quarters of the earth
See the lines that stretch to the horizon
 the procession, the gifts borne
 see us feed the fire
Feel the earth's life renewed
And the circle is complete again
 and the medicine wheel is formed anew
 and the knowledge within each one of us
 made whole
Feel the great turning, feel the change

the new life runs through your blood like fire
and all of nature rises with it
greening, burgeoning, bursting into flower

At that mighty rising
do the vines rise up, do the grains rise up
and the desert turns green
the wasteland blooms like a garden
Hear the earth sing
of her own loveliness
her hillock lands, her valleys
her furrows well-watered
her untamed wild places
She arises in you
as you in her
Your voice becomes her voice
Sing!
Your dance is her dance
of the circling stars
and the ever-renewing flame
As your labor has become her labor

Out of the bone, ash
Out of the ash, pain
Out of the pain, the swelling
Out of the swelling, the opening
Out of the opening, the labor
Out of the labor, the birth
Out of the birth, the turning wheel
the turning tide
This is the story we like to tell ourselves
In the night
When the labor is too hard, and goes on too long
When the fire seems nothing but dying embers winking
out
We say we remember

a time when we were free
We say
    that we are free, still, and always
And the pain we feel
    is that of labor
And the cries we hear
    are those of birth

And so you come to the fire
    where the old ones sit
You are young
    just on the edge of ripening
They are ancient
    their faces lined
    with spiderwebs of wrinkle
Their faces brown, bronze, cream, black
    their eyes are wells of memory
They say
    Listen child
    For this is your night of passage
    And it is time to learn
    Your history
    Tonight you will run free, out into the wild
    Fearing only the spirit of your own power
    And no one in this world would harm you or lay
        a hand on you
But there was a time
    When children were not safe

STARHAWK

from Dancing at the Edge of the World

BUT we heard a hint of something else from Oliphant; and here (thanks, Tillie) is the painter Käthe Kollwitz:

> I am gradually approaching the period in my life when work comes first. When both the boys were away for Easter, I hardly did anything but work. Worked, slept, ate, and went for short walks. But above all I worked.
>
> And yet I wonder whether the 'blessing' isn't missing from such work. No longer diverted by other emotions, I work the way a cow grazes.

That is marvelous – 'I work the way a cow grazes.' That is the best description of the 'professional' at work I know.

> Perhaps in reality I accomplish a little more. The hands work and work, and the head imagines it's producing God knows what, and yet, formerly, when my working time was so wretchedly limited, I was more productive, because I was more sensual; I lived as a human being must live, passionately interested in everything. . . . Potency, potency is diminishing.

This *potency* felt by a woman is a potency from which the Hero-Artist has (and I choose my words carefully) cut himself off, in an egoism that is ultimately sterile. But it is a potency that has been denied by women as well as men, and not just women eager to collude with misogyny.

Back in the seventies Nina Auerbach wrote that Jane Austen was able to write because she had created around her 'a child-free space.' Germ-free I knew, odor-free I knew, but child-free? And Austen? who wrote in the parlor, and was a central figure to a lot of nieces and nephews? But I tried to accept what Auerbach said, because although my experience didn't fit it, I was, like many women, used to feeling that my experience was faulty, not right – that it was *wrong*. So I was probably wrong to keep on writing in what was then a fully child-filled space. However, feminist thinking evolved rapidly to a far more complex and realistic position, and I, stumbling along behind, have been enabled by it to think a little for myself.

The greatest enabler for me was always, is always, Virginia Woolf. And I quote now from the first draft of her paper 'Professions for Women,' where she gives her great image of a woman writing.

> I figure her really in an attitude of contemplation, like a fisher-woman, sitting on the bank of a lake with her fishing rod held over its water. Yes that is how I see her. She was not thinking; she was not reasoning; she was not constructing a plot; she was letting her imagination down into the depths of her consciousness while she sat above holding on by a thin but quite necessary thread of reason.
>
> Ursula Le Guin

Poppy

2

Scarlet poppy
grows
out of cracked
earth
in Gethsemane.

Inside, hidden
by petals,
folded – the one
upon the other –
a secret.

A shining
ebony

cross, dusted
with yoke-yellow
pollen. Ashes
to carry life.

Scarlet poppy
keeping vigil
over the honeyed
walls
of Jerusalem.

Wild 'common poppy'
special, unique,
ordinary amidst
the promiscuous crowd
of mustard and daisies.

Scarlet poppy
steadfastly keeping
a dawn watch
over tousled olive trees
outcast from the city

Waiting for the feathered
sky to part
to allow the sun
to rise, blazing
in glory above the graves.

HEATHER LAWTON

from The Sea Around Us

FOR the sea as a whole, the alternation of day and night, the passage of the seasons, the procession of the years, are lost in its

vastness, obliterated in its own changeless eternity. But the surface waters are different. The face of the sea is always changing. Crossed by colors, lights, and moving shadows, sparkling in the sun, mysterious in the twilight, its aspects and its moods vary hour by hour. The surface waters move with the tides, stir to the breath of the winds, and rise and fall to the endless, hurrying forms of the waves. Most of all, they change with the advance of the seasons. Spring moves over the temperate lands of our Northern Hemisphere in a tide of new life, of pushing green shoots and unfolding buds, all its mysteries and meanings symbolized in the northward migration of the birds, the awakening of sluggish amphibian life as the chorus of frogs rises again from the wet lands, the different sound of the wind which stirs the young leaves where a month ago it rattled the bare branches. These things we associate with the land, and it is easy to suppose that at sea there could be no such feeling of advancing spring. But the signs are there, and seen with understanding eye, they bring the same magical sense of awakening.

RACHEL CARSON

Integrity

the quality or state of being complete; unbroken condition; entirety

Webster

A wild patience has taken me this far

as if I had to bring to shore
a boat with a spasmodic outboard motor
old sweaters, nets, spray-mottled books
tossed in the prow
some kind of sun burning my shoulder-blades.
Splashing the oarlocks. Burning through.

Your fore-arms can get scalded, licked with pain
in a sun blotted like unspoken anger
behind a casual mist.

The length of daylight
this far north, in this
forty-ninth year of my life
is critical.

The light is critical: of me, of this
long-dreamed, involuntary landing
on the arm of an inland sea.
The glitter of the shoal
depleting into shadow
I recognize: the stand of pines
violet-black really, green in the old postcard
but really I have nothing but myself
to go by; nothing
stands in the realm of pure necessity
except what my hands can hold.

Nothing but myself? . . . My selves.
After so long, this answer.
As if I had always known
I steer the boat in, simply.
The motor dying on the pebbles
cicadas taking up the hum
dropped in the silence.

Anger and tenderness: my selves.
And now I can believe they breathe in me
as angels, not polarities.
Anger and tenderness: the spider's genius
to spin and weave in the same action
from her own body, anywhere –
even from a broken web.

The cabin in the stand of pines
is still for sale. I know this. Know the print
of the last foot, the hand that slammed and locked that door,
then stopped to wreathe the rain-smashed clematis
back on the trellis
for no one's sake except its own.
I know the chart nailed to the wallboards
the icy kettle squatting on the burner.
The hands that hammered in those nails
emptied that kettle one last time
are these two hands
and they have caught the baby leaping
from between trembling legs
and they have worked the vacuum aspirator
and stroked the sweated temples
and steered the boat here through this hot
misblotted sunlight, critical light
imperceptibly scalding
the skin these hands will also salve.

ADRIENNE RICH

Life's Gifts

I SAW a woman sleeping. In her sleep she dreamt Life stood before her, and held in each hand a gift – in the one Love, in the other Freedom. And she said to the woman, 'Choose!'

And the woman waited long: and she said, 'Freedom!'

And Life said, 'Thou hast well chosen. If thou hadst said, "Love," I would have given thee that thou didst ask for; and I would have gone from thee, and returned to thee no more. Now, the day will come when I shall return. In that day I shall bear both gifts in one hand.'

I heard the woman laugh in her sleep.

OLIVE SCHREINER, from Dreams

The fresh roses are such a lovely
company, in beauty and splendor,
They surpass the celebrated
paintings of the inimitable Mani.

The roses have put on the fairest
colors from Leila's face;
For not otherwise would the eyes
of Majnoon behold them from the clouds.
Night has so filled the tulips with
her wine, that in the dawn
Flush they sway like ruby chalices.

The narcissus blooms carry the
tint of silver and gold,
Each of them looking like a crown
fit to adorn a princely head.

The frail violets appareled in
their delicate hues,
Look like a company of nuns
receiving their ordination from nature.

RABIAH BALKHI

from A Writer's Diary

Tuesday June 19th 1923

I TOOK up this book with a kind of idea that I might say something about my writing – which was prompted by glancing at
what K. M. said about her writing in *The Dove's Nest*. But I only
glanced. She said a good deal about feeling things deeply: also
about being pure, which I won't criticise, though of course I very
well could. But now what do I feel about *my* writing? – this book,
that is, *The Hours*,[1] if that's its name? One must write from deep
feeling, said Dostoievsky. And do I? Or do I fabricate with words,

loving them as I do? No, I think not. In this book I have almost too many ideas. I want to give life and death, sanity and insanity; I want to criticise the social system, and to show it at work, at its most intense. But here I may be posing. I heard from Ka[2] this morning that she doesn't like *In the Orchard*. At once I feel refreshed. I become anonymous, a person who writes for the love of it. She takes away the motive of praise, and lets me feel that without any praise I should be content to go on. This is what Duncan said of his painting the other night. I feel as if I slipped off all my ball dresses and stood naked – which as I remember was a very pleasant thing to do. But to go on. Am I writing *The Hours* from deep emotion? Of course the mad part tries me so much, makes my mind squirt so badly that I can hardly face spending the next weeks at it. It's a question though of these characters. People, like Arnold Bennett, say I can't create, or didn't in *Jacob's Room*, characters that survive. My answer is – but I leave that to the *Nation*: it's only the old argument that character is dissipated into shreds now; the old post-Dostoievsky argument. I daresay it's true, however, that I haven't that 'reality' gift. I insubstantise, wilfully to some extent, distrusting reality – its cheapness. But to get further. Have I the power of conveying the true reality? Or do I write essays about myself? Answer these questions as I may, in the uncomplimentary sense, and still there remains this excitement. To get to the bones, now I'm writing fiction again I feel my force glow straight from me at its fullest. After a dose of criticism I feel that I'm writing sideways, using only an angle of my mind. This is justification; for free use of the faculties means happiness. I'm better company, more of a human being. Nevertheless, I think it most important in this book to go for the central things. Even though they don't submit, as they should, however, to beautification in language. No, I don't nail my crest to the Murrys, who work in my flesh after the manner of the jigger insect. It's annoying, indeed degrading, to have these bitternesses. Still, think of the 18th Century. But then they were overt, not covert, as now.

I foresee, to return to *The Hours*, that this is going to be the devil of a struggle. The design is so queer and so masterful. I'm always having to wrench my substance to fit it. The design is certainly original and interests me hugely. I should like to write away and away at it, very quick and fierce. Needless to say, I can't. In three weeks from today, I shall be dried up.

[1] Subsequently this title was altered to *Mrs Dalloway*.
[2] Mrs Arnold-Forster.

VIRGINIA WOOLF

Psalm 92: *Bonum est confiteri*

O lovely thing
To sing and praises frame
To thee, O Lord, and thy high name;
With early spring
Thy bounty to display,
Thy truth when night hath vanquished day:
Yea so to sing,
That ten-stringed instrument
With lute, and harp, and voice consent.

For, Lord, my mind
Thy works with wonder fill;
Thy doings are my comfort still.
What wit can find,
How bravely thou hast wrought,
Or deeply sound thy shallow'st thought?
The fool is blind,
And blindly doth not know,
How like the grass the wicked grow.

The wicked grow
Like frail though flow'ry grass;
And fall'n, to wrack past help do pass.

But thou not so,
But high thou still dost stay:
And lo thy haters fall away.
Thy haters lo,
Decay and perish all;
All wicked hands to ruin fall.

Fresh oiled I
Will lively lift my horn,
And match the matchless unicorn:
Mine eye shall spy
My spies in spiteful case;
Mine ear shall hear my foes' disgrace.
Like cedar high
And like date-bearing tree,
For green, and growth the just shall be.

Where God doth dwell
Shall be his spreading place:
God's courts shall his fair boughs embrace.
Even then shall swell
His blossoms fat and fair,
When aged rind the stock shall bear.
And I shall tell
How God my Rock is just,
So just, with him is nought unjust.

MARY HERBERT, Countess of Pembroke

2

AIMING AT THE HIGHEST

The Spirit lurks within the Flesh
Like Tides within the Sea
That make the Water live, estranged
What would the Either be?

EMILY DICKINSON

My peace, O my brothers, is in solitude,
And my Beloved is with me always,
For His love I can find no substitute,
And His love is the test for me among mortal beings,
When-e'er His Beauty I may contemplate,
He is my 'mihrab,' towards Him is my 'qibla'
If I die of love, before completing satisfaction,
Alas, for my anxiety in the world, alas for my distress,
O Healer (of souls) the heart feeds upon its desire,
The striving after union with Thee has healed my soul,
O my Joy and my Life abidingly,
Thou wast the source of my life and from Thee also came
    my ecstasy.
I have separated myself from all created beings,
My hope is for union with Thee, for that is the goal of my desire.

RABI'A THE MYSTIC

from The Golden Fountain

IT cannot possibly be said, that in ecstasy we see God: it is a question of 'knowing' Him through the higher part of the soul in lesser or in deeper degrees [. . . finding God is] encounter with the Supreme Spirit. It is life at its perfection point – a stupendous felicity, and that repose in bliss for which all souls secretly long. It is the meeting of the Wisher and the Wished; of Desire with the Desired. And yet being unthinkable fulfilment it is above all, or any wishes, and beyond desire [. . .] In this Spirit-life we meet the ideas of God uncrystallized into any form. They penetrate the soul. She flashes to them, she becomes them, she reaches unimaginable heights of bliss [. . .] God is life itself to us – the air, the bread, and the blood of the soul. No one can live without, at every moment, drawing upon Him, however unconscious they may be that they are.

ANONYMOUS

from The Interior Castle

THE spiritual espousal is different, for this is often dissolved, and so also is union; for though 'union' is the joining of two things into one, they may at last be divided, and may subsist apart. We generally see that this favour of our Lord quickly passes away, and the soul afterwards does not enjoy that company, that is, so as to know it. But in that other favour of our Lord this is not the case, for the soul always remains with her God in that centre.

Let us suppose 'union' to be like two *tapers*, so exactly joined together, that the light of both makes but one; or that the wick, light, and wax, are all one and the same, but that, afterwards, one taper may be easily divided from the other, and then two distinct tapers will remain, and the wick will be distinct from the wax. But here (in the spiritual espousals) it is like water descending from heaven into a river or spring, where one is so mixed with the other, that it cannot be discovered which is the river-water, and which the rain-water. It is, also, like a small rivulet running into the sea, whose waters cannot be separated from each other; or as if there were two windows in a room, at which one great light entered; but which, though entering in divided, yet makes but one light within. This is, perhaps, that which St. Paul means, where he says: 'He who adheres to God, is one with Him,' alluding to this sublime marriage, which presupposes that God is united to the soul by union. He likewise says: 'Mihi vivere Christus est, et mori lucrum' (To me to live is Christ, and to die is gain). I think the soul may say the same here; for here the butterfly dies – of which we have spoken, and this with very great joy – because now her life is Christ. This in time is best known by the effects, for it is clearly seen, by certain secret inspirations, that it is God who gives life to the soul; and these inspirations are often so very lively, that they cannot in any way be doubted, because the soul perceives them very well, though they cannot be expressed. But the feeling is so great, that sometimes it produces certain amorous words, which, it appears, one cannot help uttering; as for example: 'O life of my life! my support which upholdest me!' together with other like expressions. From those divine breasts, wherewith it seems God continually supports the soul, streams of milk issue, which comfort all the people of the castle; for it seems our Lord wishes them to enjoy, in some manner, that abundance which the soul enjoys; and that, from this vast river, in which the little spring is swallowed up, there should, sometimes, flow a quantity of that water, in order to support those who are to serve these two spouses, in that which relates to the body. And just as if a person, who should be suddenly plunged in this water, without thinking of any such thing, could not help feeling himself wet; so, in the same manner, but with more certainty, are these operations I am speaking about discerned; because as a great quantity of water could not fall upon us, if there were no principle whence it descended; so here we clearly see, that there is one in our interior who sends forth these darts, and gives life to this life; and that there is a sun, from which proceeds that great light, which is conveyed to the powers from the interior of the soul.

She does not, as I have said, stir from this centre, nor does she lose her peace, for He Himself who gave it to the apostles, when they were assembled together, can give it to her also.

ST TERESA OF AVILA

[1576]

The Spirit lasts – but in what mode –
Below, the Body speaks,
But as the Spirit furnishes –
Apart, it never talks –
The Music in the Violin
Does not emerge alone
But Arm in Arm with Touch, yet Touch
Alone – is not a Tune –
The Spirit lurks within the Flesh

Like Tides within the Sea
That make the Water live, estranged
What would the Either be?
Does that know – now – or does it cease –
That which to this is done,
Resuming at a mutual date
With every future one?
Instinct pursues the Adamant,
Exacting this Reply –
Adversity if it may be, or
Wild Prosperity,
The Rumor's Gate was shut so tight
Before my Mind was sown,
Not even a Prognostic's Push
Could make a Dent thereon –

EMILY DICKINSON

from The One Work

THE path around the Mountain, which all who go to Bhagavan have to tread, is nine miles long. We set out at five o'clock when the sun is still very bright. Hansa goes with me. We walk for a long time without speaking, trying to shield our faces from the powerful rays with the folds of our cotton sarees. Speech is unnecessary, so intense is the communion between us. Hansa, as she walks, becomes all Beauty, and as she raises her hand to shield her eyes from the sun, the tinkle of her gold bracelets is the only sound on earth.

I begin to think about the evening before, but as I look to the Mountain on my right, thoughts fall away. I begin to feel my smallness, and at the same time, strangely, my greatness. All solutions are inadequate. I cannot as I am eliminate suffering and despair from the world, nor even solve my own problems. I am not free to think or act in the way that an arrow speeds to its target. My only concern should be to learn how to apply what I have been taught, what has at last been opened to my understanding. Has not Bhagavan said that the greatest form of service one can render the world is one's own Self-realization? 'Aim at the highest and thereby all lower aims are achieved.'

With this thought comes a flow of energy that makes my feet speed over the ground like Hermes', hardly seeming to touch it. The golden plain stretches away to the left towards a line of violet hills. We speed past the five different faces of the mountain and our path is lit by the sun and the moon. We feel no fatigue. For each of us, no landscape has ever held such beauty nor any day such joy. Four hours after we have started, exultant, laughing, we run into Ma's garden, up the steps of her house, and into the inner room where she smilingly awaits us.

There is no further going.

ANNE GAGE

from The Joy of the Snow

WE cannot understand – not yet – but we can see how the more we lose our sense of separateness in the knowledge of the one-ness of all living creatures, millions of small leaves on the one single tree of life, the more we shall lose our sense of self-importance, and so be liberated from our self-pity; a bondage so horrible that I believe it can bring us at last to a state not unlike that of Gollum, the dreadful creature Tolkien created, living alone in the dark, talking to himself, murmuring, 'My preciouss. My preciouss.'

But if that 'my preciouss' were to be the song of the leaves on the tree, each leaf delighting in all the others, there could be no love of self, no hatred and no sin, and none of the suffering that springs from sin. And since a tree has no voice but the wind, and the leaves know it, they would soon know who it was who was singing their song with them and through them, and lifting and swinging them in the dance. If we can find a little of our one-ness with all other creatures, and love for them, then I believe we are half-way towards finding God.

ELIZABETH GOUDGE

Last Lines

No coward soul is mine,
No trembler in the world's storm-troubled sphere;
I see Heaven's glories shine,
And faith shines equal, arming me from fear.

O God within my breast,
Almighty, ever-present Deity!
Life – that in me has rest
As I – undying Life – have power in Thee!

Vain are the thousand creeds
That move men's hearts: unutterably vain;
Worthless as wither'd weeds,
Or idlest froth amid the boundless main,

To waken doubt in one
Holding so fast by Thine infinity;
So surely anchor'd on
The steadfast rock of immortality

With wide-embracing love
Thy spirit animates eternal years,
Pervades and broods above,
Changes, sustains, dissolves, creates and rears.

Though earth and man were gone,
And suns and universes cease to be,
And Thou were left alone,
Every existence would exist in Thee.

There is not room for Death
Nor atom that his might could render void:
Thou – Thou art Being and Breath,
And what Thou art may never be destroyed.

EMILY BRONTË

from Journey within the Crystal

THEN, the beautiful Laura spoke to me in this manner:

'You are aware that there are in each of us who lives on earth two manifestations which are really very distinct, although they may be confused in the concept of our earthly life. If we believe our restricted senses and our incomplete appreciation, we have only one soul, or to speak as Walter does, a certain animism destined to be extinguished with the functions of our organs. If, on the contrary, we rise above the sphere of the positive and the palatable, an invincible, nameless, and mysterious sense tells us that our *self* is not only in our organs, but it is linked in an indissoluble manner to universal life, and that it must survive intact at the time of what we call death.

'What I am calling to your attention here is not new: under all religious or metaphysical forms, men always have believed and always will believe in the persistence of the *self*. But my idea, as I speak to you in the region of the ideal, is that this immortal *self* is only partially contained in visible man. Visible man is only an emanation of invisible man, and the true unity of the soul, the real, enduring, and divine face of the latter, remains hidden from him.

'Where is this flower, this essence of the eternal spirit, and what does it do while the soul of the body goes through its painful and austere daily existence? It is somewhere in time and in space, since space and time are the conditions of all life. In time, if it has preceded human life and if it must survive, it accompanies and directs it up to a certain point, but, it is not dominated by it and does not number its days and its hours by the same instrument.

In space, it is also certainly in a possible and frequent relationship with the human *self*; but it is not the slave of it, and its expansion floats in a sphere the limits of which man does not know. Have you understood me?'

'I think so,' I replied to her, 'and in order to summarize your revelation in a more common fashion, I would say that we have two souls: one which lives within us and does not leave us, the other which lives outside of us and is unfamiliar to us. The first one lives in us transitorily and dies apparently with us; the second one lives in us eternally and is continually renewed in us, or rather it is that which renews us, and which provides, without ever exhausting itself, for every series of our successive existences.'

GEORGE SAND

from The Interior Castle

IT is as if a raindrop fell from heaven into a stream or fountain and became one with the water in it so that never again can the raindrop be separated from the water of the stream; or as if a little brook ran into the sea and there was thenceforward no means of distinguishing its water from the ocean; or as if a brilliant light came into a room through two windows and though it comes in divided between them, it forms a single light inside.

ST TERESA OF AVILA

Moon-faced, my Saqi carries,
Two ruby-shaded chalices of wine in hand;
From His lips two kisses I steal,
From His palm two flasks.

O, my inner state and my Beloved
Are as one soul cast into two bodies.

How fantastic this fleshly difference,
One individual called by two names!

Your tresses, hanging from either side,
Share the bird of my heart.
How hard it is to accept
A single prey caught in two snares!

I have come here to discourse on Love:
Myself, a soldier, and a Mulla
Yet how can I respond to them?
One of us is well-done, while two are half-baked.

LADY SAKINA SHIRAZ

from Birth and Evolution of the Soul

BUT that he may achieve immortality. Immortal in the essence of
the Soul? Yes; but not in its developed self-conscious intelligence.
For intelligence has to be worked out and built up by slow
degrees; intelligence has to be evolved by this spark, working
through the matter into which it has come, and unless it works
successfully, acquires experience slowly, and gradually builds it
up into faculty in the course of that pilgrimage of the Soul that
lies in front of our thought, immortality will not be achieved.
For it is necessary, in order that immortality may be achieved,
that this which is to acquire experience and build up accumulated
experiences shall regain unity. That which is compounded does
not last; that which is compounded will be at some time disinte-
grated: only the unit persists. The individual begins at this point,
and he is a compound. He will weave into his own existence all
these endless experiences, and will become, so to speak, more
and more compound, a more and more complex combination.
But this has in itself the seed of destruction; everything that thus
goes on combining has in it the conditions of disintegration, and
the compound disintegrates. How then can this compound

achieve immortality? By a process of unification that will form the last stages of its pilgrimage; by that Yoga, or union, which will make it again the One. Having achieved individuality by many, many incarnations, through which this individuality will be built up, it then unifies all these experiences, and by a subtle alchemy extracts as it were a unit experience out of the multiplicity, and in a way beyond words – beyond words because it is beyond brain-experience and thought, but which is not beyond the 'sensing' of some who have at least begun the process – this individual evolves into a unity higher than its own combined nature; and while it may be said to lose individuality as we know it, it gains something which is far greater. Without losing the essence of individuality, it re-becomes a unit consciousness, and by that becomes incapable of disintegration and achieves its final immortality. But here is the beginning point – and on that I want to lay a good deal of stress – that it begins then, that before that the Ego which is now in each of you was not in existence as Ego, any more than the plant which will develop from a germ, if the germ be fertilised, is in existence before that fertilisation takes place. True, that which will form it exists, because there is no increase either of energy or of matter; but the combination which makes the new individual does not exist until the junction has taken place, and the Ego does not exist before this union has taken place.

ANNIE BESANT

A Letter to her Husband, absent upon Publick employment

My head, my heart, mine eyes, my life, nay more,
My joy, my magazine of earthly store,
If two be one, as surely thou and I,
How stayest thou there, whilst I at Ipswich lie?
So many steps, head from the heart to sever;
If but a neck, soon should we be together:
I, like the earth this season, mourn in black,

My sun is gone so far in's zodiac,
When whilst I 'joyed, nor storms, nor frosts I felt,
His warmth such frigid colds did cause to melt.
My chilled limbs now numbed lie forlorn;
Return, return sweet Sol from Capricorn;
In this dead time, alas, what can I more
Than view those fruits which through thy heat I bore?
Which sweet contentment yield me for a space,
True living pictures of their father's face.
O strange effect! now thou art southward gone,
I weary grow, the tedious day so long;
But when thou northward to me shalt return,
I wish my sun may never set, but burn
Within the Cancer of my glowing breast,
The welcome house of him my dearest guest.
Where ever, ever stay, and go not thence,
Till nature's sad decree shall call thee hence;
Flesh of thy flesh, bone of thy bone,
I here, thou there, yet both but one.

ANNE BRADSTREET

from Chasm of Fire

HE went inside and I remained alone in the garden. A yellow sunset dramatically lit the sky; everything around was glowing with gold . . . Oh, to merge in all this wonderful gold, the colour of joy! Disappear in it for ever, to forget, not to think, not to doubt, not to suffer any more! The western sky . . . liquid azure and aquamarine between the delicate feathers of shining gold, shimmering through the foliage. A feeling of magic as in dimly-remembered dreams . . . The air was so pure, the earth so fragrant. All the objects around – the trees, the leaves, the stones, the whole town, seemed to breathe.

Suddenly, crystal-clear, a thought floated into my mind: a belief which is taken up can be given up; after all, you were not born with this idea of karma. You accepted it; what is accepted can be rejected. This is the way the mind is made . . .

Well, I thought; that's that. And went home.

Put up my *charpoy* [rope bed] in the courtyard and lay on my back looking at the sky.

Then it happened. It was as if something snapped inside my head, and the whole of me was streaming out ceaselessly, without diminishing, on and on. There was no 'me' – just flowing. Just being. A feeling of unending expansion, just streaming forth . . . But all this I knew only later, when I tried to remember it. When I first came back, the first clear, physical sensation was of intense cold.

It was shattering. But what was it? Was it prayer? Not in the ordinary sense. For a prayer there must be somebody to pray. But I was not. I did not exist.

IRINA TWEEDIE

'. . . That Passeth all Understanding'

An awe so quiet
I don't know when it began.

A gratitude
had begun
to sing in me.

Was there
some moment
dividing
song from no song?

When does dewfall begin?

When does night
fold its arms over our hearts
to cherish them?

When is daybreak?

DENISE LEVERTOV

from The Rose-Garden Game

THE appetite for the symbolic is never satiated. Whether this implies the existence of a supernatural reality, or not, is not a matter one can argue about. If one at least admits supernatural reality – or whatever one may call it – as a hypothesis, one may more easily consider why it is that purely aesthetic symbolism and ritual can increase the hunger for the numinous to a point where it becomes raging. The reason appears to lie in the difference between the candles lighted on the dinner-table and the candles lighted on the altar. The difference is none the less real because either may provoke, from someone lacking all sacramental sense, or rather, fiercely suppressing it, the question: 'What are all the pretty candles for?' Either set of candles can, of course, be beautifully justified as being no damned use to anyone. But that is not quite the point. The one symbol is undefined, non-committal, and the other refers explicitly to the pattern of man's condition, which is grounded in the desire and pursuit of the whole. Regardless of one's 'believing in God' or otherwise, symbols are more satisfying the more explicitly they refer to the ultimate, to the whole.

We cast around for some means of crystallising ourselves inwardly, of becoming more of one piece with everything. Each of us says: *ut unum sim*. Such techniques as the various Far-Eastern methods of attaining spiritual enlightenment are, even now, not readily available to most people in Europe, nor, for that matter, is depth-psychological analysis, and these undertakings, some of which (one gathers) have their dangers, cannot be pursued at home, at work, anywhere and at any time. But there is no reason why anyone should not play with the rosary instead of, or as well as, with mandalas. For the rosary is not only a tool for cultivating the interior garden in terms of specific doctrine. It is also a mysterious toy and a kind of nursery-rhyme, a singing-game, just as liturgy (as a distinguished modern theological writer has elaborated) is also play. And it has a full load of symbolism. If the word 'load' is reminiscent of electric cables and a supply of domestic current, so much the better. Anyone can find at least some of the switches even in a strange house in the dark, and turn on some light, even if no one can explain – least of all when he receives a shock – what electricity 'is'.

EITHNE WILKINS

from Chasm of Fire

MEMORIES come crowding in. Unexpectedly I hear his voice again, remember his kindness.

I recalled particularly, on a day of trembling luminosity, of sparkling transparency, that he was already seated outside when an Indian village woman came to him.

She was small, very thin, her face wrinkled and shrunken, as if dried up by the merciless sun and the hot winds of the plains.

She was telling an endless, sorrowful litany of her troubles. Illnesses, misery, the death of her husband and most of her children. Now she was alone, useless, nobody needed her, she had nothing to hope for, nothing to live for . . .

And she came out with the question which seemed to burn, scorching her trembling lips:

'Maharaj, why did God create this world so full of troubles? Why did He create me to endure all these sufferings?'

I saw him lean forward, a shimmering light in his eyes, the light of compassion I knew and loved so well. His voice was soft when he answered:

'Why has He created the world? That you should be in it! Why has He created you? He is alone; He needs you!'

Never will I forget the broad, blissful smile on that lined emaciated face when she was walking away. She went happy in the knowledge that she was not alone, not really, for God needed her to keep Him company because He too was alone . . .

Never will I forget the love that I felt then. Only a very Great Soul could have expressed so simply and convincingly one of the greatest Mysteries to a naive, childlike village woman. The Ultimate Metaphysical Truth; that He who is Alone and Perfect, in order to realize His Perfection, created the Universe . . .

Mid-November
Since I have been here in Kausani, from the beginning when the states of consciousness began to change considerably, I felt that I was nearing the end of the road. I mean the end of the road to the Real Home. There is nothing else to do. He takes over. When the devotee becomes His, everything ends there. Yes, I am only at the beginning of this state; there will be many ups and downs. But this is really the beginning of the end. This feeling of belonging to Him, every breath, every pore of the body, every thought, every little cell – it is wonderful! There is such security in it, such tenderness; and yet it is Nothingness itself. Like a perfume rising from the innermost sweetness is this still joy . . .

December
The Realization that every act, every word, every thought of ours not only influences our environment but mysteriously forms an integral part of the Universe, fits into it as if by necessity, in the very moment we do or say or think it, is an overwhelming and even shattering experience.

If we only knew deeply, absolutely, that our smallest act, our smallest thought, has such far-reaching effects; setting forces in motion; reaching out to the galaxy; how carefully we would act and speak and think. How precious life would become in its integral oneness.

It is wonderful and frightening. The responsibility is terrifying and fascinating in its depth and completeness, containing as it does the perplexing insecurity of being unique and the profound consolation of forming part of the Eternal Undivided Whole. And we all have the right to, and can achieve, the realization of this wonderful meaning of life; one is *quite simply* part of it all; a single vision of Wholeness.

Very acute it became after Guruji's passing away. And I could not reconcile the torment of the heat, the mangy dogs, the filthy children, the sweat, the smells; for they were THAT too . . .

But it was here, in the stillness of the mountains, that it gradually crystallized; distilled itself from a different dimension into the waking consciousness. And now I must live with the Glory and the Terror of it . . . It is merciless, inescapable; an intensely virile, intoxicating Presence, so utterly joyous, boundless and free. It is blasphemy to attempt to put it into words.

I know that the states of Nearness will increase, will become more permanent; but also the state of separation will become more painful, more lonely, the nearer one comes to Reality.

I know that I go back to a life of fire; for you, dear Guruji, told me what to expect. I know that sometimes my health will fail, and that I shall be burned. But I know also that I can never be alone any more, for you are with me always. I know that God is Silence, and can be reached only in silence; the Nearness to Thee will remain and give me the strength to go on.

Goodbye days of peace; and days of wrestling with myself. Days of incredible beauty with Nature at its best; days of glorious states of consciousness, wherein the divine heart within myself was the Divine Heart within the cosmos. When I knew the meaning of Oneness because I lived it. You did not deceive me, Guruji. You pointed out the Way, and now the Way has taken hold of me . . . fully . . . irrevocably.

IRINA TWEEDIE

from The Color Purple

I BELIEVE God is everything . . . Everything that is or ever was or ever will be. And when you can feel that, and be happy to feel that, you've found It . . . My first step from the old white man was trees. Then air. Then birds. Then other people. But one day when I was sitting quiet and feeling like a motherless child, which I was, it come to me: that feeling of being part of everything, not separate at all. I knew that if I cut a tree, my arm would bleed. And I laughed and I cried and I run all round the house. I knew just what it was. In fact, when it happen, you can't miss it.

ALICE WALKER

Fire

a woman can't survive
by her own breath alone
she must know
the voices of mountains
she must recognize
the foreverness of blue sky
she must flow
with the elusive
bodies
of night wind women
who will take her into
her own self
look at me
i am not a separate woman
i am a continuance
of blue sky
i am the throat
of the sandia mountains
a night wind woman

who burns
with every breath
she takes

JOY HARJO

Song of the Earth at the Century's End

Melodies thread upwards
Through the stars
Stairways climbed by grief
With a touch so light
That joy cries to the traveller
'This is your home!'
And the black sun
Rolls in the dust
In a cartwheel of light.

The cohort rain drove all before it
And fell like lead amid the corn,
Trampling the land.
The bodies of men were sloughed off.

Or else,
Or else, the blue mountain
Must be hewn
From a lake of glass
By giant hands, centuries old,
Its huge heart beating light.

The forests now are bristling
The day is dark as night.
The strange fields are livid
With the light of revelation.
Steam rises from the river.

A ribbon of smoke
Twists through the violet wood.
Sky meets sky
Without a sound
In an embrace of light
Before the gracious appearance
Of the star.

The apple trees of the Caucasus
Flare from a red furrow.
The fruit is given to the knife.
Lift out the seed of light:
Stone lids, stone eyes
And a star at the core,
Arms eternally outstretched,
Embedded in this disc.

O lantern Earth, swing
Through the firmament of night.

FRANCES HOWARTH

from Initiations and Initiates in Tibet

NO 'rapture' awaits the sober thinker in his hermitage, his hut or cave, amid the immensity of Tibetan solitudes. Ecstasy, however, will be his for him to plunge himself therein. What will keep him in a state of attentive immobility day after day, month after month, and year after year, will be the contemplation of the working of his thought in self-analysis, effacing its own functionings according as they are discovered to be untrue, until the time comes when reasoning ceases because it has been replaced by direct perception.

Then, the storms raised by thought-creating theories and speculations having calmed down, the ocean of the mind becomes

tranquil and smooth, without a single ripple disturbing its surface. In this faultlessly smooth mirror things are reflected without
their image becoming distorted – and this is the starting-point of
a series of states which comprise neither ordinary consciousness
nor unconsciousness. This is the entrance into a sphere different
from that in which we habitually move; hence, after making a certain number of reservations as to the meaning of the term, we
may speak of Tibetan 'mysticism'.

ALEXANDRA DAVID-NEEL

The lover whose lust
And longing and leisure
Are rooted in trust,
Is lucky beyond measure.

PERNETTE DU GUILLET

from Experiences Facing Death

IN my search for the technique of the subjective approach to that
Immaterial Reality, intimations of which have always haunted
the soul of man, I had to conclude that Jesus could not be studied as an average man, nor as an intellectual. He was a genius; a
genius whose field was spiritual subjectivity; he was perhaps the
greatest spiritual genius who ever lived. It is characteristic of
geniuses that they arrive at their goal by methods that are so far
submerged in the deep-self that they are difficult to describe,
almost impossible to communicate. Jesus arrived at the high spiritual state described as 'union with God' – he called it 'abiding in
the Father' – as directly, as securely as the musical genius arrives
at absolute pitch. He struck into his own spiritual way as easily as
a man with an ear for music strikes into a tune. And like all
geniuses, he had difficulty often in getting past the lack of such
genius in his hearers. He would say to them, 'I have more to tell

you, but you cannot bear it now.' There is reason to believe that in John, the beloved disciple, he found a more receptive aptitude, which gives to the Gospel of St. John its special value of the supposedly more intimate revelation. But in fact, the rest of his disciples were ordinary men who, if they could not plunge into the absolute pitch of their teacher's spiritual song, could presumably sing as taught, and devoutly wished to be so taught.

Jesus believed in the power of prayer. But aside from the note of his own practise in going apart 'on a mountain' to pray, and his explicit use of affirmation as a mode of prayer, and his denial of the pertinence of inordinate public petition he left very little by way of personal technique. In the only formalized prayer model which he left the psychological progressions are:

Acknowledgment	Our Father . . . in Heaven
Worship	Hallowed be Thy Name
Affirmation	Thy Kingdom come
Petition	Give us this day . . . bread
Reaffirmation	Thine be the Power
Affirmation of everlastingness	For ever and ever . . .
Affirmation of decision	Amen

This firm commitment of the intuitive and intellectual judgments to the content of the prayer is an important item in practically all formal prayer . . . Amen . . . Waiting happily upon fulfilment . . . May I be placed in a state of perfect Buddhahood . . .

Probably the manner of Jesus' own death, tortured and violent, prevented a public approach such as would have served as an example. Allowing the utmost to tradition, he expected for the repentant thief a release at once swift and secure, and saying *Father into Thy hands* . . . gave up the ghost. It was as easy as that for him at the last, therefore requiring no particular technique. But such a passage predicated a whole life spent in that state of consciousness which he called 'abiding in the Father.' The mystics among his later followers were so much at a loss for a technique which would enable them to maintain that state, that the chief objective of Medieval Christianity was to work it out with immense and heroic pains and much stumbling. More than half the ritual of the Church of Rome is the crystallized residue of that search.

The disciples of Jesus, besides being ordinary men, were Jews. There is no traditional mystical lore among the Jews except for those states which are emotionally induced. Something could be attained by going through agonies of depression – usually brought on by objective difficulties – repentance and abasement, followed by reactions of relief, recovered confidence and reversion to the evidence of history; but that was not much. To this day it is difficult to make a Jew understand that mysticism is of the subjective self rather than of the emotions. He leans to the belief that mystical revelation when rationalized is, by that process, caused to disappear out of existence. It is true St. Paul had intuitive flashes: that one about faith as the evidence of things not seen, and his notion of a 'spiritual body' which seems to have been something like the 'astral body' of the Orient, or the 'animal soul' of Aristotle. He realized a meaning in the death of Jesus deeper than the fact, but he saw no deeper actually than the Jewish tradition of sacrifice.

All of which explains why the early Christian world was obliged to bolster up its own situation with spiritual practise salvaged from discarded 'beliefs' of its pagan past. It was a *belief* that Christianity maintained itself; its practise was eclectic.

This was the discovery that turned my study from the historic Jesus to the experienceable paganism that I knew.

MARY AUSTIN

Remember

Remember me when I am gone away,
   Gone far away into the silent land;
   When you can no more hold me by the hand,
Nor I half turn to go yet turning stay.
Remember me when no more day by day
   You tell me of our future that you planned:

Only remember me; you understand
It will be late then to counsel or to pray.
Yet if you should forget me for a while
   And afterwards remember, do not grieve:
   For if the darkness and corruption leave
   A vestige of the thoughts that once I had,
Better by far you should forget and smile
   Than that you should remember and be sad.

CHRISTINA ROSSETTI

from Smile at Time

IT was lovely, – the crystal clarity of air, the silent spaces, the pallid grass and the shining loops of the burns winding away like glittering threads that one looked down upon from the tops of hills. We ate our sandwiches sitting by one of those hurrying little brooks, all limpid swirls, and smooth flowing with the gravelly bottom glassy clear. And such place-names! I made a list of names culled from this part of the world which seem to me as memorable as 'Wuthering Heights.' Bloody Bush Edge, Heathery Tops, Windy Walls, Blow Weary, Foulmire Heights; aren't they wonderful? – and all have a sombre northern sound.

Yes; it was another lovely day to add to life's rich pattern. 'How to find life lovely, or even worthwhile,' you ask me, and I reply,

> 'I know not what my secret is,
> I know but – it is mine.'

But since you ask me I suppose I must try, as I have before, to say what I feel about it. Don't you ever have the conviction that the true nature of Reality is very different and something far more substantially real than this impermanent attenuated version of it we see around us here? This, after all, is based on invisible things; some might say spiritual things. I wonder why we have allowed ourselves to be jockeyed into thinking spiritual reality is something thin, formless, vague? It seems to me that those who know, who have had experience of it (however momentarily), – the Dantes, the Bunyans, the St. Theresas, the A.Es and Blakes of this world, – those who have glimpsed one or other of the many mansions, report them as something very different, in their living strength, beauty and wholeness, – nature perfected, and shining inhabitants.

That being so, one has a different ground to one's thoughts; things are not lost for ever but only lost here, which robs sadness of much of its sting. I don't mean that I can always feel this, but I hope to: even as it is, faith is my waking life, and unbelief a darkening, a form of lifelessness of the mind. Experiences here are for me promises, hints of a greater perfection elsewhere, but that carries with it the energising (and frightening) thought that to deserve it one must grow in perfection too.

Anyhow, whichever way I take life the sense of wonder remains. It is so surprising in its twists and turns. These letters to you, for instance, – surprising, don't you think, as a result of a chance meeting?

It is time for sleep; for a few minutes longer I will hang out of the window and watch for the far lights flashing, and then turn from the mysterious spaces to the smallness, the cosiness, of the room. You can turn that into an allegory if you want to; I'm too sleepy.

CONSTANCE SITWELL

Music stirs me, for you
Sea and
Cloud
Mountain and Star
touch me for you.
Alien things only turn
the whole prayer of my heart
to you
All noble paintings
wake the dream of you
All singing lines
lead home to your memory –
Beauty is everywhere kin.

RICARDA HUCH

from The Flowing Light of the Godhead

Now my sorrow and Thine
Have rested in peace together
Now is our love made whole . . .
Risen from the dead
Thou comest in to me,
Comfort me, O my Beloved
And hold me in Thy Presence
In continual joy . . .
In all ways I must die for love
That is all my desire.
Give me and take from me
What thou wilt, but leave me this,
In loving, to die of love!

MECHTILD OF MAGDEBURG

O my joy, my longing,
O my sanctuary, my companion,
O provision of my way
O my ultimate aim!
You are my spirit;
You are my hope;
You are my friend,
My yearning, my welfare.
Without you, O my life and love,
Never across these endless countries
Would I have wandered.
How much grace, how many gifts,
Favors and bounty have you shown me
Your love I seek; in it I am blessed,
O radiant eye of my yearning heart!
You are my heart's captain!
As long as I live, never from You
Shall I be free. Be satisfied with me,
O my heart's desire, and I am fortunate, blessed.

RABI'A THE MYSTIC

Umai

THE first people were the Wogè. The world was the same in
Wogè times as it is today; it has always been the same. And
Umai, who was one of the Wogè, was much as our girls are now,
that is to say, she was young and beautiful. But she was lonely and
restless, too.

Umai's home was on the far edge of the earth by Upriver
Ocean where the river begins. She liked to stand on the river
bank and look out across the world. She could see down the full
length of the river, from one side of the world to the other, and
across Downriver Ocean to where the sun sets. She liked to wait
on clear evenings for the little silver flash that follows the setting of the sun, making a brief crescent of light no thicker than

the crescent of a fingernail along the horizon line. When darkness settled over the earth, Umai turned away from the river and went inside her house. She thought about the crescent of light, wondering what it was, and she thought she would like to go all the way down the river if only she could find some way to do it.

She searched here and there in her house until she found an old toy dugout canoe, no longer than her foot, no wider than her hand. She took it to the river and dipped it into the water. Then she patted its sides lightly and put a hand in and stretched the little canoe until it was two hands wide. She patted it front and back and put her foot into it and stretched it until it was long enough for both of her feet, one ahead of the other. She continued to pat the canoe and to sing to it and to stretch it a little at a time, until at last it was large enough for her to sit in.

At first dawn, Umai settled herself in her canoe and pushed off from the bank. Only then did she remember about a paddle. Having none, she held on to the sides of the canoe and swayed gently back and forth, and after a moment the canoe started down the river. In smooth water, she repeated the swaying, rocking motion. When she came to rough water or to riffles or rapids or falls, she sat still, and the canoe went safely over or around them without help from her.

She passed the Centre of the World. Here, the big tributaries join the river, and the water becomes much deeper and swifter. Umai went faster and faster so that soon she was all the way downstream and at the river's mouth where it empties into Downriver Ocean.

The surf, rough and forbidding, was breaking over the rocks along the shore. But Umai looked past the breakers, out across the blue ocean and she saw where the rim of the sky meets the water. And she thought she would like to ride on the ocean, too. So she sat and counted eleven waves. As the twelfth – always the smallest wave – rolled in to shore, Umai patted the sides of her canoe and sang a song to it and swayed forward and back. The canoe rode the twelfth wave out, carrying her safely on to the open ocean. During the rest of the day she went on and on across it and farther and farther away from the earth.

The sun was low in the sky when Umai came at last to the very edge of the world. She sat in her canoe alongside the world's edge, watching quietly. She saw that the sky does not rest solidly on the ocean, but that it lifts and dips and lifts and dips in an even rhythm, except that the twelfth is a slower, gentler rise and fall. And she saw that it is this dipping sky that causes the waves in Downriver Ocean which forever beat against the shores of the earth.

The sun went down behind the edge of the world and was followed by the familiar silver flash. But from so much closer up, Umai saw that it was not at all a narrow crescent but a waving, moving something with a centre of living brightness.

Umai thought: her boat had taken her easily past the pounding surf and across the great ocean – might it not carry her out beyond the world as far as this brightness?

She patted her canoe and sang to it again while she counted eleven liftings and dippings of the sky. At the beginning of the twelfth and slower rise, Umai held tightly to the sides of the boat with both hands and rocked forward. The canoe went, straight and swift, through the gap. When the rim of the sky dipped again to the water, she was already some distance away in the Ocean-Outside-the-World.

Far away in the ocean which encircles the world, water gives way to pitch, and beyond the ocean of pitch, there is nothing at all. But where Umai went under the sky, she had only to cross a narrow stretch of water to find herself coming near the shore of the Land-Beyond-the-World.

On the shore of this land, a young girl stood waving to her – Laksis, Shining One, she was. And Umai saw that the silver brightness that follows the setting sun is Laksis waving from this far shore. She waved till Umai's canoe scraped bottom; then she helped her beach her canoe and welcomed her to her home and to the Land-Beyond-the World.

Laksis was young like Umai and she too was lonely. Neither of them had had a friend before they found each other. They walked together over the barren and empty land and talked together as young girls talk. Umai told Laksis how from her home on Upriver Ocean she watched each night at sundown for the silver crescent behind the dipping sky. And Laksis told Umai how she came to the shore of her land each night at sundown to wave to the distant earth.

When it was time for Umai to go home, they said goodbye as friends do who will see each other again before the day is done. Together they counted eleven liftings of the sky. At the beginning of the twelfth, Laksis launched the canoe with a strong push which sent Umai back into the world under the lifted rim.

The trip home seemed very short to Umai because she was busy and happy with her thoughts. She saw that from the far side of the ocean, the earth itself looks no wider than the shore of Laksis' home. She came close to her own shore and recognized its rocks and the wide mouth of the river. It was good to see these familiar things again. Without trouble, swaying gently and singing a little, she rode a low wave through the surf and went on up the river; past its falls and rapids and riffles and into its quiet water; on to its source and her own home.

Umai belongs up where the river begins; she is known as Upriver Ocean Girl. She made no more trips in her canoe, and it shrank until it was a toy again, and Umai stored it carefully in her house. But each evening at sundown, she goes to the riverbank and she and Laksis face each other across the width of the world, and Laksis, Shining One, signals to her friend from behind the moving sky. You may see her for yourself after the sun has set – a silver streak where the sky meets the ocean, seeming no wider than the crescent of one of your fingernails.

When you are going out on the river or the ocean, it is well to sing to Umai, up there by Upriver Ocean. Put your hands on the sides of your canoe and pat it as you sing:

> *Umai!*
> *You rode the rapids.*

> *You crossed the Ocean.*
> *Lend me your canoe –*
> *This is your canoe!*
> *Now I too*
> *Shall have no trouble*
> *From the River.*
> *No trouble*
> *From the Ocean.*
> *Thank you, Umai!*

You will then go safely anywhere: on the river or through the surf or out on the ocean; to the edge of the world if you want to. It will take you longer than it took Umai: many days instead of one. And you will need a paddle, for these are not the ancient Wogè times and you are not a Wogè. But you will go safely and you will come home safely: if you have followed the customs and the rules; and your heart is pure.

from *The Inland Whale*, ed. THEODORA KROEBER

To My Dear and Loving Husband

If ever two were one, then surely we.
If ever man were lov'd by wife, then thee;
If ever wife was happy in a man,
Compare with me ye women if you can.
I prize thy love more than whole Mines of gold,
Or all the riches that the East doth hold.
My love is such that Rivers cannot quench,
Nor ought but love from thee give recompence.
Thy love is such I can no way repay,
The heavens reward thee manifold I pray.
Then while we live, in love lets so persever,
That when we live no more, we may live ever.

ANNE BRADSTREET

from Revelations of Divine Love

WOULDST thou witten thy Lord's meaning in this thing? Learn it well: love was his meaning. Who shewed it thee? Love. What shewed he thee? Love. Wherefore shewed it he? For love. Hold thee therein, and thou shalt learn and know more in the same. But thou shalt never know nor learn therein other thing without end. Thus was I learned that love was our Lord's meaning. And I saw full surely that ere God made us he loved us; which love was never slacked nor ever shall be. And in this love he hath done all his works; and in this love he hath made all things profitable to us; and in this love our life is everlasting. In our making we had beginning; but the love wherein he made us was in him from without beginning: in which love we have our beginning. And all this shall we see in God, without end.

JULIAN OF NORWICH

XXIX

I think of thee! – my thoughts do twine and bud
About thee, as wild vines, about a tree,
Put out broad leaves, and soon there's nought to see
Except the straggling green which hides the wood.
Yet, O my palm-tree, be it understood
I will not have my thoughts instead of thee
Who art dearer, better! Rather, instantly
Renew thy presence; as a strong tree should,
Rustle thy boughs and set thy trunk all bare,
And let those bands of greenery which insphere thee
Drop heavily down, – burst, shattered, everywhere!
Because, in this deep joy to see and hear thee
And breathe within thy shadow a new air,
I do not think of thee – I am too near thee.

ELIZABETH BARRETT BROWNING

from The Story of a Soul

I STREW flowers. Not one shall I find without scattering its petals before Thee . . . and I will sing . . . I will sing always, even if my roses must be gathered from amidst thorns; and the longer and sharper the thorns, the sweeter shall be my song.

But of what avail to thee, my Jesus, are my flowers and my songs? I know it well: this fragrant shower, these delicate petals of little price, these songs of love from a poor little heart like mine, will nevertheless be pleasing unto Thee. Trifles they are, but Thou wilt smile on them. The Church Triumphant, stooping towards her child, will gather up these scattered rose leaves, and, placing them in Thy Divine Hands, there to acquire an infinite value, will shower them on the Church Suffering to extinguish its flames, and on the Church Militant to obtain its victory.

O my Jesus, I love Thee! I love my Mother, the Church; I bear in mind that 'the least act of pure love is of more value to her than all other works together.'

But is this pure love really in my heart? Are not my boundless desires but dreams – but foolishness? If this be so, I beseech Thee to enlighten me; Thou knowest I seek but the truth. If my desires be rash, then deliver me from them, and from this most grievous of all martyrdoms. And yet I confess, if I reach not those heights to which my soul aspires, this very martyrdom, this foolishness, will have been sweeter to me than eternal bliss will be, unless by a miracle Thou shouldst take from me all memory of the hopes I entertained upon earth. Jesus, Jesus! if the mere desire of Thy Love awakens such delight, what will it be to possess it, to enjoy it for ever?

How can a soul so imperfect as mine aspire to the plentitude of Love? What is the key of this mystery? O my only Friend, why dost Thou not reserve these infinite longings to lofty souls, to the eagles that soar in the heights? Alas! I am but a poor little unfledged bird. I am not an eagle, I have but the eagle's eyes and heart! Yet, notwithstanding my exceeding littleness, I dare to gaze upon the Divine Sun of Love, and I burn to dart upwards unto Him! I would fly, I would imitate the eagles; but all that I can do is to lift up my little wings – it is beyond my feeble power to soar. What is to become of me? Must I die of sorrow because of my helplessness? Oh, no! I will not even grieve. With daring self-abandonment there will I remain until death, my gaze fixed upon that Divine Sun. Nothing shall affright me, nor wind nor rain. And should impenetrable clouds conceal the Orb of Love, and should I seem to believe that beyond this life there is darkness only, that would be the hour of perfect joy, the hour in which to push my confidence to its uttermost bounds. I should not dare to detach my gaze, well knowing that beyond the dark clouds the sweet Sun still shines.

So far, O my God, I understand Thy Love for me. But Thou knowest how often I forget this, my only care. I stray from Thy side, and my scarcely fledged wings become draggled in the muddy pools of earth; then I lament *'like a young swallow,'* and my lament tells Thee all, and I remember, O Infinite Mercy! that *'Thou didst not come to call the just, but sinners.'*

Yet shouldst Thou still be deaf to the plaintive cries of Thy feeble creature, shouldst Thou still be veiled, then I am content to remain benumbed with cold, my wings bedraggled, and once more I rejoice in this well-deserved suffering.

O Sun, my only Love, I am happy to feel myself so small, so frail in Thy sunshine, and I am in peace . . . I know that all the eagles of Thy Celestial Court have pity on me, they guard and defend me, they put to flight the vultures – the demons that fain would devour me.

St Teresa of Lisieux

from Smile at Time

How exquisite the country looked in that crystalline noonday! Far up upon the hillsides little birch trees stood in groups with a nimbus of light around them, delicate and lovely; the flocks of mountain-sheep scattered over the swelling shoulders of green looked like pearls; the grey rocks glistened, and in the distance the shining little burns could be seen threading down from the high ground; no wandering breeze ruffled the air. Silence and stillness sometimes appear to halt the hours and in this timeless moment – this moment which belonged to us, – I seemed to be walking with him again, 'innocent frequenters of beauty', in Plotinus' phrase – the essence of our friendship in flower, the essence of its meaning captured, and finally shut away in the chambers of memory to be renewed in some other form in some other state. There are such strange levels of life just out of reach; the feeling was so unstained that, as I went on my journey I felt I had been bathed in peace and yet the scene was the homely earth I knew. Could death be something like that, changing everyday things to that degree?

But here, in this room, it grows dark, there is only the firelight left, the glow of the sunset is over; I must move, and walk through the dim rooms of the house in the fading light, 'blacking out', and drawing the curtains; perhaps to-morrow, when the past is not so insistent, I will look for that old batch of letters and live again that year.

CONSTANCE SITWELL

THE only instance in Egyptian annals of the personal description of a woman given by herself is in the case of Hatshepsut, who uses no measured terms.

'His Majesty herself put with her own hands oil of ani on all her limbs. Her fragrance was like a divine breath, her scent reached as far as the land of Punt; her skin is made of gold, it shines like the stars in the hall of festival, in the view of the whole land . . . They celebrate Kamara, in her divine doings, as she is such a great marvel. She had no equal among the gods who were before since the world was. She is living Ra eternally. He hath selected her for protecting Egypt and for rousing bravery among men . . . Horus, the avenger of her father, the first-born of his mother's husband, whom Ra has engendered to be his glorious seed upon earth and to give happiness to future generations, being his living image, the King of Upper and Lower Egypt, Kamara, the electrum (gold) of kings.

'By my life, by the love of Ra and the favour of my father Amen, . . . I bear the white crown, I am diademed with the red crown, . . . I rule over this land like the son of Isis, I am mighty like the son of Nu, . . . I shall be for ever like the star which changeth not. He gave me my royal power over Egypt and the red country, all the foreign lands are under my feet . . . all the marvels and the precious things of this land, they are presented to my palace altogether . . . (turquoise) of the land of Reshut they bring to me the choicest things from the oasis of Testesu (Dakhel), acacia, juniper, *mer*-wood . . . all the good woods of the divine land . . . Tribute is brought to me from the land of the Tahennu in ivory, seven hundred tusks . . . She lives, she is stable, she is in good health, she is joyous as well as her double on the throne of Horus of the living like the sun, for ever and ever.'

HATSHEPSUT

Passionate, with longing in my eyes,
Searching wide, and seeking nights and days,
Lo! I beheld the Truthful One, the Wise,
Here in mine own house to fill my gaze.

Just for a moment a flower grows,
Bright and brilliant on a green-clad tree
Just for a moment a cold wind blows
Through the bare thorns of a thicket free.

LALLESWĀRI OR LĀL DIDDI OF KASHMIR

from The Story of a Soul

FOR once a soul has been captivated by the odour of Your oint-
ments, she cannot run alone; by the very fact of being drawn to
You herself, she draws all the souls she loves after her. Just as a
mighty river carries with it all it meets into the ocean's depth, so,
my Jesus, a soul which plunges into the boundless ocean of Your
love bears all her treasures with her. You know what my treasures
are; they are the souls You made one with mine, treasures which
You Yourself have given me, so that I even dare to make my own
the very words You used on the last evening You spent as a
mortal traveller on earth. I do not know my Jesus, when my exile
will come to an end. Many an evening yet may find me singing
Your mercies here below, but sometime my last evening too will
come.

ST TERESA OF LISIEUX

AND Hannah prayed, and said, My heart rejoiceth in the LORD,
mine horn is exalted in the LORD: my mouth is enlarged over
mine enemies; because

1 Rejoice in thy salvation.

2 There is none holy as the LORD: for there is none beside
thee: neither is there any rock like our God.

3 Talk no more so exceeding proudly; let not arrogancy come
out of your mouth: for the LORD is a God of knowledge, and by
him actions are weighed.

4 The bows of the mighty men are broken, and they that
stumbled are girded with strength.

5 They that were full have hired out themselves for bread;
and they that were hungry ceased: so that the barren hath born
seven; and she that hath many children is waxed feeble.

6 The LORD killeth, and maketh alive: he bringeth down to the
grave, and bringeth up.

7 The LORD maketh poor, and maketh rich: he bringeth low,
and lifteth up.

8 He raiseth up the poor out of the dust, and lifteth up the beggar from the dunghill, to set them among princes, and to make them inherit the throne of glory: for the pillars of the earth are the LORD's and he hath set the world upon them.

9 He will keep the feet of his saints, and the wicked shall be silent in darkness; for by strength shall no man prevail.

10 The adversaries of the LORD shall be broken to pieces; out of heaven shall he thunder upon them: the LORD shall judge the ends of the earth; and he shall give strength unto his king, and exalt the horn of his anointed.

I SAMUEL 2:1–10

from To the Lighthouse

'YES, of course, if it's fine tomorrow,' said Mrs Ramsay. 'But you'll have to be up with the lark,' she added.

To her son these words conveyed an extraordinary joy, as if it were settled the expedition were bound to take place, and the wonder to which he had looked forward, for years and years it seemed, was, after a night's darkness and a day's sail, within touch. Since he belonged, even at the age of six, to that great clan which cannot keep this feeling separate from that, but must let future prospects, with their joys and sorrows, cloud what is actually at hand, since to such people even in earliest childhood any turn in the wheel of sensation has the power to crystallize and transfix the moment upon which its gloom or radiance rests, James Ramsay, sitting on the floor cutting out pictures from the illustrated catalogue of the Army and Navy Stores, endowed the picture of a refrigerator as his mother spoke with heavenly bliss. It was fringed with joy. The wheelbarrow, the lawn-mower, the sound of poplar trees, leaves whitening before rain, rooks cawing, brooms knocking, dresses rustling – all these were so coloured and distinguished in his mind that he had already his private code, his secret language, though he appeared the image of stark and uncompromising severity, with his high forehead and his fierce blue eyes, impeccably candid and pure, frowning slightly at the sight of human frailty, so that his mother, watching him guide his scissors neatly round the refrigerator, imagined him all red and ermine on the Bench or directing a stern and momentous enterprise in some crisis of public affairs.

'But,' said his father, stopping in front of the drawing-room window, 'it won't be fine.'

VIRGINIA WOOLF

Soul-Shrine

Thou angel of God who hast charge of me
From the fragrant Father of mercifulness,
The gentle encompassing of the Sacred Heart
To make round my soul-shrine this night,
  Oh, round my soul-shrine this night.

Ward from me every distress and danger,
Encompass my course over the ocean of truth,
I pray thee, place thy pure light before me,
O bright beauteous angel on this very night,
  Bright beauteous angel on this very night

Be Thyself the guiding star above me,
Illume Thou to me every reef and shoal,
Pilot my barque on the crest of the wave,
To the restful haven of the waveless sea,
  Oh, the restful haven of the waveless sea.

ANN MACDONALD

from The Dean's Watch

WHAT should she do . . . ?

She never knew what put it into her head that she, unloved, should love. Religion for her parents, and therefore for their children, was not much more than a formality and it had not occurred to her to pray about her problem, and yet from somewhere the idea came as though in answer to her question, and . . . she dispassionately considered it. Could mere loving be a life's work? Could it be a career like marriage or nursing the sick or going on the stage? Could it be adventure? Christians were commanded to love, it was something laid upon them that they had to do whether they liked it or not. They had to love . . . But what was love? Was there anything or anybody that she herself truly loved?

A rather shattering honesty was as much a part of her as her strong will and her humour, and the answer to this question was that she loved the cat and Blanche's bower . . . She was concerned for them both and had so identified herself with them that they seemed part of her. Making a start with the cat, was it possible to make of this concern and identification a deliberate activity that should pass out in widening circles, to her parents and the servants and the brothers and sisters and their families, to the city and its people, the Cathedral, even at last perhaps to God himself? It came to her in a flash that it must be wonderful to hold God and be held by him, as she held the cat in her arms rubbing her cheek against his soft fur, and was in turn held within the safety and quietness of the bower. Then she was shocked by the irreverence of her thought, and tried to thrust it away. But she did not quite succeed. From that day onwards it remained warm and glowing at the back of her mind.

So she took a vow to love. Millions before her had taken the same simple vow but she was different from the majority because she kept her vow, kept it even after she had discovered the cost of simplicity. Until now she had only read her Bible as a pious exercise, but now she read it as an engineer reads a blueprint and a traveller a map, unemotionally because she was not emotional, but with a profound concentration because her life depended on it. Bit by bit over a period of years, that seemed to her long, she began to get her scaffolding into place. She saw that all her powers, even those which had seemed to mitigate against love, such as her shrewdness which had always been quick to see the faults of others, her ambition and self-will, could by a change of direction be bound over in service to the one overmastering purpose. She saw that she must turn from herself, and began to see something of the discipline that that entailed, and found too as she struggled that no one and nothing by themselves seemed to have the power to entirely hold her when she turned to them.

It was then that the central figure of the gospels, a historical figure whom she deeply revered and sought to imitate, began at rare intervals to flash out at her like live lightning from their pages, frightening her, turning the grave blueprint into a dazzle of reflected fire. Gradually she learned to see that her fear was not of the lightning itself but what it showed her of the nature of love, for it dazzled behind the stark horror of Calvary. At this point, where so many vowed lovers faint and fail, Mary Montague went doggedly on over another period of years that seemed if possible longer and harder than the former period. At some point along the way, she did not know where because the change came so slowly and gradually, she realized that he had got her and got everything. His love held and illumined every human being for whom she was concerned, and whom she served with the profound compassion which was their need and right, held the Cathedral, the city, every flower and leaf and creature, giving it reality and beauty. She could not take her eyes from the incredible glory of his love. As far as it was possible for a human being in this world she had turned from herself. She could say, 'I have been turned,' and did not know how very few can speak these words with truth.

ELIZABETH GOUDGE

from Flaubert – Sand: The Correspondence

Sand to Flaubert

Nohant, 12 January 1876

Mon chéri Cruchard,

I've been meaning to write to you every day but have had absolutely no time. At last there's a space, though; we're buried in snow. I adore this kind of weather: the whiteness is like a universal purification, and indoor amusements are even more cosy and pleasant. How can anyone hate winter in the country? Snow is one of the most beautiful sights in the whole year!

It seems my sermons aren't very clear. I have that in common with the orthodox, but I'm not one of them: I have no fixed plan about either equality or authority. You seem to think I want to convert you to some doctrine or other. Not at all – I wouldn't dream of it. Everyone sees things from his own point of view, which I acknowledge should be chosen freely. I can summarize my own point of view in a few words: not to stand in front of a misted window which shows one nothing but the reflection of one's own nose. And to see as much as possible – good, evil, near, far, around, about; and to perceive how everything, tangible or intangible, constantly gravitates towards the necessity of goodness, kindness, truth and beauty.

I don't say humanity's on the way to the heights. I happen to think it is, in spite of everything, but I don't argue about it – there's no point, because everyone judges according to what he sees, and at the moment the general prospect is meagre and ugly. In any case, I don't need to be sure that the world will be saved in order to believe in the necessity of goodness and beauty. If the world departs from this law it will perish; if its citizens reject it they will be destroyed. Other planets and other souls will trample them underfoot – no matter! But for my part, I want to tend upwards till my last gasp, not because I either expect or need to find a 'haven' for myself elsewhere, but because my only pleasure is to stay with the people I love on the path that leads upward.

In other words, I shun the sewer and seek what is dry and clean, in the conviction that this is the law of my existence. Being human doesn't amount to much; we're still very close to the apes from whom we're said to descend. So be it. All the more reason to distinguish ourselves from them, and at least be worthy of the relative truth which our species has been permitted to understand: a very poor, limited, humble truth, at that! But still let us grasp it as well as we can, and not suffer it to be taken away from us.

I think you and I really agree; but I practise this simple religion and you do not, since you let yourself be got down; your heart is not convinced of it, since you curse life and wish for death like some Catholic looking for recompense, if not for eternal rest. You can't be sure, any more than anyone else, of that recompense. Life may be eternal, in which case toil is eternal too. If that's the case, let us run our course bravely. If it's otherwise and the self perishes completely, let's earn the honour of having performed our task, our duty – for we have no clear duties but towards ourselves and our fellow-creatures. What we destroy in ourselves we destroy in them. Our abasement degrades them, our falls drag them down; we owe it to them to remain upright so that they may not be laid low. The wish for a speedy death, like the desire for long life, is a weakness, and I don't want you to go on thinking of it as a right. I once thought I had that right too, though I believed then what I believe now. But I lacked strength and said, like you, 'I can't help it.' I was lying to myself. One can do anything. One discovers unsuspected strength when one really wants to 'climb upward', to go a rung higher every day, to say to oneself, 'The Flaubert of tomorrow has got to be better than the Flaubert of today, and the Flaubert of the day after tomorrow must be stronger and more lucid still.' Once you feel you're on the ladder you'll soon start to mount it. Before long you will gradually be entering upon the happiest and most propitious part of life: old age. It's then that art reveals itself in all its sweetness; in our youth it manifests itself in anguish. You prefer a well-written sentence to the whole of metaphysics. I too like to see that which elsewhere fills volumes reduced to a few words; but a writer has to have understood the true content of those volumes, whether he accepts or rejects it, before he can produce the sublime summary that is the pinnacle of literary art. So we shouldn't despise the efforts the human mind has made in order to arrive at the truth.

I say this because you are extremely prejudiced as far as mere *words* are concerned. In reality, however, you read and ponder and work at things much harder than I and many another. You have acquired a degree of learning which I shall never attain. So you are a hundred times richer than any of us – and yet you howl as if you were poor. Give alms to a beggar whose mattress is stuffed with gold, but who will eat nothing but well-written sentences and carefully chosen words? Foolish fellow, dig into your mattress and eat your gold. Feed on the ideas and feelings you've amassed in your head and heart; the words and phrases, the *form* you attach such importance to, will emerge of themselves. You regard form as an end when it is only an effect. The best visible effects emerge only from emotion, and emotion comes only from conviction. No one is ever moved by something he doesn't ardently believe in.

I don't say you don't believe. On the contrary: one aspect of your life is all affection, protection of others, graceful and simple kindness, which shows that you're a more convinced believer than anyone. But as soon as you're dealing with literature you insist for some reason or other on being a different person, one who has to disappear or even annihilate himself – one who doesn't exist! What a strange obsession! What misguided 'good taste'! Our work can never be better than we are ourselves.

Who's saying anything about putting your *self* on the stage? Of course that's no good, unless one's actually writing a first-person story or recording a personal experience. But to withdraw one's *soul* from what one writes – what kind of morbid fancy is that? If a writer conceals his opinion of his characters, and so leaves the reader uncertain what *he's* to make of them, then that writer is asking to be misunderstood, and the reader is bound to abandon him. For if your reader is to want to understand the story you're telling him, he must be shown clearly which of the characters are supposed to be strong and which are supposed to be weak.

GEORGE SAND

from Mirror of an Eastern Moon

'We went away from your town
    and had not seen you enough,
We fell, alas, from your tree:
    fruits, unripe, deprived of your sap . . .
We went to the ruins and hoped
    to find a treasure like you;
Like serpents creeping in dust,
    that is how we went from your door . . .'
Reduced now to shadows, we passed
    from hopelessness and from hope.
The thorns turned to roses. No word.
    The desert was filled with black light.

ANNE MARIE SCHIMMEL

3

A Constant Source
of Pleasure

Grasmere was very solemn in the last glimpse of
twilight; it calls home the heart to quietness

DOROTHY WORDSWORTH

To Be in Rain

The lush and lull of now the lapsing rain
The beautiful drench and flood is all about
On branch and sparkled sprawl of dripping bough
And diamond dangle slipping from the twigs,
And things of slumbered ivory huddled under
Break up from sleeping with a tender prong.
Unhushable and quiet drills the rain,
Each pointed spangle spats and pushes down
Into the little vats where lilies brew,
Into the silver cellars of the slug,
Between the jointed pillars, sheen and clean,
That lift the grass above the tremulous ant.
With shift, twist, twirl and peck of pebble under
The liquid fern, now dips the pale and spinning tip
Of rain, rain, rain into the swelling earth,
And here beneath the poise and strip
Of tactile waters tapping to get in,
The mind, the mortal soil gone bleak and sere
Goes green, puts up a candid flower, a sleek
Sweet bud, first bud, the firstling crisp and sheer.

HILDEGARDE FLANNER

from The Land of Journey's Ending

NOT all mountains are so, though to me they all have personality as much as ever they have to the Navajo. Even the new mountains not yet worn down to the smoothed contours of maturity, that crop out of the scorched *abras* to the south of Mt. Taylor, west of the Rio Grande, mountains unnamed and never lived in, blind cinder-heaps, cupped craters, wedged-shaped dikes surviving the cleft sandstone walls that shaped them. Dead mountains, dead and dreaming. Mostly it is water they dream of, as women unfulfilled are said to dream of the sea. Any way you look, traveling across that country, the dream comes stealing. It comes flowing toward you like a river, down the road you travel, almost to the fore wheels of your car from under which it slips to reappear as far behind you. Sometimes it lies like spilled quicksilver, cupped in the land's hollows; or spreads in one wide mirage like a lake on the surface of which the mountains float. Now and then a mountain fronts you, stark stone, uncomforted; but look behind you as you go and you see the dream creep back about its base. Toward evening, such mountains dream of fire, taking the light along their western faces, glowing with it as when they burst up molten from earth's core.

I knew a mountain once, over toward Lost Borders, which could both glow and pale, pale after the burning, like a lovely neglected woman who burned to no purpose, a dark mountain, whose bareness was like a pain. After some thousand years nothing grew there but sparse tufted grass, round-branched, rusted cacti and the knee-high creosote. Occasionally, in hollows where the seldom rains would catch, astragalus ripened a few papery pods, and slim spears of painted-cup. So dry it was, not even lizards darted, nor lichens grew upon the rocks. Then after several seasons of less frequent rains, a solitary rabbit found its way there. If by chance I saw it in my visits, I turned quickly and went another way; not for worlds would I have scared it from the mountain. And the second season after, I went there with a man of my acquaintance, and in my excitement to discover that the rabbit had found a mate, I cried out. Unhappily, the man was of the sort in whom a mountain wakes only the love of killing, and after he showed me the rabbits dangling bloody from his hand, I felt I could never go there again. But sometimes I have dreamed of it, and in my dream the mountain has a face, and on that face a look of hurt, intolerably familiar.

There is always something purposeful in the way a mountain

changes with the changing light, as if from within. Going up from the valley of Jemez, between the Rio Puerco and the Rio Grande, there is a magic mountain, a rounded basalt head, probably an old volcanic plug from which time has eaten away the crater, Cerro de la Cabeza, which has the property of becoming air, pure and shadowless, hanging suspended between thin gildings of the morning sun, like the Curtain of the Doorway of the Dawn which was lifted by the Elder Brother when he came from Carrizal. Forty or fifty miles to the east, the peaks of Jemez are blown blue against the morning and the evening light, deep trumpet blueness, against which, if you should see it from the Sangre de Cristo side in the spring twilight, the tops of the potreros vibrate lilac and lavender, and the green of the piedmont passes into the luminous air in thin trebles of French horns. There must have been a time, for man, when the impact of the mountain on his sense was too direct for clear distinctions of seeing or hearing – oh, long before he was able to make poetry without melody, or to separate the singing and the verse from the motions of the self that made it. It comes back here for definite, memorable moments, as when, in the early winter months, the sunset light has a way of passing invisibly through space, to break on the first object it encounters, tree-tops or the clinkered crests of extinct craters, into a glory of gold and hyacinthine color. Thus the whole Sangre de Cristo fills with secret fire, rose flame, shadowed with violet, deepening at its base to the hue of the spirit's most poignant mystery . . . holy, holy, holy. . . .

The moment comes and goes. Not beauty only, for there is a special kind of beauty for every hour the mountain knows, beauty which man perceives without participating, beauty to which he feels himself a stranger. There is the beauty of the structureless gloom of gathering storms, beauty with terror of the milling maelstroms of the air, beauty edged with intolerable loneliness of the moon-bow flung on the fluffy, silver-flecked floor of cloud observed from peaks above the tree line. There is beauty of the mountain meadows, to which the response is a joyous sense of well-being, lakes like jade, jeweled with water-lilies, long bajadas

thick with the plumes of bear-grass bowing like white ladies to
the royal wind. From all these we come back, knowing that long
before men set up an anthropomorphic deity there was a state,
easily met among mountains, called holy, being whole with the
experienceable universe.

Curiously, one of these moments of complete and happy
abandonment to wholeness, comes, for me, with the birth, in
the air before me, of the fragile, six-parted flowers of the snow. It
is only at very high altitudes that it is possible to see snowflakes
shaping level with your eyes, coming out of the thick grayness as
a star comes out of the twilight. There is a falling flash that
gathers whiteness as it falls, and suddenly on the black cloth of
your coat you catch a cluster of stemless, feathery blooms that
under your breath dissolve and regather, always six-sided but
never twice the same. Snowflakes forming under such conditions are unusually large, probably because they cannot form at
all except in the absence of all motion but their own. Those that
come sliding down the long slopes of mountain being almost
always clogged together, shattered in particles, or whipped by the
wind into round, icy grains. Sometimes on the surface of heavy
falls after warm days divided by cold nights, will be found a still
more varied bloom of snow flowers in the form of hoar-frost,
mingled with ice spicules which the Tewas call 'seed-of-the-
snow.' It is, I think, of some such shape of matter is made the
thin shell that far beyond the reach of man's highest flight of air,
shuts in our world against the invasive universe. Well! What if
science has not yet found it? Very clear spring and winter morn-
ings, after long falls of snow or heavy rain, from heaven-reaching
cumbres I have seen it, straining the blue out of the sun shafts,
breaking and scattering them as heat and light. Now, I remember
that when we were very young, the German housemaid used to
bring us clear sugar eggs for Easter, with a peep-hole at one end,
to an inclosed colored picture; so the earth ball within its shell
might look, should there be seraph or any other creature to peep
in.

Mountains are the only things we know to grow beautiful in

aging. Young mountains are all terrible, hard from the moment
they are cold, angular and graceless. There must be peaks of volcanic origin, in Arizona, which cannot be more than fifteen or
twenty thousand years old. Not old enough to have anything
growing on them but lichens of lovely rich colors and seaweed
patterns. Ever since Mac, to whom this book is dedicated, told
me that a lichen is the perfect coöperation of two living and unlike
plant organisms, grown into one the better to compass the rock's
devouring, I have been afraid of lichens; and the little stone crops
and saxifrages that live in the crevices of the rocks, by their power
of extracting sustenance from minerals, seem terrible in their frail
prettiness, as to men must seem certain sorts of women.

MARY AUSTIN

from Pilgrim at Tinker Creek

IT was sunny one evening last summer at Tinker Creek; the sun
was low in the sky, upstream. I was sitting on the sycamore log
bridge with the sunset at my back, watching the shiners the size
of minnows who were feeding over the muddy sand in skittery
schools. Again and again, one fish, then another, turned for a
split second across the current and flash! the sun shot out from its
silver side. I couldn't watch for it. It was always just happening
somewhere else, and it drew my vision just as it disappeared:
flash, like a sudden dazzle of the thinnest blade, a sparking over
a dun and olive ground at chance intervals from every direction.
Then I noticed white specks, some sort of pale petals, small,
floating from under my feet on the creek's surface, very slow and
steady. So I blurred my eyes and gazed towards the brim of my
hat and saw a new world. I saw the pale white circles roll up, roll
up, like the world's turning, mute and perfect, and I saw the
linear flashes, gleaming silver, like stars being born at random
down a rolling scroll of time. Something broke and something
opened. I filled up like a new wineskin. I breathed an air like
light; I saw a light like water. I was the lip of a fountain the creek

filled forever; I was ether, the leaf in the zephyr; I was flesh-
flake, feather, bone.

When I see this way I see truly. As Thoreau says, I return to
my senses.

ANNIE DILLARD

Immanence

I come in the little things,
Saith the Lord:
Not borne on morning wings
Of majesty, but I have set My Feet
Amidst the delicate and bladed wheat
That springs triumphant in the furrowed sod.
There do I dwell, in weakness and in power:
Not broken or divided, saith our God!
In your straight garden plot I come to flower:
About your porch my Vine
Meek, fruitful, doth entwine;
Waits, at the threshold, Love's appointed hour.

I come in the little things,
Saith the Lord:
Yea! on the glancing wings
Of eager birds, the softly pattering feet
Of furred and gentle beasts, I come to meet
Your hard and wayward heart. In brown bright eyes
That peep from out the brake, I stand confest.
On every nest
Where feathery Patience is content to brood
And leaves her pleasure for the high emprize
Of motherhood –
There doth My Godhead rest.

I come in the little things,

Saith the Lord:
My starry wings
I do forsake,
Love's highway of humility to take:
Meekly I fit My stature to your need.
In beggar's part
About your gates I shall not cease to plead –
As man, to speak with man –
Till by such art
I shall achieve My Immemorial Plan.
Pass the low lintel of the human heart.

EVELYN UNDERHILL

from Bright Morning

I USED to think, if I was given a choice of one thing to take away
from the world with me, it would be my diaries, but now I should
choose the flowers of earth instead, for they would almost form a
diary – England and India, Italy and Baluchistan, Egypt and
Ireland, Ceylon, Scotland, Brazil, Switzerland. I would look at the
flowers and shut my eyes, and then there would rise up the lovely
tumbling brooks of the Highlands on a summer's day; a striped
tulip – and there would be the stone wastes of Baluchistan or
Persia in the blinding light of midday; I would smell jasmine and
the hot scents of India would come too; the honey smell of lupins
and there are the tawny hills one sees from the Nile. I have read
of an old Irish greeting, 'What blossom is on you to-day?' What
blossom have I thought of, or seen, to-day? Where has it taken
me to? How many years has it bridged? Is it only to a few that
flowers make a focus to a place; the 'scraps of joy their wander-
ings find', as John Clare wrote?

I wonder how many times I have walked to the garden here at
home? Whenever I come back fresh to the place and go to the
garden I seem to feel and see down the other years, a longer and
longer vista, with richer and richer honey stored. It does seem

sometimes as though one should almost rejoice in growing older; there is more store, more added to this ever-living panorama; there will be more to relive, thousands more beautiful moments put away for future use when our 'time' is transcended. I always felt this, even as a child; the day will come, I used to feel, when I shall be able to unroll this coloured scroll and look at, and live out, all its pictures again, catch again the sweetness run to waste. It was an intuition, I suppose, but now, with later years and deeper thought, it has become a settled conviction – almost a proved science – that even the filmiest perception can be recalled from the subconscious, given certain conditions.

How I seized on Tagore's line about a parting glance! 'In the immense world where shall I keep that single glance? Where is the place that is beyond the silent footsteps of seconds, minutes, hours? . . . I touch not the kingly crown, nor the gold of the rich; but trifles like that glance are my sole treasure. With them I make a garland for eternity.'

A.E. walked to this garden, too; he only wanted things he could 'take to Paradise with him'; he, too, echoed Tagore's words, 'What shall I do with that which will not make me immortal!' I put aside the idea that everything seen or said or thought is there for ever; that in the divine economy nothing is lost, that no 'idle word' is really gone, because it becomes almost overpowering. It becomes too pressing – there is so little time – so little time to really look at and see the countless myriad forms of beauty.

Sometimes I go out into the sun and pick a few flowers; white periwinkles in December, a scarlet geranium from the greenhouse, marigolds on a warm autumn day – and look at them through a magnifying glass in the sunlight. One must be prepared beforehand for the miracle, otherwise it is startling. There is the homely flower one has passed a thousand times, dully, blindly, unaware. Take it and look at it through something that changes it even slightly and one shrinks back at the incredible beauty revealed, the unbelievable creation, the glistening shining petals, petals dusted over with silver and gold, the living bloom of them; the whole perfection of the form. Yes; it is mine now, for ever and ever. For ever I possess in myself that transparent white autumn-crocus, a chalice of pearl, that bit of fringed moss, those ruby berries of the yew.

It is flowers that wake this sense of heaven more than anything, I think, because their beauty is such that it seems as though it couldn't conceivably be greater; I look at an aconite on a rough, icy winter's day; the earth, the rain, the air have conspired together to produce this purity of yellow and green; I kneel down and look at the shining crocuses piercing through the hard ground in glowing bunches.

And when I thought, half in fun, of writing down the distinct memories of other years, I found that they were mostly linked to, and remembered by, flowers. Clearly we shall each have our own Paradise and 'yours', as A.E. said to me with a laugh, and perhaps also a little bored by the idea, 'will be all flowers'.

And so perhaps it will be only to those to whom the subtle and marvellous forms, the scents and fragrancies of flowers, seem important, that these light chapters will have any appeal. I have already written some small books; all their names contain flowers; and this is only another addition to the setting down of hours spent in watching, in company or alone, 'that bright procession on its way' through the years.

CONSTANCE SITWELL

from The Story of My Life

EVERYTHING that could hum, or buzz, or sing, or bloom, had a part in my education – noisy-throated frogs, katydids and crickets held in my hand until, forgetting their embarrassment, they trilled their reedy note, little downy chickens and wildflowers, the dogwood blossoms, meadow-violets and budding fruit trees. I felt the bursting cotton-bolls and fingered their soft fibre and fuzzy seeds; I felt the low soughing of the wind through the cornstalks, the silky rustling of the long leaves, and the indignant snort of my pony, as we caught him in the pasture and put the bit in his mouth – ah me! how well I remember the spicy, clovery smell of his breath!

Sometimes I rose at dawn and stole into the garden while the heavy dew lay on the grass and flowers. Few know what joy it is to feel the roses pressing softly into the hand, or the beautiful motion of the lilies as they sway in the morning breeze. Sometimes I caught an insect in the flower I was plucking, and I felt the faint noise of a pair of wings rubbed together in a sudden terror, as the little creature became aware of a pressure from without.

Another favourite haunt of mine was the orchard, where the fruit ripened early in July. The large, downy peaches would reach themselves into my hand, and as the joyous breezes flew about the trees the apples tumbled at my feet. Oh, the delight with which I gathered up the fruit in my pinafore, pressed my face against the smooth cheeks of the apples, still warm from the sun, and skipped back to the house!

HELEN KELLER

Better than Love

Are you there? Can you hear?
Listen, try to understand,
O be still, become an ear,
For there is darkness on this land.
Stand and hearken, still as stone,
For I call to you alone.

Who can be what the weed was
In the empty afternoon?
Who can match me the wild grass,
Sighing its forgotten tune:
Who is equal to that shell,
Whose spiral is my parable?

No human eye reflects the weed
Burning beneath the lonely sun:
The wild hard grass spangled with seed
Is still unmatched by anyone;
The justice of the shell is still
Above the mind, above the will.

Since love and beauty, blown upon,
Are not desired, not spoken of,
Hear me, you solitary one,
Better than beauty or than love,
Seen in the weed, the shell, the grass,
But never in my kind, alas!

The ragged weed is truth to me,
The poor grass honour, and the shell
Eternal justice, till I see
The spirit rive the roof of hell
With light enough to let me read
More than the grass, the shell, the weed.

RUTH PITTER

from Peig: The Autobiography of Peig Sayers of the Great Blasket Island

ONE day, I had buried my fourth child and it was no wonder that I was troubled in my mind. As the evening was fine I decided to go out so I took up a stocking from the window in order to be knitting, but to tell you the truth, I hadn't much mind for work that same evening. I drove the cow back before me and let her into the field for I reckoned that I could do no better than sit down for a while herding her.

I sat on the bank above the beach where I had a splendid view all around me. Dead indeed is the heart from which the balmy air of the sea cannot banish sorrow and grief. The passage between the Great Blasket and Beginnis is like a little harbour and it looks most attractive when the weather is calm. As I had no interest in the work I put down my stocking on a tussock and began to look away out to sea at the thousands of seabirds flying here and there in search of a bite to eat. Every bird from the stormy petrel to the cormorant, from the sand-snipe to the gannet was there and each variety of bird had its own peculiar call. There were many thousands of small seagulls; some, hovering lightly, were searching for little sprat or other morsels of food. Whenever one of them found a mouthful she'd utter a call and straightaway thousands of others were down on top of her. Such scuffling and pecking no one ever saw before! They were all entangled in one another trying to snatch the morsel from her.

At last I grew tired of watching the gulls and I turned my gaze to the south – towards Iveragh and Dingle Bay. It was a beautiful view. The whole bay was as calm as new milk, with little silver spray shimmering on its surface under a sunlight that was then brilliant. To the south Slea Head stood boldly in view as if it would stand there for ever – not a stir out of the water at the edge of the rocks nor in the creek itself so that even an old woman need not be troubled if she were sitting in a sheltered nook by the edge of a rock – for there was no fear of her being drowned! Dunmore stood out before me and Liúir too, like its watchdog, its crest covered with seagulls and cormorants resting at their ease; the Seanduine – Old Man Rock himself – was grinning beside them, his skull covered with a fleece of seaweed – though a person might say that it was high time for that same skull to be shaken and stripped by the mighty and insolent ocean waves that were forever crashing down upon it. Maol, or Baldie Bank, looked so peaceful and mild-tempered that you wouldn't think he ever did hurt or harm, though the old people said that it was on that rock the King of Spain's ship was wrecked along ago. And that finished the vessel and all on board – God save those who hear the tale!

Out before me stood Dunquin – the fresh colour of summer

on its fields and gardens – this was where I had spent my early days. Many the fine evening I was on top of that hill, Mount Eagle, when I was young and airy and with no responsibility whatsoever to carry. Away to the north stood the headland of Ceann Sratha and there also lay the mouth of Ferriter's Cove and Dún an Óir. Binn Diarmada appeared both triumphant and stately; the sunlight glistened brightly on its sides and on the deep scars the mighty ocean had wrought upon it. From Fiach to Barra Liath was one great sea harbour; it resembled a single sheet of glass and indeed, an observer might see it as a great city lying under a magic spell.

A sigh welled up from my heart and I said aloud: 'God! isn't it an odd person indeed who would be troubled in mind with so much beauty around him and all of it the work of the Creator's hand?'

PEIG SAYERS

from Domestic Manners of the Americans

OUR autumn walks were delightful; the sun ceased to scorch; the want of flowers was no longer peculiar to Ohio; and the trees took a colouring, which in richness, brilliance, and variety, exceeded all description. I think it is the maple, or sugar-tree, that first sprinkles the forest with rich crimson; the beech follows, with all its harmony of golden tints, from pale yellow up to brightest orange. The dog-wood gives almost the purple colour of the mulberry; the chestnut softens all with its frequent mass of delicate brown, and the sturdy oak carries its deep green into the very lap of winter. These tints are too bright for the landscape painter; the attempt to follow nature in an American autumn scene must be abortive. The colours are in reality extremely brilliant, but the medium through which they are seen increases the effect surprisingly. Of all the points in which America has the advantage of England, the one I felt most sensibly was the clearness and brightness of the atmosphere. By day and by night this exquisite purity of air gives tenfold beauty to every object. I could hardly believe the stars were the same; the Great Bear looked like a constellation of suns; and Jupiter justified all the fine things said of him in those beautiful lines, from I know not what spirited pen, beginning,

> *I looked on thee, Jove! till my gaze*
> *Shrunk, smote by the pow'r of thy blaze.*

I always remarked that the first silver line of the moon's crescent attracted the eye on the first day, in America, as strongly as it does here on the third. I observed another phenomenon in the crescent moon of that region, the cause of which I less understood. That appearance which Shakespeare describes as 'the new moon, with the old moon in her lap', and which I have heard ingeniously explained as the effect of *earth light*, was less visible there than here.

Cuyp's clearest landscapes have an atmosphere that approaches nearer to that of America than any I remember on canvas; but even Cuyp's *air* cannot reach the lungs, and, therefore, can only give an idea of half the enjoyment; for it makes itself felt as well as seen, and is indeed a constant source of pleasure.

FRANCES TROLLOPE

Living

The fire in leaf and grass
so green it seems
each summer the last summer.

The wind blowing, the leaves
shivering in the sun,
each day the last day.

A red salamander
so cold and so
easy to catch, dreamily

moves his delicate feet
and long tail. I hold
my hand open for him to go.

Each minute the last minute.

DENISE LEVERTOV

from The Professor's House

I'LL never forget the night I got back. I crossed the river an hour
before sunset and hobbled my horse in the wide bottom of Cow
Canyon. The moon was up, though the sun hadn't set, and it had
that glittering silveriness the early stars have in high altitudes.
The heavenly bodies look so much more remote from the bottom
of a deep canyon than they do from the level. The climb of the
walls helps out the eye, somehow. I lay down on a solitary rock
that was like an island in the bottom of the valley, and looked up.
The grey sage-brush and the blue-grey rock around me were
already in shadow, but high above me the canyon walls were dyed
flame-colour with the sunset, and the Cliff City lay in a gold
haze against its dark cavern. In a few minutes it, too, was grey,
and only the rim rock at the top held the red light. When that was
gone, I could still see the copper glow in the piñons along the
edge of the top ledges. The arc of sky over the canyon was silvery
blue, with its pale yellow moon, and presently stars shivered into
it, like crystals dropped into perfectly clear water.

I remember these things, because, in a sense, that was the first
night I was ever really on the mesa at all – the first night that all
of me was there. This was the first time I ever saw it as a whole.
It all came together in my understanding, as a series of experi-
ments do when you begin to see where they are leading.

Something had happened in me that made it possible for me to co-ordinate and simplify, and that process, going on in my mind, brought with it great happiness. It was possession. The excitement of my first discovery was a very pale feeling compared to this one. For me the mesa was no longer an adventure, but a religious emotion. I had read of filial piety in the Latin poets, and I knew that was what I felt for this place. It had formerly been mixed up with other motives; but now that they were gone, I had my happiness unalloyed.

What that night began lasted all summer. I stayed on the mesa until November. It was the first time I'd ever studied methodically, or intelligently. I got the better of the Spanish grammar and read the twelve books of the *Æneid*. I studied in the morning, and in the afternoon I worked at clearing away the mess the German had made in packing – tidying up the ruins to wait another hundred years, maybe, for the right explorer. I can scarcely hope that life will give me another summer like that one. It was my high tide. Every morning, when the sun's rays first hit the mesa top, while the rest of the world was in shadow, I wakened with the feeling that I had found everything, instead of having lost everything. Nothing tired me. Up there alone, a close neighbour to the sun, I seemed to get the solar energy in some direct way. And at night, when I watched it drop down behind the edge of the plain below me, I used to feel that I couldn't have borne another hour of that consuming light, that I was full to the brim, and needed dark and sleep.

All that summer, I never went up to the Eagle's Nest to get my diary – indeed, it's probably there yet. I didn't feel the need of that record. It would have been going backward. I didn't want to go back and unravel things step by step. Perhaps I was afraid that I would lose the whole in the parts. At any rate, I didn't go for my record.

During those months I didn't worry much about poor Roddy. I told myself the advertisements would surely get him – I knew his habit of reading newspapers. There are times when one's vitality is too high to be clouded, too elastic to stay down.

Hurrying from my cabin in the morning to the spot in the Cliff City where I studied under a cedar, I used to be frightened at my own heartlessness. But the feel of the narrow moccasin-worn trail in the flat rock made my feet glad, like a good taste in the mouth, and I'd forget all about Blake without knowing it. I found I was reading too fast; so I began to commit long passages of Vergil to memory – if it hadn't been for that, I might have forgotten how to use my voice, or gone to talking to myself. When I look into the *Æneid* now, I can always see two pictures: the one on the page, and another behind that: blue and purple rocks and yellow-green piñons with flat tops, little clustered houses clinging together for protection, a rude tower rising in their midst, rising strong, with calmness and courage – behind it a dark grotto, in its depths a crystal spring.

Happiness is something one can't explain. You must take my word for it. Troubles enough came afterward, but there was that summer, high and blue, a life in itself.

WILLA CATHER

from Grasmere Journal

[May 16th] Friday Morning

Warm and mild, after a fine night of rain. Transplanted radishes after breakfast, walked to Mr Gell's with the books, gathered mosses and plants. The woods extremely beautiful with all autumnal variety and softness. I carried a basket for mosses, and gathered some wild plants. Oh! that we had a book of botany. All flowers now are gay and deliciously sweet. The primrose still pre-eminent among the later flowers of the spring. Foxgloves very tall, with their heads budding. I went forward round the lake at the foot of Loughrigg Fell. I was much amused with the business of a pair of stone-chats; their restless voices as they skimmed along the water following each other, their shadows under them, and their returning back to the stones on the shore, chirping with the same unwearied voice. Could not cross the water, so I went round by the stepping-stones. The morning clear but cloudy, that is the hills were not overhung by mists. After dinner Aggy weeded onions and carrots. I helped for a little – wrote to Mary Hutchinson – washed my head – worked. After tea went to Ambleside – a pleasant cool but not cold evening. Rydale was very beautiful, with spear-shaped streaks of polished steel. No letters! – only one newspaper. I returned by Clappersgate. Grasmere was very solemn in the last glimpse of twilight; it calls home the heart to quietness. I had been very melancholy in my walk back. I had many of my saddest thoughts, and I could not keep the tears within me. But when I came to Grasmere I felt that it did me good. I finished my letter to M.H. Ate hasty pudding and went to bed. As I was going out in the morning I met a half crazy old man. He shewed me a pin-cushion and begged a pin, afterwards a half-penny. He began in a kind of indistinct voice in this manner: 'Matthew Jobson's lost a cow. Tom Nichol has two good horses strayed. Jim Jones's cow's brokken her horn, etc. etc.' He went into Aggy's and persuaded her to give him some whey, and let him boil some porridge. She declares he ate two quarts.

DOROTHY WORDSWORTH

from The Land of Journey's Ending

THE first sound of spring in the Rio Grande country is the sound of snow-water. In the March-April Moon, the Moon of the Rabbit Brush Disappearing, when the Indians take down their wind-breaks and shelters, snow may still fall. Lodging like fluffs of cloud on the flat roofs and the finely divided foliage of the piñon pines, it begins at once to sparkle with the dew of the drip. The drip quickens to a gurgle. Pools, yellow but mirror-bright, collect in the hollows of the road, so that your car seems every moment about to plunge into an abyss of basalt cliff and cambric sky. Lacy hummocks on the sage and the cedars are undercut by the warm breath of the earth, and the trickle of snow-water is intermittent with the swish of dropping wreaths and straightening boughs.

By this time the rabbit-brush has lost its veil of winter fluff; its pale stalks, passing insensibly into light along the banks of washes, are defined only by the green smudge at the base of its dry fascicles. Bluebirds flutter in the chaparral like flecks of falling sky; the willows are lacquered orange and vermilion. Now the wind has a growing smell, but along the wooded tops of the ranges snow still filters delicately through the rarefied air. The diffused, shut-in light of the snow is like the whiteness of rapid vibration, the earth envelop disappearing in a mist of its own motion. Farther south, where snow is made rain midway of the vault, the storm, seen moving across the *abras* from the inclosing hills, has the effect of emanating from the ground, as if the earth exhaled it, and by a gentle, down-streaking motion, drew it to its breast again.

Between the last snows and the coming of the green, broken-winged cold winds play between the ranges. The dried watercourses are picked out by lifting veils of dust as the wind struggles woundedly with the returning sun. Around the Little Colorado, which was once called Rio de Lino because of the flax that grew there, and on the *plan del Zuñi* and all sandy washes toward the west, there is a Bigelovia which at this season gathers a silvery lint along stems that are milky blue with the cold, and on a day are suddenly, definitely green. About this time, walking among the junipers, still sticky yellow and friable like discarded Christmas trimmings, first one and then another pricks itself on your attention. As if all the vitality of the tree, which during the winter had been withdrawn to the seat of the life processes underground, had run up and shouted, 'Here I am.' Not one of all the ways by which a tree strikes freshly on your observation, – with a greener flush, with stiffened needles, or slight alterations of the axis of the growing shoots, accounts for this flash of mutual awareness. You walk a stranger in a vegetating world; then with an inward click the shutter of some profounder level of consciousness uncloses and admits you to sentience of the mounting sap.

But it is only in the low growths of the New Mexico highlands, where, as you walk, your head comes level with the forest crown, that it happens with authority. What can we know of trees whose processes of elongation toward the light go on a hundred feet or more overhead? Only occasionally, after a long time in the tall forest, doing nothing and thinking very little, a sense of the alien and deeply preoccupied life of the tree shakes our less experienced human consciousness with a touch called Panic.

There is an exceeding subtlety about the spring in New Mexico, at once virginal and experienced, like Mona Lisa's smile. The planted orchards hold aloof, the wild-plum thickets are tiptoe for flight. Suddenly at the end of May, from painted-cup and filmy cactus-flower blazons forth the secret of that country, the secret of fire that gave it birth.

MARY AUSTIN

from An Old Woman's Reflections

THE weather is beautiful and the sun is shining brightly on sea and on land. There is freshness and brightness in everything God created. The sea is polished, and the boys are swimming down at the shore. The little fishes themselves are splashing on the top of the water and even the old people are sitting out here and there sunning themselves. Poor humans are overcome after the winter because we have a hard life of it on the island for that part of the year – hemmed in like a flock of sheep in a pen, buffeted by storm and gale, without shade or shelter but like a big ship in the middle of a great sea, cut off from the land without news coming to us or going from us. But God does the ordering, praise for ever to Him, when He sees our hardship. He abates the storm, and gives us the opportunity to go among the people, and when the summer and fine weather like this come He takes from us the memory and the gloom of winter.

PEIG SAYERS

San Ysidro Cabezon

We went up the pass, she and I,
to see the mountain turning,
watched it discover
its golden light
rejoicing
we followed a rutted road
center blooming and filled with rocks,
yellow, magenta and pale brown,
that kept us twisting, unable to see
what was ahead, climbing
until the valley opened wide below
fading into simple blue as the sky
revealing distance to our astounded eyes.
we were reminded of an old wanderer's dream,
a stream fizzing and bubbling among the hills,
the blooming, smokable trees –
the kind and perfect ease anyone would wish for,
going so unbelieved.
I want to tell you this:
the notion of how it ought to be,
name of an Eskimo god who sits,
content, grinning. He understands.
And so do you, and I,
if only we could remember
the banks are steep,
the peaks so far away,
but in between
a careful space of perfect springs
and all we'd ever need,
and swift winds on the peaks
where the light is clear.

PAULA GUNN ALLEN

from The Continuum Concept

THE incident happened during a nature walk in the Maine woods where I was at summer camp. I was last in line, I had fallen back a bit and was hurrying to catch up when, through the trees, I saw a glade. It had a lush fir tree at the far side and a knoll in the center covered in bright, almost luminous, green moss. The rays of the afternoon sun slanted against the blue-black green of the pine forest. The little roof of visible sky was perfectly blue. The whole picture had a completeness, an all-there quality of such dense power that it stopped me in my tracks. I went to the edge and then, softly, as though into a magical or holy place, to the center, where I sat then lay down with my cheek against the freshness of the moss. 'It is here,' I thought, and I felt the anxiety which colored my life fall away. This, at last, was where things were as they ought to be. Everything was in its place – the tree, the earth underneath, the rock, the moss. In autumn, it would be right; in winter under the snow, it would be perfect in its wintriness. Spring would come again and miracle within miracle would unfold, each at its special pace, some things having died off, some sprouting in their first spring, but all of equal and utter rightness.

I felt I had discovered the missing center of things, the key to rightness itself, and must hold on to this knowledge which was so clear in that place. I was tempted for a moment to take a scrap of moss away with me, to keep as a reminder; but a rather grown-up thought prevented me. I suddenly feared that in treasuring an amulet of moss, I might lose the real prize: the insight I had had – that I might think my vision safe as long as I kept the moss, only to find one day that I had nothing but a pinch of dead vegetation.

So I took nothing, but promised myself I would remember The Glade every night before going to sleep and in that way never be far from its stabilizing power. I knew, even at eight, that the confusion of values thrust upon me by parents, teachers, other children, nannies, camp counselors and others would only worsen as I grew up. The years would add complications and steer me into more and more impenetrable tangles of rights and wrongs, desirables and undesirables. I had already seen enough to know that. But if I could keep The Glade with me, I thought, I would not get lost.

That night in my camp bed I brought The Glade to mind and was filled with a sense of thankfulness, and renewed my vow to preserve my vision. And for years its quality was undiminished as I saw the knoll, the fir, the light, the wholeness, in my mind every night.

JEAN LIEDLOFF

A Nocturnal Reverie

In such a night, when every tender wind
Is to its distant cavern safe confined;
And only gentle Philomel, still waking, sings,
Or from some tree, famed for the owl's delight,
She, hollowing clear, directs the wand'rer right;
In such a night, when passing clouds give place,
Or thinly veil the heaven's mysterious face;
When in some river, overhung with green,
The waving moon and trembling leaves are seen;
When freshened grass now bears itself upright,
And makes cool banks to pleasing rest invite,
Whence springs the woodbind and the bramble-rose,
And where the sleepy cowslip sheltered grows;
Whilst now a paler hue the foxglove takes,
Yet chequers still with red the dusky brakes;
When scattered glow-worms, but in twilight fine,
Show trivial beauties, watch their hour to shine;
Whilst Salisb'ry stands the test of every light,
In perfect charms and perfect virtue bright;
When odours, which declined repelling day,
Through temp'rate air uninterrupted stray;
When darkened groves their softest shadows wear,

And falling waters we distinctly hear;
When through the gloom more venerable shows
Some ancient fabric, awful in repose,
While sunburnt hills their swarthy looks conceal,
And swelling haycocks thicken up the vale;
When the loosed horse now, as his pasture leads,
Comes slowly grazing through th'adjoining meads,
Whose stealing pace and lengthened shade we fear,
Till torn-up forage in his teeth we hear;
When nibbling sheep at large pursue their food,
And unmolested kine rechew the cud;
When curlews cry beneath the village walls,
And to her straggling brood the partridge calls;
Their short-lived jubilee the creatures keep,
Which but endures whilst tyrant man does sleep;
When a sedate content the spirit feels,
And no fierce light disturbs, whilst it reveals,
But silent musings urge the mind to seek
Something too high for syllables to speak;
Till the free soul to a compos'dness charmed,
Finding the elements of rage disarmed,
O'er all below a solemn quiet grown,
Joys in th'inferior world and thinks it like her own:
In such a night let me abroad remain,
Till morning breaks, and all's confused again:
Our cares, our toils, our clamours are renewed,
Or pleasures, seldom reached, again pursued.

ANNE FINCH, Countess of Winchilsea

from Bright Morning

IT was rather a late love that I brought to Scotland, and even now it is only the West Coast and the green hills of Dumfriesshire that I feel are at all my own through the force of imagination and affection. But it would be a hard heart indeed that was not melted by the West Coast in June; specially coming to it for the first time by sea. It is the constant changing of the sky and weather which makes it so lovely, so exasperating and so exciting. For two days there is nothing but cloud and mist and a chill greyness; then the veil lifts on to a radiant scene, and only the words used for precious stones are the right ones – sapphire, aquamarine, crystal, chrysoprase. Those azure levels of sea, those turquoise waves which have the transparency and depth of jewels! If Holland is a country for painters, then surely the West Coast is for poets, for it is a country of moods, of moments, of changes, of lights that wax and wane, of winds that shift and veer, of sunlight that transforms and transfigures, of rain that swerves and passes, of weather that rings the changes constantly and gives a new colour to each hour of the day.

CONSTANCE SITWELL

I Taught Myself to Live Simply

I taught myself to live simply and wisely,
to look at the sky and pray to God,
and to wander long before evening
to tire my superfluous worries.

When the burdocks rustle in the ravine
and the yellow-red rowanberry cluster droops
I compose happy verses
about life's decay, decay and beauty.

I come back. The fluffy cat
licks my palm, purrs so sweetly,
and the fire flares bright
on the saw-mill turret by the lake.

Only the cry of a stork landing on the roof
occasionally breaks the silence.
If you knock on my door
I may not even hear.

ANNA AKHMATOVA

from The Professor's House

THERE was one fine thing about this room that had been the
scene of so many defeats and triumphs. From the window he
could see, far away, just on the horizon, a long, blue, hazy smear –
Lake Michigan, the inland sea of his childhood. Whenever he
was tired and dull, when the white pages before him remained
blank or were full of scratched-out sentences, then he left his
desk, took the train to a little station twelve miles away, and spent
a day on the lake with his sail-boat; jumping out to swim, floating on his back alongside, then climbing into his boat again.

When he remembered his childhood, he remembered blue
water. There were certain human figures against it, of course;
his practical, strong-willed Methodist mother, his gentle,
weaned-away Catholic father, the old Kanuck grandfather, various brothers and sisters. But the great fact in life, the always
possible escape from dullness, was the lake. The sun rose out of
it, the day began there; it was like an open door that nobody
could shut. The land and all its dreariness could never close in on
you. You had only to look at the lake, and you knew you would
soon be free. It was the first thing one saw in the morning, across
the rugged cow pasture studded with shaggy pines, and it ran
through the days like the weather, not a thing thought about, but
a part of consciousness itself. When the ice chunks came in of a

winter morning, crumbly and white, throwing off gold and rose-coloured reflections from a copper-coloured sun behind the grey clouds, he didn't observe the detail or know what it was that made him happy; but now, forty years later, he could recall all its aspects perfectly. They had made pictures in him when he was unwilling and unconscious, when his eyes were merely open wide.

When he was eight years old, his parents sold the lakeside farm and dragged him and his brothers and sisters out to the wheat lands of central Kansas. St. Peter nearly died of it. Never could he forget the few moments on the train when that sudden, innocent blue across the sand dunes was dying for ever from his sight. It was like sinking for the third time. No later anguish, and he had had his share, went so deep or seemed so final. Even in his long, happy student years with the Thierault family in France, that stretch of blue water was the one thing he was home-sick for. In the summer he used to go with the Thierault boys to Brittany or to the Languedoc coast; but his lake was itself, as the Channel and the Mediterranean were themselves. 'No,' he used to tell the boys, who were always asking him about *le Michigan*, 'it is altogether different. It is a sea, and yet it is not salt. It is blue, but quite another blue. Yes, there are clouds and mists and sea-gulls, but – I don't know, *il est toujours plus naïf.'*

WILLA CATHER

Dartmoor

I shall not return again the way I came,
Back to the quiet country where the hills
Are purple in the evenings, and the tors
Are grey and quiet, and the tall standing stones
Lead out across the moorland till they end
At water's edge.
It is too gentle, all that land,
It will bring back

Such quiet dear remembered things,
There, where the longstone lifts its lonely head,
Gaunt, grey, forbidding,
Ageless, however worn away;
There, even, grows the heather . . .
Tender, kind,
The little streams are busy in the valleys,
The rivers meet by the grey Druid bridge,
So quiet,
So quiet,
Not as death is quiet, but as life can be quiet
When it is sweet.

AGATHA CHRISTIE

Vignette – By the Sea

LYING thus on the sand, the foam washing over my hands, I am spellbound by the sea.

Behind the golden hills the sun is going down, a flaming jewel in a lurid setting, and there is a faint flush everywhere, on sea and land. To my right the sky has blossomed into a vivid rose, but, to my left, the land is hidden by a grey mist, lightened now here, now there, by the sun colour . . . It is like land seen from a ship, very far away, dreamland, mirage enchanted country.

Two sea birds, high in the air, fly screaming towards the light. It beats upon their white breasts, it flames upon their dull wings. Far away, a little boat is sailing upon the sweet water, a golden butterfly upon the dainty bosom of a mystic blossom . . .

And now the Italian fishermen are sailing in, their white sails bellying in the breeze. Several come rowing in a little boat. They spring ashore, the light shines upon their crisp, black hair, it shines on their faces, so that their skin is the colour of hot amber, on their bare legs and strong brown arms. They are dragging towards them the boat, the long, black, wet rope running through their fingers and falling in a bold pattern on the foam-blown sand . . . They call to one another – I cannot hear what they say – but against the long, rhythmic pulsing of the sea their voices sound curiously insignificant, like voices in a dream . . .

And there are exquisite golden-brown sprays and garlands of sea weed, set about with berries, white and brown. Are they flowers blown from the garden of the sea king's daughter? Does she wander through the delicate coral forests, seeking them, playing upon a little silver shell, her long hair floating behind her?

And near me there is a light upon the blue coast – steadily, tenderly it burns – a little candle set upon the great altar of the world.

The glow pales in the sky, on the land, but ever the long rhythmic pulsing of the sea. Oh, to sail and sail into the heart of the sea. Is it darkness and silence there, or is it a great light? . . .

So the grey sand slips, drifts through my fingers.

Night comes swiftly . . .

KATHERINE MANSFIELD, from *Poems*

from The Chasm of Fire

October 1966
Dearest,

This letter comes to you from a solitary retreat in the Himalayan hills. I am writing seated on my doorstep, facing the snows. They are clear this morning. And last evening too; the whole range was coral pink, the glow after the setting sun dying gently away on the glaciers. And so near they seem . . .

It is a glorious morning. The ashram garden is a riot of colours. Sunflowers, zinnias, dahlias and, above all, cosmos and marigolds. The air is vibrating with the hum of the bees and the crickets are busy filling the garden with the gay monotonous sound which seems to belong to the sunshine. Sheer joy of living, bringing back childhood memories of summer days, blue sky and much hot, lovely sunshine.

Everything grows so tall here; as if the vegetation is trying to compete with the high hills around and the huge mountains. Sunflowers are nine to ten feet high; the nearest one to my door has thirty-two blooms and at least the same amount of buds. There are shrub-like zinnias covered with large blooms rather like dahlias, four inches across. And cosmos! I have never seen anything like it! They grow wild here on the slopes, and in the clearings of the jungle, and in our garden we must have several thousand plants in crimson, white, deep pink, pale pink, and pink with a crimson heart. There is a marigold six feet tall near the veranda!

Our ashram garden looks like a valley of flowers just now. The other day I went into the pine forest on the opposite hill, from where there is an enchanting view into the three valleys. The valley of Garur with the snows behind it; then of Kausani and of the Chenoda river. All round are high hills, the famous Kumaon Hills, covered with pine forests at this altitude and with jungle lower down on the slopes. The ashram is at 6,075 feet above sea level. Kausani, a village of only one thousand inhabitants, is in the centre, about six hundred feet below. Once a week I go down to the village to do my shopping, although at present most things come from the ashram garden.

I seem to live on my doorstep lately, since the snows are clearly visible. Every morning I am up long before sunrise. The green, livid transparency of the sky changes gradually into a pale yellow, the harbinger of dawn. It is perfectly still. The snows are sombre, forbidding. No sound from anywhere. Nature is waiting. Then from the village below sounds begin to come, of life awakening. Children's voices, laughter, dogs barking, an occasional snatch of song. The sound of water running into the buckets. Smoke begins to rise, the lovely acrid smell of wood fire.

But the forest and jungle are still. Then suddenly, as if obeying the signal of an unseen conductor, the birds begin to sing on the slopes and in the valleys. At first hesitantly, a lonely sound, a soft modulation. Then all join in. As in the West, the blackbirds are the first to begin; and here in the Himalayas they have yellow bills as our own blackbirds do.

And I sit and listen and the sky is orange with shafts of light behind the peaks. Each day these shafts are more to the south. Now the most dramatic moment arrives: the tips of the snows get the first glow. It is as if a Deva lights a crimson lantern on the tip of the highest mountain and, one by one, all the other tips begin to glow. The deep, red light slides lower and lower, and the tips of the peaks become coral-red. Then by magic, the whole range becomes coral-red, then deep gold, then brilliant yellow, and, becoming paler and paler, they will stand white, glistening, unreal in their purity; first against a livid, yellowish sky and later as though suspended in the blue. Seemingly so light and ethereal that one cannot believe one's eyes.

The nights are completely windstill; and there is something very special about the silence of the Himalayas. I have never experienced anything quite like it. I mean the Sound . . . Everywhere I went, in Darjeeling, in Kashmir on the borders of Nepal, and here of course, I have heard it louder than ever. The Sound, like a distant melodious roar. Something between the whistle of a bat and the singing of telegraph wires. It seems to come from afar, and at the same time it is very near, outside one and inside the head also. When the Silence is Absolute, it has Sound. It must be the same with Light. For it is said that Absolute Light represents Absolute Darkness. So the Rishis call God 'The Dark Light'. I call it the Roar of Silence, *Nada*, the first and the last Sound of Creation.

As soon as I arrived here from the plains on the 5th August I heard it. I woke up in the night; it was pitch dark. There was stillness and the Sound. And my heart was suddenly glad; it was like a greeting from the homeland . . . The silence is so compact, so dense, almost physically felt; it seems to descend on and envelop one; one is lost, immersed in it, drowned; and there is nothing else beside it in the whole wide world . . . The Sound is deep, endless, eternal.

The Yogis in Rishikesh say that it is the *Nada*, the Breath of Brahma, who can never sleep, can never rest, otherwise the Creation will disappear into Nothingness. And they also say that you can hear it in the Himalayas much more easily than anywhere else in the world, because so many Rishis have meditated in those hills for thousands of years, creating a special, favourable atmosphere. Perhaps it is true; certainly the Sound is true and very real. It is impossible to say from where it comes; from very far; from very near and yet from all around.

I am so deeply happy here, a happiness never before experienced. That peace which Guruji left with us all. Prayer is easy and God is near . . .

My Love to you . . .

8 November
I have been here for three months. Almost sixteen weeks have passed since Guruji's death. So much has happened within me; slowly, gradually, by degrees the world begins to look differently, to change imperceptibly.

The sunrise, the sunset, the garden, the people, the whole daily life seems outwardly the same. But the values have changed. The meaning underlying it all is not the same as before. Something which seemed intangible, unattainable, slowly, very slowly becomes a permanent reality. There is nothing but Him. At the beginning it was sporadic; later of shorter or longer duration, when I was acutely conscious of it. But now . . . The infinite, endless Him . . . Nothing else is there. And all the beauty of nature which surrounds me is as if only on the edge of my consciousness. Deep within I am resting in the peace of His Heart. The body feels so light at times. As if it were made of the pure, thin air of the snow peaks. This constant vision of the One is deepening and increasing in the mind, giving eternal peace.

IRINA TWEEDIE

Thoughts on my Sick-Bed

And has the remnant of my life
Been pilfered of this sunny spring?
And have its own prelusive sounds
Touched in my heart no echoing string?

Ah! say not so – the hidden life
Couchant within this feeble frame
Hath been enriched by kindred gifts,
That, undesired, unsought-for, came

With joyful heart in youthful days
When fresh each season in its round
I welcomed the earliest celandine
Glittering upon the mossy ground

With busy eyes I pierced the lane
In quest of known and *un*known things,
– The primrose a lamp on its fortress rock,
The silent butterfly spreading its wings,

The violet betrayed by its noiseless breath,
The daffodil dancing in the breeze,
The carolling thrush, on his naked perch,
Towering above the naked trees.

Our cottage-hearth no longer our home,
Companions of Nature were we,
The stirring, the still, the loquacious, the mute –
To all we gave our sympathy.

Yet never in those careless days
When spring-time in rock, field, or bower
Was but a fountain of earthly hope
A promise of fruits and the *splendid* flower.

No! then I never felt a bliss
That might with *that* compare
Which, piercing to my couch of rest,
Came on the vernal air.

When loving friends an offering brought,
The first flowers of the year,
Culled from the precincts of our home,
From nooks to memory dear.

With some sad thoughts the work was done,
Unprompted and unbidden,
But joy it brought to my *hidden* life,
To consciousness no longer hidden.

I felt a power unfelt before,
Controlling weakness, languor, pain;
It bore me to the terrace walk
I trod the hills again; –

No prisoner in this lonely room,
I *saw* the green banks of the Wye,
Recalling thy prophetic words,
Bard, brother, friend from infancy!

No need of motion, or of strength,
Or even the breathing air:
– I thought of Nature's loveliest scenes;
And with memory I was there.

DOROTHY WORDSWORTH

To Maggie Lukens

Feb. 5th [1884]

My Dear Maggie.

I hope I never shall be too busy or too old to answer letters like yours as far as I can, for to all of us comes this desire for something to hold by, look up to, & believe in. I will tell you my experience & as it has stood the test of youth & age, health & sickness, joy & sorrow, poverty & wealth I feel that it is genuine, & seem to get more light, warmth & help as I go on learning more of it year by year.

My parents never bound us to any church but taught us that the love of goodness was the love of God, the cheerful doing of duty made life happy, & that the love of one's neighbor in its widest sense was the best help for oneself. Thier lives showed us how lovely this simple faith was, how much honor, gratitude & affection it brought them, & what a sweet memory they left behind for, though father still lives his life is over as far as thought or usefulness are possible.

Theodore Parker & R. W. Emerson did much to help me to see that one can shape life best by trying to build up a strong & noble character through good books, wise people's society, an interest in all reforms that help the world, & a cheerful acceptance of whatever is inevitable. Seeing a beautiful compensation in what often seems a great sacrifice, sorrow or loss, & believing always that a wise, loving & just Father cares for us, sees our weakness & is near to help if we call. Have you read Emerson? He is called a Pantheist or believer in Nature instead of God. He was truly *Christian* & saw God *in* Nature, finding strength & comfort in the sane, sweet influences of the great Mother as well as the Father of all. I too believe this, & when tired, sad, or tempted find my best comfort in the woods, the sky, the healing solitude that lets my poor, weary soul find the rest, the fresh hope, or the patience which only God can give us.

People used to tell me that when sorrow came I should find my faith faulty because it had no name, but they were wrong, for when the heavy loss of my dear, gifted sister found me too feeble to do anything but suffer passively, I still had the sustaining sense of a love that never failed even when I could not see why this lovely life should end when it was happiest.

As a poor, proud, struggling girl I held to the belief that if I *deserved* success it would surely come so long as my ambition was not for selfish ends but for my dear family, & it did come, far more fully than I ever hoped or dreamed tho youth, health & many hopes went to earn it. Now when I might enjoy rest, pleasure & travel I am still tied by new duties to my baby, & give up my dreams sure that something better will be given me in time.

Freedom was always my longing, but I have never had it, so I am still trying to feel that this is the discipline I need & when I am ready the liberty will come.

I think you need not worry about any name for your faith but simply try to be & do good, to love virture [i.e., virtue] in others & study the lives of those who are truely worthy of imitation. Women need a religion of thier own, for they are called upon to lead a quiet self sacrificing life with peculiar trials, needs, & joys, & it seems to me that a very simple one is fitted to us whose hearts are usually more alive than heads, & whose hands are tied in many ways.

Health of body helps health of soul, cheerful views of all things keep up the courage & brace the nerves. Work for the mind *must* be had, or daily duty becomes drudgery & the power to enjoy higher things is lost. Change of scene is sometimes salvation for girls or women who out grow the place they are born in, & it is thier duty to go away even if it is to harder work, for hungrey minds prey on themselves & ladies suffer for escape from a too pale or narrow life.

I have felt this, & often gone away from Concord to teach, (which I never liked) because there was no food for my mind in that small conservative town, especially since Mr Emerson died.

Food, fire & shelter are not *all* that women need, & the noble discontent that asks for more should not be condemned but helped if possible.

At 21 I took my little earnings ($20) & a few clothes, & went to seek my fortune tho I might have sat still & been supported by rich friends. All those hard years were teaching me what I afterward put into the books, & so I made my fortune out of my seeming *mis* fortunes; I speak of myself because what one has *lived* one really knows & so can speak honestly. I wish I had my own house (as I still hope to have) so that I might ask the young women who often write to me as you do, to come & see me, & look about & find what they need, & see the world of wise, good people to whom I could introduce them as others did me thirty years ago. I hope to have it soon, & then you must come & have our talk, & see if any change can be made without neglecting duty.

When one cannot go away one can travel in spirit by means of books. Tell me what you read & like, & perhaps I can send you a key that will at least open a window through which your eyes can wander while the faithful hands & feet are tied by duty at home.

Write freely to me, dear girl, & if I can help in any way be sure I gladly will. A great sorrow often softens & prepares the heart for a new harvest of good seed, & the sowers God sends are often very humble ones, used only as instruments by him because being very human they come naturally & by every day ways to the help of those who are passing through trials like thier own.

I find one of the compensations for age in the fact that it seems to bring young people nearer to me, & that the experiences so hard to live through now help me to understand others. So I am always glad to do what I can, remembering how I wrote to my father for just such help as you ask, & how he answered as I have tried to answer you.

Let me know if it does comfort you any.

With love to my other girls

I am always your friend
L. M. A.

The simple Buddha religion is very attractive to me, & I believe in it. God is enough for me, & all the prophets are only stepping stones to him. Christ is a great reformer to me not God.

from The Selected Letters of Louisa May Alcott

The Seasons

Very early in the morning sunlight runs
  Plucking at the grassblades with the spheres' music,
  And the silver-candled moon in the dawn
  Kindles in each dewdrop a reflected song.
  The trees catch the young light playing,
  Flinging this shower of green laburnum gold,
  A seamless robe.

The noiselessness which lives in the summer air
  Is borne from interstellar spaces
  Free as the winged seed on the wind,
  Implanted as a gift in quiet hearts.

And when in the maturing year in autumn mists
  The elms loom a golden shadow in the mind
  (Forgetting fine detail of loved leaf and bark)
  We know they are foreshadowings of our own dissolving
  (O burnished cloud) –
  Both are indwelling and a dispossessing.

For when night falls with the stars unsphered
  (Crystal frosts burning the windowpane)
  And lips are dumb and our house derelict,
  From the interlunar caverns the Word will run
  Swift as light and speak for us from the thick cloud.
  Then we will hope for the silver nails
  To splinter the dark for us again –
  See them turning in the vast door of heaven –
And open wide new worlds.

                              M.L., a nun of Burnham Abbey

from A Writer's Diary

Saturday, September 22nd [1928]
This has been the finest, and not only finest, but loveliest, summer in the world. Still, though it blows, how clear and bright it is; and the clouds are opalescent; the long barns on my horizon mouse-coloured; the stacks pale gold. Owning the field has given a different orient to my feelings about Rodmell.

VIRGINIA WOOLF

from Smile at Time

YES, I should say, I do know what Eden might feel like, I have known days when, walking, out of doors, I have had to keep my eyes on the ground for the beauty around has been too exhausting to look at any longer, each oakleaf an unique work of art, each fern or flower a miracle of beauty, and when everything fell into a marvellous composition. I have known a face which, if placed in imagination in any country or age, woke that place into vivid life, and my heart beat with excitement over it. In imagination we were in a boat lying in a harbour of Crete ages ago, or listening in the philosophic schools of Alexandria in the first centuries, where I could almost see the sun beating down on marble terraces and stone steps, and hear the many tongues spoken. No poetry has seemed to be more beautiful than that which I have experienced in my own life, and none, except the mystics, seemed to say more than I myself have felt. But these things cannot be told, so, with this *credo amantis*, I will turn to the life lived here between the two great wars.

CONSTANCE SITWELL

Morning Glory

With a pure colour there is little one can do:
Of a pure thing there is little one can say.
We are dumb in the face of that cold blush of blue,
Called glory, and enigmatic as the face of day.

A couple of optical tricks are there for the mind;
See how the azure darkens as we recede:
Like the delectable mountains left behind,
Region and colour too absolute for our need.

Or putting an eye too close, until it blurs,
You see a firmament, a ring of sky,
With a white radiance in it, a universe,
And something there that might seem to sing and fly.

Only the double sex, the usual thing;
But it calls to mind spirit, it seems like one
Who hovers in brightness suspended and shimmering,
Crying Holy and hanging in the eye of the sun.

And there is one thing more; as in despair
The eye dwells on that ribbed pentagonal round,
A cold sidereal whisper brushes the ear,
A prescient tingling, a prophecy of sound.

RUTH PITTER

COOL are the rays of the moon; cooler still is sandal paste, coolest
are the pleasant words of the gracious who have love, learning and
patience.

AVVAIYĀR, from *Nīti Venbā*

from Smile at Time

THE longer I live the more I am struck by the different facets one involuntarily shows to different people; for each different friend pulls out diverse stops of the organ, so to speak. Someone said that each separate person was a separate door to Beauty – an unique world revealed by companionship, or kinship of mind. Real beauty, as Plato said, is not for us here and now, of course, but if we can't use moments which seem perfect and timeless, what directions have we? You know the line I am so fond of, – 'Eternity is in love with the productions of Time?' How marvellous it would be if you did even feel it honest to believe in these things! It does seem to me that modern scientific ideas fit in wonderfully with what occultists have said down the centuries. I believe they have exact knowledge which goes beyond ours, but doesn't contradict it. I remember having a talk along those lines once with an Indian doctor of medicine at a dinner-party at Lahore. 'Western science,' he said, 'is legitimate knowledge; but ignorant knowledge.' Perhaps limited knowledge would be a fairer phrase?

There has been an early snowfall to everyone's surprise. When we woke up to-day it was astonishing to look out of the window on to such an exquisite world; utterly silent, and fashioned, it seemed, of crystal and ebony and gold, for when the rising sun shone on the trees each branch and twig shone with frozen snow and the gulls flying landward had gold under-wings. But that only lasted a short hour and now we are almost snowed-up and the skies have turned sombre and ponderous, and there is no shining world to be gazed at. Jim cuts wood and helps to thin a little plantation, and I have plunged like a thirsting plant into a stream of occult literature. For nearly four whole days I had not given a thought to the destiny of the soul, if you can credit it. But how happy I could be, hour after hour, day after day, to go farther and farther into these mysteries of the 'inner man' – that being that seems to shine brighter and brighter the deeper he is quarried for. All these metaphors of light, radiance, shining which are used, – they must surely correspond to some reality and they make me very envious of those who really see.

CONSTANCE SITWELL

Villeggiature

My window, framed in pear-tree bloom,
    White-curtained shone, and softly lighted:
So, by the pear-tree to my room
    Your ghost last night climbed uninvited.

Your solid self, long leagues away,
    Deep in dull books, had hardly missed me;
And yet you found this Romeo's way,
    And through the blossom climbed and kissed me.

I watched the still and dewy lawn,
    The pear-tree boughs hung white above you;
I listened to you till the dawn,
    And half forgot I did not love you.

Oh, dear! what pretty things you said,
    What pearls of song you threaded for me!
I did not – till your ghost had fled –
    Remember how you always bore me!

EDITH NESBIT

4

Burning with Fire

I am and am not, I freeze and yet am burned

Elizabeth I

Sonnet VIII

I live, yet die; I burn, and yet I drown;
I faint with heat, yet shiver with the cold;
My bitter griefs still sweeter joys enfold;
My life is hard as rock, yet soft as down.
I'm quick to foolish giggles, sudden tears,
And in my joy nurse many a grievous pain,
My bliss eternal swiftly fades again;
My leaves die off, and green bud reappears.
Thus Love unkindly leads me by the nose;
And when my breast can bear such pain no more,
Without my knowing how or why, it goes.
Then, when the heights of joy my longing knows,
And of my longed-for bliss I feel secure,
Love hurls me down, back where I wept before.

Louise Labé

from The Swan in the Evening

WHERE are the three little girls whose laughing portraits, sketched with such tenderness and such technical grace of light long lines and short, and printed in *Punch*, made us appear so cherished, comical and attractive? Polly. Molly. Betsy. What has happened to them?

Quick said the bird find them, find them . . .

. . . They are only prints and echoes, all that is recapturable, among the other echoes inhabiting the garden; lost paradise within which one master echo still reverberates, as vibrant now as then.

Once upon a time, but when, in actual time, I have no idea, a sudden searching convulsion of my whole ground of being overtakes me in the garden. I am mooching alone along the gravel path that runs between the lawn and Lovers' Walk. It is autumn, and the sun has dropped. I am not Amaranth Aurora or Beryl Diamond, or that obsessive spell-maker, murmuring as I stroll or crawl around OM MANI PADME HUM. I am almost no one, kicking up amber drifts of chestnut leaves, aware of the dark green thickets of laurel on my left, and on my right of the hoary expanse of lawn, ringed by blue deodars and cedars and already crisping with frost and sparkling in the opalescent haze of dusk. I look up and see the moon quite high in the sky, a moon nearly at the full, singular in its lucence. I stop to stare at it. Then something extraordinary happens. . . . A flash . . . as if an invisible finger had pressed a master switch and floodlit my whole field of vision. At the same time the world starts spinning, and I am caught up in the spin, lifted, whirled. A voice splits the sky, splits my head. . . . And yet there is absolutely not a sound in the garden, not a barking dog, not a shunting train, not even a late robin; and although the detonation is within me it is also immeasurably distant, as far beyond the moon as I in the spinning garden am immeasurably below it. It is the Voice of God, of this I am certain. He has addressed me, he has pierced me with a word, an arrow with my name on it, imperative. . . .

All over in a second. I am put down again; dropped out. I hurry back into the house, hoping not to be seen because I must look different. I dash upstairs and seek the mirror in my bedroom; scrutinize my poorly lit reflection. . . . Not changed.

God has pointed at me. He has not touched me.

ROSAMOND LEHMANN

from West-Eastern Divan

Zuleika

What does this commotion mean?
Will the East good news impart?
Of its pinions the fresh motion
Cools the deep wounds of the heart.

With the dust it sports caressing,
Blows it up in fleecy cloud,
Drives towards the safe vine-arbour
Insects in their happy crowd.

Renders mild the sun's hot fervour,
Cools these heated cheeks of mine,
Kisses, as it passes by,
On the hills and plains the vine.

And its gentle whisper brings me
Thousand greetings from my friend,
And before the hills grow darker
Greet me kisses without end.

So thou canst now farther go!
Serve thy friends and those that sorrow.
There, where lofty towers glow,
Shall I find my love to-morrow.

Ah! glad tidings for the heart,
Love's breath that makes it joy to live,
Come to me only from his mouth,
For these his breath alone can give.

MARIANNE WILLEMER

The Force of Love

THESE are some of the affections of the soul which I have been obliged to speak about. I have been unable to explain otherwise its sentiments and its dispositions. These are given to the soul in such great abundance that it would be impossible to speak about all of them. But, above all, what cannot be expressed is how they are infused into the soul, and the intimate and loving way in which this happens! O, how many times have I been constrained, through the force of the respect and love I felt in the presence of the majesty of God, to throw myself at full length on the ground, for I would have wished to lose myself in any abyss and vanish utterly, right down to the centre of the world! And in that state, doing nothing but crying and sighing, I would have wished by my tears and my sighs to embrace even more ardently that fire with which I felt myself burning, desiring nothing more than to die in the violence of those passions, beseeching the saints of Paradise to procure for me this happy death, to kindle it with such force that I might be able to burn from it and be consumed by it entirely.

It seems to me that in this state the soul is always empty and always full! Always empty in that everything is erased from it, be it the external works it performs or the internal affections it receives, neither retaining nor conserving any idea or memory of them; and always full on account of the loving affections which God pours incessantly into it! Always empty in that it has a simple, sweet, but strong impression of its own nothingness and that of all created things, which empties it of itself and of all creatures. Always full, in that it has a simple impression, sweet, but also strong, of God who fills it, and of all its powers which it gathers together completely! In effect, these powers no longer function naturally. For the imagination, no matter how mad and extravagant it might be, does not rove any more! It is enchained and imprisoned in some port which it leaves no more! Sometimes I thought that I no longer had any imagination, or at least that I no longer had any use for it! Then at other times I heard it said that 'one represents things to oneself and imagines many things'. This surprises me and I cannot understand it; for I have neither image, figure, species or representation, be it corporeal or spiritual, even of the divinity and humanity of our Lord. And when images of them appear and begin to form themselves, something in me rejects and destroys them in a moment, because I desire God, and not his image or a representation of him! The memory does not return to the past and does not think about the future. The understanding comes neither from discourse, nor reasoning; or at least so little that it is negligible. And with regard to the will – it is all on fire; and all its powers are in some unknown satiety and repose. The whole soul, in a forgetfulness of self and of all things, is not troubled about itself, its good or its evil, its salvation or its loss. This it doesn't think about! But all its aspirations and desires tend towards and result in carrying out the will of God and in being in the state in which it pleases him. This is what it asks of him incessantly.

Two things I have asked in particular from God. The first, that it might please him to grant me the grace of never seeing, touching or feeling as in any way belonging to me any of his gifts and his graces; but that, returning them to him with the same purity with which it pleased him to give them to me, and not having sullied them by appropriating them to myself, I give them back to him faithfully. The second, that it might please him to grant me also the grace of never seeing, seeking or finding anything in myself; but that, in attaching myself entirely and perfectly to him, I seek nothing but his glory! It pleased him, through his goodness, not to reject my prayers. For truly, there is nothing which humbles me more than the knowledge of his gifts; and, no matter what, I hardly ever think about myself or any creature.

The soul's impression of God surges back and also influences the body, placing its senses in an honourable and modest posture, banishing entirely all frivolity and unseemliness from it, no matter how little.

The soul, it seems to me, simply looks at God, bearing itself in his presence with great respect and great modesty. It does not continue in that exercise of interior acts as it did in the beginning, but looks only at God with that attention and respect. It does not act, or very little, except when those affections of which I have spoken are infused into it, and even then it does not operate through its natural power. The soul is moved, without itself being the agent; it yields itself rather than act on its own.

There is one thing which troubles me and causes me fear. This is when it is a question of forming one's intentions. It is done in this state by a single glance at God, a simple sentiment so sweet and so delicate that often the soul is not even aware of it. Being as swift as it is subtle, this happens in a moment, and no longer or seldom by a formal act. When one thinks of adjusting one's intentions in this way, this troubles the repose and peace of the soul somewhat; and it appears to me that the will is displeased when it is drawn from the place of its repose in order to be employed in those things. I have not been able yet to express myself well in this, so as to know what I must do about it. For I fear more than I can say any thought, word, action or the slightest operation of the body and of the soul that is produced through the movement and instinct of nature, and even of reason itself; because the soul cannot act or operate except through the movement and spirit of God and of Jesus Christ and his love. I have always had a pure intention, together with its sentiment. But for a year now this sentiment has been taken away from me, if not absolutely, at least from day to day. This means that sometimes I know neither where I am, nor why, nor through what movement I do these things. Nevertheless, if I enter into myself and examine my heart, I always find it in the disposition in which I would much prefer to die than do anything that – I do not say offend God, but – would not be in conformity with his will and for its pure accomplishment.

CLAUDINE MOINE, from *You Looked at Me*

On Monsieur's Departure

I grieve and dare not show my discontent,
I love and yet am forced to seem to hate,
I do, yet dare not say I ever meant,
I seem stark mute but inwardly do prate.
    I am and am not, I freeze and yet am burned,
    Since from myself another self I turned.

My care is like my shadow in the sun,
Follows me flying, flies when I pursue it,
Stands and lies by me, doth what I have done.
His too familiar care doth make me rue it.
    No means I find to rid him from my breast,
    Till by the end of things it be suppressed.

Some gentler passion slide into my mind,
For I am soft and made of melting snow;
Or be more cruel, love, and so be kind.
Let me float or sink, be high or low.
    Or let me live with some more sweet content,
    Or die and so forget what love e'er meant.

Elizabeth I

from The Fire of Love

What things I should like to tell you, reverend father, so that you might have a better chance of understanding me a little! Sometimes I am forced to cry out – Where am I? What has become of me? I feel myself burning without fire, bound down without fetters; sheets of flame lick me up, making me live and die. I suffer, I live, and I die, endlessly, but I would not exchange this life with a dozen other temporal lives for anything. I can't keep still: I want to fly, to chatter, to call out to people 'Love Jesus and nothing else!' I am often alone, but Jesus is good company.

Here is a curious thing: the more I wish to be free the more I feel taken up with and bound to Him. I try to renounce all temporal things as much as possible, and find in return an extreme satisfaction which makes me very happy. I continually burn and suffer, and want to burn and suffer more and more. I want to live; I want to die. I tell you frankly I don't know what I want myself. I seek and I don't find, and then I don't know what I am looking for. I love a little, but I don't see or understand what I love. But for all my ignorance I feel that it is some great, huge good. It is Jesus.

My dear father, if you know any soul deeply wounded by the love of Christ, ask her what remedy she has found for the bitter pain of that burning love – and then tell me. Jesus often does not answer me; I seek Him, and He won't be found; He turns a deaf ear to my sighs and moaning. 'Tell me who you are and what you want,' I say to Him, 'Make yourself known and then let me die.' I am uncontrolled almost to the extent of being rude to Him. Why does He have to be looked for thus? Sometimes I end up by calling Him cruel, but immediately after beg His pardon: some of the things I say are prompted not by anger, but by so much love. Now, father, you can follow the example of many others and say that I am mad.

It is little enough to suffer, to be burning, to die, to be reduced to nothing . . . what then can I do for Jesus? I know nothing to say or to give to Him. But for all that I have this very day consecrated myself to Him, such as I am, without reserve.

Forgive the waste of words in this letter. I don't want to write any more to anybody; I find it difficult to put two words together, which is really disheartening. But then, Jesus comes to my help. I scribble down everything that comes into my head – and then this loathsome pride which never leaves me prevents me from reading over what I have written for fear of verifying for myself that it is all lunacy. *Vive Jésus!* Pray for me, and bless me always and from the bottom of your heart. – From poor Gemma of Jesus.

GEMMA GALGANI, from *Lettres et extases*

Remembrance

If I should leave you in the days to come
God grant that may not be –
But yet if so,
Your love for me must fade I know.
You will remember – and you will forget.
But oh! imperishable – strong
My love for you shall burn and glow
Deep in your heart – your whole life long,
Unknown, unseen, but living still in bliss
So you shall bear me with you all the days.
Forget then what you will.
I died – but not my love for you,
That lives for aye – though dumb,
Remember this
If I should leave you in the days to come.

AGATHA CHRISTIE

from Hildegard of Bingen's Book of Divine Works

THEN a wheel of marvelous appearance became visible right in the center of the breast of the above-mentioned figure which I had seen in the midst of the southern air. On the wheel there were symbols that made it look like the image I had seen twenty-eight years ago – then it took the form of an egg, as described in the third vision of my book *Scivias*. At the top of the wheel, along the curve of the egg, there appeared a circle of *luminous fire*, and under it there was another circle of *black fire*. The luminous circle was twice as large as the black one. And these two circles were so joined as to form but a single circle. Under the black circle appeared another circle as of *pure ether*, which was as large as the two other circles put together. Under this ether circle was seen a circle of *watery air*, which in size was the same as the circle of luminous fire. Beneath this circle of watery air appeared another

circle of *sheer white clear air*, which looked to be as tough as a
sinew of the human body. This circle was the same size as the
circle of black fire. Both circles, too, were so joined as to appear to
be but a single circle. Under this sheer white clear air, finally,
there appeared still another *thin stratum of air*, which at times
seemed to raise up high, light clouds and then again deep-hang-
ing dark clouds. At times the stratum of air seemed to extend over
this entire circle. All six circles were joined together without a
wide space between them. While the topmost circle exceeded the
other spheres in light, the circle of watery air moistened all the
other circles with dampness.

From the edge of the wheel's eastern side a line separating the
northern zone from the other areas extended in a northerly direction as far as the edge of the western side. In addition, in the
middle of the sphere of thin air was seen a sphere, which was
equally distant all around from the sheer white and luminous air.
The radius of the sphere had the same depth as the space extending from the top of the first circle to the outermost clouds, or we
might say that this space extended from the distant clouds as far
as the top of this sphere.

In the middle of the giant wheel appeared a human figure.
The crown of its head projected upward, while the soles of its feet
extended downward as far as the sphere of sheer white and luminous air. The fingertips of the right hand were stretched to the
right, and those of the left hand were stretched to the left, forming a cross extending to the circumference of the circle. This is
the way in which the figure had extended its arms.

At the four sides appeared four heads: those of a leopard, a
wolf, a lion, and a bear. Above the crown of the figure's head, in
the sphere of pure ether, I saw from the leopard's head that the
animal was exhaling through its mouth. Its breath curved somewhat backward to the right of the mouth, became extended, and
assumed the shape of a crab's head with a pair of pincers that
formed its two feet. At the left side of the mouth the leopard's
breath assumed the shape of a stag's head. Out of the crab's
mouth there emerged another breath that extended to the middle

of the space between the heads of the leopard and the lion. The breath from the stag's head extended as far as the middle of the space remaining between the leopard and the bear. All of these exhalations had the same length: the breath extending from the right side of the leopard's head to the crab's head; the breath stretching from the left side of the same mouth as far as the stag's head; the breath reaching from the stag's head to the middle of the space between the heads of the leopard and lion; and finally, the breath emerging from the mouth of the stag's head to the midst of the space between the heads of the leopard and lion.

All these heads breathed toward the above-mentioned wheel and the human figure.

[In like manner the exhalations of the other animals are described. After the leopard come the wolf, and lion, and the bear; after the stag and the crab, the serpent and the lamb. And all of them breathe concentrically toward the human figure in the center.]

Above the head of this human figure the seven planets were sharply delineated from each other. Three were in the circle of luminous fire, one was in the sphere of black fire beneath it, while another three were farther below in the circle of pure ether . . . [All the planets shone their rays at the animal heads as well as at the human figure] . . . Within the circumference of the circle that looked like luminous fire, there now appeared sixteen major stars: four between the heads of the leopard and the lion, four between the heads of the lion and the wolf, four between the heads of the wolf and the bear, and four between the heads of the bear and the leopard. Eight of them, which as medium-sized stars helped one another, were between the heads in such a way that two of them between two of the heads shone their rays toward one another at the image of the thin layer of air. But the other eight stars, which were neighbors of the other animal heads, directed their radiance at the circle of black fire.

The circle of pure ether and the circle of sheer white luminous air were completely full of stars which shone their rays at the opposite clouds. From this point one could see at the right of the above-described image, as it were, two separate tongues flowing like streams toward the above-mentioned wheel and the human figure. Also to the left of the previously mentioned clouds similar tongues emerged from time to time and were turned toward the wheel and the human figure as if to give rise to small streams. Thus the figure was entwined and surrounded by these symbols. I saw also that from the breath of the figure in whose breast the wheel appeared, there emerged a light with many rays that was brighter than the brightest day. In these rays were measured to an accurate and most precise standard the symbols of the circles and the symbols of all the other figures that were seen on this wheel as well as the individual marks of articulation of the human figure – I am speaking here of the image in the midst of the cosmic wheel.

The Hidden Dream

O, hey, man who has burned
My lips with the sparkling flames of kisses,
Have you seen anything in the depth of
My two silent eyes of the secret of this madness?

Do you have any idea that, in my heart, I
Hid a dream of your love?
Do you have any idea that of this hidden love
I had a raging fire on my soul?

They have said that that woman is a mad woman
Who gives kisses freely from her lips;
Yes, but kisses from your lips
Bestow life on my dead lips.

May the thought of reputation never be in my head.
This is I who seeks you for satisfaction in this way.

I crave a solitude and your embrace;
I crave a solitude and the lips of the cup.

An opportunity far from the eyes of others
To pour you a goblet from the wine of life,
A bed I want of red roses so that one night
I might give you intoxication.

O, hey, man who has burned my lips
With the flames of kisses,
This is a book without conclusion,
And you have read only a brief page from it.

FURUGH FARRUKHZAD

from The Golden Fountain

IN answer to a question as to whether God did not feel like fire
she replied: 'Yes, and no, for we feel we shall be consumed, and
yet it is not a burning which is experienced, but a blissful energy
of the most inexpressible and unbearable intensity, which seems
to disintegrate or disperse the flesh. So long as this is given with
certain limits the experience is blissful to heart and mind. Beyond
that limit it is bliss-agony. Beyond this again it would soon be
death to the body – a very terrible feeling which does not bear
remembering or thinking about.'

ANONYMOUS

from The Lamentations of Isis and Nephthys

Isis: Come thou to me quickly,
   Since I desire to see thy face after not having seen thy face . . .
   My heart is hot at thy wrongful separation;
   I yearn for thy love toward me.
   Come! Be not alone! Be not far off!

Nephthys: Draw nigh, so please you, to us;
   We miss life through lack of thee.

FROM *SOPHIA: GODDESS OF WISDOM*

from Mirror of an Eastern Moon

'See, I tried everything, went everywhere,
But never found a friend as dear as you;
I drank from all the fountains, tried the grapes,
But never tasted wine as sweet as you.'

I studied hundred learned manuscripts:
In every letter I saw only you.
I washed away the letters with my tears:
A mirror was the shining page for you.

I heard your voice in every rustling breeze;
The snow, the grass were lovely veils for you;
I dived into the ocean without shore:
The lustrous pearls reflected only you.

Then came the storm.
The garden of my heart
Was shiv'ring in the cold, all leaves were shed.
There was the desert.
And the barren cloud.
And silence. And

   the sun at midnight – you.

ANNE MARIE SCHIMMEL

The Beauty of God

UPON a certain time when I was at prayer and my spirit was
exalted, God spake unto me many gracious words full of love.

And when I looked, I beheld God who spake with me. But if thou seekest to know that which I beheld, I can tell thee nothing, save that I beheld a fullness and a clearness, and felt them within me so abundantly that I can in no wise describe it, nor give any likeness thereof. For what I beheld was not corporal, but as though it were in heaven. Thus I beheld a beauty so great that I can say naught concerning it, save that I saw the Supreme Beauty, containeth within Itself all goodness. And all the saints were standing before this beauteous Majesty, praising it.

Methought, however, that I stayed in this trance but a very brief while; then said God unto me, 'My beloved daughter, dear unto Me, all the saints of Paradise do bear an especial love toward thee, and likewise doth My mother, and they will bring thee unto Me.' And albeit these words were spoken unto me, all concerning His mother and all the saints seemed unto me but a small thing. For so great was my joy in Him that I took no heed of looking at the angels and the saints, because all their goodness and all their beauty was from Him and in Him; He was the whole and Supreme Good, with all beauty, and so great a joy had I in His words that I paid no heed to any creature.

Again He said unto me, 'Infinite is the love which I bear thee, but I do not reveal it unto thee – yea, I do even conceal it.'

Then answered my soul, 'Wherefore hast Thou such love and joy in me, who am hateful, inasmuch as I have offended Thee all the days of my life?'

To this did He make answer, 'So great is the love I bear thee that I no more remember thy sins, albeit Mine eyes do see them; for in thee have I much treasure.'

Then did my soul feel an assurance so true that it doubted no more. It felt and saw that the eyes of God were searching within it, and it had such joy in those eyes that neither man nor saint come down from heaven could declare it. When He told me that He concealed much love, because I was not able to bear it, my soul answered: 'If Thou art God omnipotent, make Thou me able to bear it.'

Then He made answer finally and said: 'If I were to do as thou askest, thou wouldst have here all that thou desirest, and wouldst no longer hunger after Me. For this reason will I not grant thy request, for I desire that in this world thou shouldst hunger and long after Me and shouldst ever be eager to find Me.'

ST ANGELA OF FOLIGNO

Like a silkworm weaving
her house with love
from her marrow,
                          and dying
in her body's threads
winding tight, round
and round,
               I burn
desiring what the heart desires.

Cut through, O lord,
my heart's greed,
and show me
your way out,

O lord white as jasmine.

MAHĀDĒVIYAKKA

from The Flowing Light of the Godhead

O soaring eagle! darling lamb!
O glowing spark! Set me on fire!
How long must I endure this thirst?
One hour is already too long,

A day is as a thousand years
When Thou art absent!
Should this continue for eight days
I would rather go down to Hell –
(Where indeed I already am!)
Than that God should hide Himself
From the loving soul;
For that were anguish greater than human death,
Pain beyond all pain.
The nightingale must ever sing
Because its nature is love;
Whoso would take that from it
Would bring it death.
   Ah! Mighty Lord! Look on my need!
Then the Holy Spirit spoke to the soul –
'Come, noble maid! Prepare thyself
Thy Lover comes!'
   Startled but inwardly rejoicing
She said: 'Welcome, faithful messenger,
Would that it were ever so!
I am so evil and so faithless
That I can find no peace of mind
Apart from my Love.
The moment it seems that I cool
But a little from love of Him,
Then am I in deep distress
And can do nothing but seek for Him lamenting.'
   Then the messenger spoke:
'Thou must purify thyself,
Sprinkle the dust with water,
Scatter flowers in thy room.'
   And the exiled soul replied:
'When I purify, I blush,
When I sprinkle, I weep,
When I pray, then must I hope,
When I gather flowers, I love.

When my Lord comes
I am beside myself
For there cometh with Him such sweet melody
That all carnal desire dieth within me:
And His sweet music puts far from me
All sorrow of heart.
    The mighty voice of the Godhead
Has spoken to me in powerful words
Which I have received
With the dull hearing of my misery –
A light of utmost splendour
Glows on the eyes of my soul
Therein have I seen the inexpressible ordering
Of all things, and recognized God's unspeakable
  glory –
That incomprehensible wonder –
The tender caress between God and the soul,
The sufficiency in the Highest,
Discipline in understanding,
Realization with withdrawal,
According to the power of the senses,
The unmingled joy of union,
The living love of Eternity
As it now is and evermore shall be.'

    Then were seen four rays of light
Which shot forth all at once
From the noble cross-bow of the Trinity
From the Divine Throne through the nine Choirs.
There none is so poor nor so rich
That he is not met by Love;
The rays of the Godhead illuminate him
With inconceivable light;
The humanity of the Son greets him
In brotherly love;
The Holy Spirit flows through him

With the miraculous creative power
Of everlasting joy!
The undivided Godhead welcomes him
With the glory of His Divine Countenance
And fills him with the blessedness
Of His life-giving breath.

Love flows from God to man without effort
As a bird glides through the air
Without moving its wings –
Thus they go whithersoever they will
United in body and soul
Yet in their form separate –
As the Godhead strikes the note
Humanity sings,
The Holy Spirit is the harpist
And all the strings must sound
Which are strung in love.

There was also seen
That sublime vessel
In which Christ dwelt nine months on earth
In soul and body,
As it ever shall remain
Only without the great glory
Which at the last day
The heavenly Father will give to all
The bodies of the redeemed.
This our Lady must also lack
So long as the earth floats above the sea.

MECHTILD OF MAGDEBURG

from Through mine own Eyes

WHEN I knew myself nothing but a prize fool in love, I took my
pain and foolishness in both hands and quite simply offered them
to God, whom I recognized through this last anguish to be the
backcloth of my life and my eternal love.

What followed was beyond me to understand.

Whether it was predestined or whether the Heavens had been
waiting with an open question to hear an uncomplaining acceptance of this last sorrow, I cannot say.

It felt as though an infinitely complex machine had in all its
parts, between one moment and the next, clicked silently into
gear and started to work with inexorable power.

I saw face to face at last.

Light streamed down from the sky such as I have never beheld.
The sun shone with a new light, as though translucent gold were at
its heart. I saw not only the physical sun but the spiritual sun also,
which poured down on me as I walked in the garden at Coombe.

The wonder was beyond anything I have ever read or imagined or heard men speak about. I was Adam walking alone in the
first Paradise. That it was a garden near the outskirts of London
in the twentieth century made no difference, for time was not, or
had come round again in a full circle. Though I was Adam, I had
no need of Eve, for both combined within me. Marriage and
maternity fulfilled and surpassed, I had run beyond womanhood
and become a human being.

Every flower spoke to me, every spider wove a miracle of intri-
cacy for my eyes, every bird understood that here was Heaven
come to earth. Turner must have been seeing the skies as I saw
them then – living cloud shapes crossing and recrossing each
other as though conversing in form or singing in color.

But there was something more wonderful than the Light
within the light – more wonderful than the standstill of time. It
was that God walked with me in the garden as He did before the
Fall. Whether I sat, whether I walked, He was there – radiant,
burningly pure, holy beyond holy.

When I breathed, I breathed Him; when I asked a question He both asked and answered it.

My heart was unshuttered to Him and He came and went at will; my head had no limit or boundary of skull, but the Spirit of God played on me as though my mind were a harp which reached the zenith.

Every prayer was fulfilled, every possible desire for the whole world consummated; for His Kingdom had come and I had beheld it with my very eyes. Never again the need to meditate for He was here, to be STOOD in, SAT in, as a child might play on the edges of a great sunny river. And, indeed, I found myself only a child, playing in Him, laughing with Him at the way He was visiting His world. When I stood within Him, He gave and was everything. The years to come, which He showed me as easily as a father shows his child a curious shell beside the great river, held in them no surprise; only wonder and joy.

KATHARINE TREVELYAN

Battle-Hymn of the Republic

Mine eyes have seen the glory of the coming of the Lord:
He is trampling out the vintage where the grapes of wrath are
     stored;
He hath loosed the fateful lightning of his terrible swift sword:
     His truth is marching on.

I have seen Him in the watch-fires of a hundred circling camps;
They have builded Him an altar in the evening dews and
     damps;
I can read His righteous sentence by the dim and flaring lamps.
   His day is marching on.

I have read a fiery gospel, writ in burnished rows of steel:
'As ye deal with my contemners, so with you my grace shall deal;

Let the Hero, born of woman, crush the serpent with his heel,
　　Since God is marching on.'

He has sounded forth the trumpet that shall never call retreat;
He is sifting out the hearts of men before his judgment-seat:
Oh! be swift, my soul, to answer Him! be jubilant, my feet!
　　Our God is marching on.

In the beauty of the lilies Christ was born across the sea,
With a glory in his bosom that transfigures you and me:
As he died to make men holy, let us die to make men free,
　　While God is marching on.

JULIA WARD HOWE

Magnificat

46 And Mary said, 'My soul doth magnify the Lord,

47 And my spirit hath rejoiced in God my Saviour.

48 For he hath regarded the low estate of his handmaiden: for, behold, from henceforth all generations shall call me blessed.

49 For he that is mighty hath done to me great things; and holy is his name.

50 And his mercy is on them that fear him from generation to generation.

51 He hath shewed strength with his arm; he hath scattered the proud in the imagination of their hearts.

52 He hath put down the mighty from their seats, and exalted them of low degree.

53 He hath filled the hungry with good things; and the rich he hath sent empty away.

54 He hath holpen his servant Israel, in remembrance of his mercy;

55 As he spake to our fathers, to Abraham, and to his seed for ever.

LUKE 1: 46–55

from The Country Beyond

Jane Sherwood describes a vision, encouraged by E.K.

[J.S.] THERE were two arcs of shining silver light and they were rapidly approaching each other in space. They were both alive and quivering with power and the sense of swift movement. I thought of powerful circuits of electricity, dangerous and beautiful. If they had collided the clash of such potent forces must have been catastrophic. As they came together they met, not with the direct impact which had seemed inevitable, but sliding harmoniously into relation with each other. It was to be felt that the forces that travelled each circuit were inviolable; they might come into relation but they could not impinge on each other. The intentness of my concentration matched the terrible power in the shining arcs. My life was almost drawn out of me. In the very moment of their meeting and sliding together I was aware that by a great effort, a plunge of re-orientation I had to leap into the opposing system. Somehow I succeeded but only at the utmost stretch of effort and with the loss of my normal consciousness. Yet all this took place in my mind alone; physically I had not moved. The sign that remained with me after this breathless adventure of the mind was that of a shining crescent riding upon an arc of light.'

[E.K.] 'There is no doubt that you were being taught something important there, although I think your vision had symbolic rather than actual meaning. What kind of feeling accompanied it?'

[J.S.] 'I was exhausted with the queer kind of non-physical effort I had made, but simply radiant with joy, and deeply satisfied as though I had achieved something very important. For some time afterwards I could not get rid of the impression of light playing round my head; a purely subjective impression, of course. I could understand nothing of the meaning of it all. In fact, I have never been able to interpret the thing at all.'

JANE SHERWOOD

PRAYER is of three sorts. The one is perpetual: it is the holy perpetual desire, which prays in the sight of God, whatever thou art
doing; for this desire directs all thy works, spiritual and corporal, to
His honour, and therefore it is called perpetual. Of this it seems that
Saint Paul the glorious was talking when he said: Pray without
ceasing. The other kind is vocal prayer, when the offices or other
prayers are said aloud. This is ordained to reach the third – that is,
mental prayer: your soul reaches this when it uses vocal prayer in
prudence and humility, so that while the tongue speaks the heart is
not far from God. But one must exert one's self to hold and establish one's heart in the force of divine charity. And whenever one felt
one's mind to be visited by God, so that it was drawn to think of its
Creator in any wise, it ought to abandon vocal prayer, and to fix its
mind with the force of love upon that wherein it sees God visit it;
then, if it has time, when this has ceased, it ought to take up the
vocal prayer again, in order that the mind may always stay full and
not empty. And although many conflicts of diverse kinds should
abound in prayer, and darkness of mind with much confusion, the
devil making the soul feel that her prayer was not pleasing to God –
nevertheless, she ought not to give up on account of those conflicts
and shadows, but to abide firm in fortitude and long perseverance,
considering that the devil so does to draw her away from prayer the
mother, and God permits it to test the fortitude and constancy of
that soul. Also, in order that by those conflicts and shadows she
may know herself not to be, and in the goodwill which she feels pre-
served within her may know the goodness of God, Who is Giver
and Preserver of good and holy wills: such wills as are not vouch-
safed to all who want them.

By this means she attains to the third and last – mental prayer, in
which she receives the reward for the labour she underwent in her
imperfect vocal prayer. Then she tastes the milk of faithful prayer.
She rises above herself – that is, above the gross impulses of the
senses – and with angelic mind unites herself with God by force of
love, and sees and knows with the light of thought, and clothes herself with truth. She is made the sister of angels; she abides with her
Bridegroom on the table of crucified desire, rejoicing to seek the

honour of God and the salvation of souls; since well she sees that for this the Eternal Bridegroom ran to the shameful death of the Cross, and thus fulfilled obedience to the Father, and our salvation. This prayer is surely a mother, who conceives virtues by the love of God, and brings them forth in the love of the neighbour. Where dost thou show love, faith, and hope, and humility? In prayer. For thou wouldst never take pains to seek the thing which thou didst not love; but he who loves would ever be one with what he loves – that is, God. By means of prayer thou askest of Him thy necessity; for knowing thyself – the knowledge on which true prayer is founded – thou seest thyself to have great need. Thou feelest thyself surrounded by thine enemies – by the world with its insults and its recalling of vain pleasures, by the devil with his many temptations, by the flesh with its great rebellion and struggle against the spirit. And thou seest that in thyself thou art not; not being, thou canst not help thyself; and therefore thou dost hasten in faith to Him who is, who can and will help thee in thine every need, and thou dost hopefully ask and await His aid. Thus ought prayer to be made, if thou wishest to have that which thou awaitest. Never shall any just thing be denied thee which thou askest in this wise from the Divine Goodness; but if thou dost in other wise, little fruit shalt thou receive. Where shalt thou feel grief in thy conscience? In prayer. Where shalt thou divest thee of the self-love which makes thee impatient in the time of insults and of other pains, and shalt clothe thee in the divine love which shall make thee patient, and shalt glory in the Cross of Christ crucified? In prayer. Where shalt thou breathe the perfume of virginity and the hunger for martyrdom, holding thee ready to give thy life for the honour of God and the salvation of souls? In this sweet mother, prayer. This will make thee an observer of thy Rule: it will seal in thy heart and mind three solemn vows which thou didst make at thy profession, leaving there the imprint of the desire to observe them until death. This releases thee from conversation with fellow-creatures, and gives thee converse with thy Creator; it fills the vessel of thy heart with the Blood of the Humble Lamb, and crowns it with flame, because with flame of love that Blood was shed.

The soul receives and tastes this mother Prayer more or less perfectly, according as it nourishes itself with the food of angels – that is, with holy and true desire for God, raising itself on high, as I said, to receive it upon the table of the most sweet Cross. Therefore I said to thee that I desired to see thee nourished with angelic food, because I see not that in otherwise thou couldst be a true bride of Christ crucified, consecrated to Him in holy religion. So do that I may see thee a jewel precious in the sight of God. And do not go about wasting thy time. Bathe and drown thee in the sweet Blood of thy Bridegroom. I say no more. Remain in the holy and sweet grace of God. Sweet Jesus, Jesus Love.

ST CATHERINE OF SIENA

O God the Holy Ghost who art Light unto Thine elect,
    Evermore enlighten us.
Thou who art Fire of Love,
    Evermore enkindle us.
Thou who art Lord and Giver of Life,
    Evermore live in us.
Thou who bestowest sevenfold grace,
    Evermore replenish us.
As the wind is Thy symbol,
    So forward our goings.
As the dove,
    So launch us heavenwards.
As water,
    So purify our spirits.
As a cloud,
    So abate our temptations.
As dew,
    So revive our languor.
As fire,
    So purge out our dross.

CHRISTINA ROSSETTI

from Doom of the Kings

THEN Saint Birgitta continued: I next saw in Heaven a house of marvellous beauty and size. And in that house was a pulpit, and on the pulpit a book. And I saw two standing before the pulpit – that is, an angel and a fiend . . .

And when I, Saint Birgitta, closely watched the same pulpit with all my powers of concentration, my understanding was insufficient to comprehend it as it was; my soul could not comprehend its fairness, nor could my tongue express it. For the pulpit looked like a sunbeam, having a red color and a white color and a shining color of gold. The golden color was like the bright sun, the white color was like snow, very white, and the red color was like a rose. And each color was seen in the other. For when I beheld the gold color I saw with it the white and the red color, when I saw the white color I saw in it the other two colors and when I beheld the red color I saw in it the white and the golden color. Each color was seen in the other, yet each was by itself and distinct from the others; and no color was in front of another, nor behind another, nor one less than another, or more than another; but taken together they seemed equal in every respect. When I looked upwards, I could not comprehend the height and the breadth of the pulpit; and looking downwards, I could not see or comprehend the thickness or the depth of it, for its totality was incomprehensible. After this I saw a book in the same pulpit, shining like very bright gold in the shape of a book. The writing in this book was not written in ink; each word in the book was alive and spoke itself, as if a man would say to do this or that and it would be done then with the speaking of the word. No one read the writing in that book, but whatever that writing said was depicted on the pulpit and in the three colors. Before this pulpit I saw a king who was alive in the world; and on the left side of the pulpit I saw another king who was dead and in Hell; and on the right side of the pulpit I saw the third king who was in Purgatory. The king who was alive sat crowned as if closed about in a vessel of glass. Above that glass hung a horrible sword with three edges, constantly drawing near to that glass as a dial in a time piece draws to the mark. On the right side of the same king stood an angel who had a vessel of gold open on his lap. And on the left side stood a fiend who had a pair of tongs and a hammer. And both the angel and the fiend competed to see whose hands would be closer to the vessel of glass when the three-edged sword would touch it and break it.

Then I heard the fiend's horrible voice saying 'How long shall it go on like this? For we both pursue the same object and we do not know who will prevail.'

ST BIRGITTA OF SWEDEN

Psalm 57: *Miserere mei, deus*

Thy mercy, Lord, Lord now thy mercy show,
 On thee I lie
 To thee I fly
 Hide me, hive me as thine own,
 Till these blasts be overblown,
Which now do fiercely blow.

To the highest God I will erect my cry,
 Who quickly shall
 Dispatch this all.
 He shall from Heaven send
 From disgrace me to defend,
His love and verity.

My soul encaged lies with lions' brood,
 Villains whose hands
 Are fiery brands,
 Teeth more sharp than shaft or spear,
 Tongues far better edge do bear
Than swords to shed my blood.

As high as highest heav'n can give thee place,
    O Lord ascend,
    And thence extend
  With most bright, most glorious show,
  Over all the earth below
The sun-beams of thy face.

Me to entangle, ev'ry way I go,
    Their trap and net
    Is ready set.
  Holes they dig, but their own holes
  Pitfalls make for their own souls:
So Lord, O serve them so.

My heart prepar'd, prepared is my heart
    To spread thy praise
    With tuned lays:
  Wake my tongue, my lute awake,
  Thou my harp the consort make,
My self will bear a part.

My self when first the morning shall appear,
    With voice and string
    So will thee sing:
  That this earthly globe, and all
  Treading on this earthly ball,
My praising notes shall hear.

For God, my only God, thy gracious love
    Is mounted far
    Above each star,
  Thy unchanged verity
  Heav'nly wings do lift as high
As clouds have room to move.

As high as highest heav'n can give thee place
   O Lord ascend
   And thence extend
  With most bright, most glorious show
  Over all the earth below,
The sun-beams of thy face.

                MARY HERBERT, Countess of Pembroke

from The Flowing Light of the Godhead

SHE is silent but longs above everything else to praise Him. And He, with great desire, shows her His Divine heart. It glows like red gold in a great fire. And God lays the soul in his glowing heart so that He, the Great God, and she, the humble maid, embrace and are one as water with wine. Then she is overcome and beside herself for weakness and can no more. And He is overpowered with love for her, as He ever was, He neither gives nor takes. Then she says, 'Lord! Thou art my Beloved! My desire! My flowing stream! My Sun! And I am Thy reflection!'

                MECHTILD OF MAGDEBURG

Love Arm'd

Love in fantastic triumph sat,
Whilst bleeding hearts around him flowed,
For whom fresh pains he did create,
And strange tyrannic power he showed;
From thy bright eyes he took his fire,
Which round about, in sport he hurled;
But 'twas from mine, he took desire,
Enough to undo the amorous world.

From me he took his sighs and tears,
From thee his pride and cruelty;

From me his languishments and fears,
And every killing dart from thee;
Thus thou and I, the god have armed,
And set him up a deity;
But my poor heart alone is harmed,
Whilst thine the victor is, and free.

APHRA BEHN

THOU, Eternal Trinity, art a sea so deep that the more I enter therein, the more I find; and the more I find, the more I seek of Thee; for when the soul is satisfied in Thine abyss, it is not satisfied, but it ever continues to thirst for Thee, Eternal Trinity, desiring to behold Thee with the light of Thy light. As the hart panteth after the water brooks, so does my soul desire to issue from the prison of the darksome body, and to behold Thee in truth. O how long shall Thy face be hidden from my eyes? O Abyss, O Eternal Godhead. O Deep Sea! Robe me with Thyself, Eternal Trinity, so that I may run this mortal life with true obedience, and with the light of Thy most holy faith.

ST CATHERINE OF SIENA

5

LOST IN THE
ABYSS

From the prison confines of darkness
From the turbid cesspool of the world
Hear my needful clamour,
O able, unique God.

FURUGH FARRUKHZAD

from Letters from Dorothy Osborne to Sir William Temple

YET you are not convinced, you say, that to be miserable is the way to be good; to some natures I think it is not, but there are many of so careless and vain a temper, that the least breath of good fortune swells them with so much pride, that if they were not put in mind sometimes by a sound cross or two that they are mortal, they would hardly think it possible; and though 'tis a sign of a servile nature when fear produces more of reverence in us than love, yet there is more danger of forgetting oneself in a prosperous fortune than in the contrary, and affliction may be the surest (though not the pleasantest) guide to heaven. What think you, might not I preach with Mr. Marshall for a wager? But you could fancy a perfect happiness here, you say; that is not much, many people do so; but I never heard of anybody that ever had it more than in fancy, so that will not be strange if you should miss on 't. One may be happy to a good degree, I think, in a faithful friend, a moderate fortune, and a retired life; further than this I know nothing to wish; but if there be anything beyond it, I wish it you.

Song

The winter being over,
　　In order comes the spring,
Which doth green herbs discover,
　　And cause the birds to sing.
The night also expired,
　　Then comes the morning bright,
Which is so much desired
　　By all that love the light.

This may learn
Them that mourn,
To put their grief to flight:
The spring succeedeth winter,
And day must follow night.

He therefore that sustaineth
Affliction or distress,
Which every member paineth,
And findeth no release:
Let such therefore despair not,
But on firm hope depend,
Whose griefs immortal are not,
And therefore must have end.
They that faint
With complaint
Therefore are to blame:
They add to their afflictions,
And amplify the same.

AN COLLINS

from The Well of Pen-Morfa

ANOTHER story which I heard of these old primitive dwellings I mean to tell at somewhat greater length:

There are rocks high above Pen-Morfa; they are the same that hang over Trê-Madoc, but near Pen-Morfa they sweep away, and are lost in the plain. Everywhere they are beautiful. The great sharp ledges, which would otherwise look hard and cold, are adorned with the brightest-coloured moss, and the golden lichen. Close to, you see the scarlet leaves of the crane's-bill, and the tufts of purple heather, which fill up every cleft and cranny; but in the distance you see only the general effect of infinite richness of colour, broken here and there by great masses of ivy. At the foot of these rocks come a rich verdant meadow or two; and then you are at Pen-Morfa. The village well is sharp down under the rocks. There are one or two large sloping pieces of stone in that last field, on the road leading to the well, which are always slippery; slippery in the summer's heat, almost as much as in the frost of winter, when some little glassy stream that runs over them is turned into a thin sheet of ice. Many, many years back – a lifetime ago – there lived in Pen-Morfa a widow and her daughter. Very little is required in those out-of-the-way Welsh villages. The wants of the people are very simple. Shelter, fire, a little oat-cake and buttermilk, and garden produce; perhaps some pork and bacon from the pig in winter; clothing, which is principally of home manufacture, and of the most enduring kind: these take very little money to purchase, especially in a district into which the large capitalists have not yet come, to buy up two or three acres of the peasants; and nearly every man about Pen-Morfa owned, at the time of which I speak, his dwelling and some land beside.

Eleanor Gwynn inherited the cottage (by the road-side, on the left-hand as you go from Trê-Madoc to Pen-Morfa), in which she and her husband had lived all their married life, and a small garden sloping southwards, in which her bees lingered before winging their way to the more distant heather. She took rank among her neighbours as the possessor of a moderate independence – not rich, and not poor. But the young men of Pen-Morfa thought her very rich in the possession of a most lovely daughter. Most of us know how very pretty Welsh women are; but from all accounts, Nest Gwynn (Nest, or Nesta, is the Welsh for Agnes) was more regularly beautiful than any one for miles around. The Welsh are still fond of triads, and 'as beautiful as a summer's morning at sun-rise, as a white sea-gull on the green sea-wave, and as Nest Gwynn,' is yet a saying in that district. Nest knew she was beautiful, and delighted in it. Her mother sometimes checked her in her happy pride, and sometimes reminded her that beauty was a great gift of God (for the Welsh are a very pious people); but when she began her little homily, Nest came dancing to her, and knelt down before her, and put her face up to be kissed, and so with a sweet interruption she stopped her mother's lips. Her high spirits made some few shake their heads, and some called her a flirt and a coquette; for she could not help trying to please all, both old and young, both men and women. A very little from Nest sufficed for this; a sweet glittering smile, a word of kindness, a merry glance, or a little sympathy, all these pleased and attracted; she was like the fairy-gifted child, and dropped inestimable gifts. But some who had interpreted her smiles and kind words rather as their wishes led them than as they were really warranted, found that the beautiful, beaming Nest could be decided and saucy enough, and so they revenged themselves by calling her a flirt. Her mother heard it and sighed; but Nest only laughed.

It was her work to fetch water for the day's use from the well I told you about. Old people say it was the prettiest sight in the world to see her come stepping lightly and gingerly over the stones with the pail of water balanced on her head; she was too adroit to need to steady it with her hand. They say, now that they can afford to be charitable and speak the truth, that in all her changes to other people, there never was a better daughter to a widowed mother than Nest. There is a picturesque old farm-house under Moel Gwynn, on the road from Trê-Madoc to Criccaeth, called by some Welsh name which I now forget; but its meaning in English is 'The End of Time;' a strange, boding, ominous name. Perhaps the builder meant his work to endure till the end of time. I do not know; but there the old house stands, and will stand for many a year. When Nest was young, it belonged to one Edward Williams; his mother was dead, and people said he was on the look-out for a wife. They told Nest so, but she tossed her head and reddened, and said she thought he might look long before he got one; so it was not strange that one morning when she went to the well, one autumn morning when the dew lay heavy on the grass, and the thrushes were busy among the mountain-ash berries, Edward Williams happened to be there, on his way to the coursing match near, and somehow his greyhounds threw her pail of water over in their romping play, and she was very long in filling it again; and when she came home she threw her arms round her mother's neck, and in a passion of joyous tears told her that Edward Williams of The End of Time had asked her to marry him, and that she had said 'Yes.'

Eleanor Gwynn shed her tears too; but they fell quietly when she was alone. She was thankful Nest had found a protector – one suitable in age and apparent character, and above her in fortune; but she knew she should miss her sweet daughter in a thousand household ways; miss her in the evenings by the fireside; miss her when at night she wakened up with a start from a dream of her youth, and saw her fair face lying calm in the moonlight, pillowed by her side. Then she forgot her dream, and blessed her child, and slept again. But who could be so selfish as to be sad when Nest was so supremely happy? She danced and sang more than ever; and then sat silent, and smiled to herself: if spoken to, she started and came back to the present with a scarlet blush, which told what she had been thinking of.

That was a sunny, happy, enchanted autumn. But the winter was nigh at hand; and with it came sorrow. One fine frosty morning, Nest went out with her lover – she to the well, he to some farming business, which was to be transacted at the little inn of Pen-Morfa. He was late for his appointment; so he left her at the entrance of the village, and hastened to the inn; and she, in her best cloak and new hat (put on against her mother's advice; but they were a recent purchase, and very becoming), went through the Dol Mawr, radiant with love and happiness. One who lived until lately, met her going down towards the well, that morning; and said he turned round to look after her, she seemed unusually lovely. He wondered at the time at her wearing her Sunday clothes; for the pretty, hooded blue-cloth cloak is kept among the Welsh women as a church and market garment, and not commonly used even on the coldest days of winter for such household errands as fetching water from the well. However, as he said, 'It was not possible to look in her face, and "fault" anything she wore.' Down the sloping stones the girl went blithely with her pail. She filled it at the well: and then she took off her hat, tied the strings together, and slung it over her arm; she lifted the heavy pail and balanced it on her head. But alas! in going up the smooth, slippery, treacherous rock, the encumbrance of her cloak – it might be such a trifle as her slung hat – something, at any rate, took away her evenness of poise; the freshet had frozen on the slanting stone, and was one coat of ice; poor Nest fell, and put out her hip. No more flushing rosy colour on that sweet face – no more look of beaming innocent happiness; – instead, there was deadly pallor, and filmy eyes, over which dark shades seemed to chase each other as the shoots of agony grew more and more intense. She screamed once or twice; but the exertion (involuntary, and forced out of her by excessive pain) overcame her, and she fainted. A child coming an hour or so afterwards on the same errand, saw her lying there, ice-glued to the stone, and thought she was dead. It flew crying back.

'Nest Gwynn is dead! Nest Gwynn is dead!' and, crazy with fear, it did not stop until it had hid its head in its mother's lap. The village was alarmed, and all who were able went in haste towards the well. Poor Nest had often thought she was dying in that dreary hour; had taken fainting for death, and struggled against it; and prayed that God would keep her alive till she could see her lover's face once more; and when she did see it, white with terror, bending over her, she gave a feeble smile, and let herself faint away into unconsciousness.

Many a month she lay on her bed unable to move. Sometimes she was delirious, sometimes worn-out into the deepest depression. Through all, her mother watched her with tenderest care. The neighbours would come and offer help. They would bring presents of country dainties; and I do not suppose that there was a better dinner than ordinary cooked in any household in Pen-Morfa parish, but a portion of it was sent to Eleanor Gwynn, if not for her sick daughter, to try and tempt her herself to eat and be strengthened; for to no one would she delegate the duty of watching over her child. Edward Williams was for a long time most assiduous in his inquiries and attentions; but by-and-by (ah! you see the dark fate of poor Nest now), he slackened, so little at first that Eleanor blamed herself for her jealousy on her daughter's behalf, and chid her suspicious heart. But as spring ripened into summer, and Nest was still bedridden, Edward's coolness was visible to more than the poor mother. The neighbours would have spoken to her about it, but she shrunk from the subject as if they were probing a wound. 'At any rate,' thought she, 'Nest shall be strong before she is told about it. I will tell lies – I shall be forgiven – but I must save my child; and when she is stronger, perhaps I may be able to comfort her. Oh! I wish she would not speak to him so tenderly and trustfully, when she is delirious. I could curse him when she does.' And then Nest would call for her mother, and Eleanor would go, and invent some strange story about the summonses Edward had had to Caernarvon assizes, or to Harlech cattle market. But at last she was driven to her wits' end; it was three weeks since he had even stopped at the door to inquire, and Eleanor, mad with anxiety about her child, who was silently pining off to death for want of tidings of her lover, put on her cloak, when she had lulled her daughter to sleep one fine June evening, and set off to 'The End of Time.' The great plain which stretches out like an amphitheatre, in the half-circle of hills formed by the ranges of Moel Gwynn and the Trê-Madoc Rocks, was all golden-green in the mellow light of sunset. To Eleanor it might have been black with winter frost, she never noticed outward things till she reached The End of Time; and there, in the little farm-yard, she was brought to a sense of her present hour and errand by seeing Edward. He was examining some hay, newly stacked; the air was scented by its fragrance, and by the lingering sweetness of the breath of the cows. When Edward turned round at the footstep and saw Eleanor, he coloured and looked confused; however, he came forward to meet her in a cordial manner enough.

'It's a fine evening,' said he. 'How is Nest? But, indeed, you're being here is a sign she is better. Won't you come in and sit down?' He spoke hurriedly, as if affecting a welcome which he did not feel.

'Thank you. I'll just take this milking-stool and sit down here. The open air is like balm after being shut up so long.'

'It is a long time,' he replied, 'more than five months.'

Mrs Gwynn was trembling at heart. She felt an anger which she did not wish to show; for, if be any manifestations of temper or resentment she lessened or broke the waning thread of attachment which bound him to her daughter, she felt she should never forgive herself. She kept inwardly saying, 'Patience, patience! he may be true and love her yet;' but her indignant convictions gave her words the lie.

'It's a long time, Edward Williams, since you've been near us to ask after Nest,' said she. 'She may be better, or she may be worse, for aught you know.' She looked up at him reproachfully, but spoke in a gentle quiet tone.

'I – you see the hay has been a long piece of work. The weather has been fractious – and a master's eye is needed. Besides,' said he, as if he had found the reason for which he sought to account for his absence, 'I have heard of her from Rowland Jones. I was at the surgery for some horse-medicine – he told me about her,' and a shade came over his face, as he remembered what the doctor had said. Did he think that shade would escape the mother's eye?

'You saw Rowland Jones! Oh, man-alive, tell me what he said of my girl! He'll say nothing to me, but just hems and haws the more I pray him. But you will tell me. You *must* tell me.' She stood up and spoke in a tone of command, which his feeling of independence, weakened just then by an accusing conscience, did not enable him to resist. He strove to evade the question, however.

'It was an unlucky day that ever she went to the well!'

'Tell me what the doctor said of my child,' repeated Mrs Gwynn. 'Will she live, or will she die?' He did not dare to disobey the imperious tone in which this question was put.

'Oh, she will live, don't be afraid. The doctor said she would live.' He did not mean to lay any peculiar emphasis on the word 'live,' but somehow he did, and she, whose every nerve vibrated with anxiety, caught the word.

'She will live!' repeated she. 'But there is something behind.

Tell me, for I will know. If you won't say, I'll go to Rowland Jones to-night and make him tell me what he has said to you.'

There had passed something in this conversation between himself and the doctor, which Edward did not wish to have known; and Mrs Gwynn's threat had the desired effect. But he looked vexed and irritated.

'You have such impatient ways with you, Mrs Gwynn,' he remonstrated.

'I am a mother asking news of my sick child,' said she. 'Go on. What did he say? She'll live –' as if giving the clue.

'She'll live, he has no doubt of that. But he thinks – now don't clench your hands so – I can't tell you if you look in that way; you are enough to frighten a man.'

'I'm not speaking,' said she in a low husky tone. 'Never mind my looks: she'll live –'

'But she'll be a cripple for life. – There! you would have it out,' said he, sulkily.

'A cripple for life,' repeated she, slowly. 'And I'm one-and-twenty years older than she is!' She sighed heavily.

'And, as we're about it, I'll just tell you what is in my mind,' said he, hurried and confused. 'I've a deal of cattle; and the farm makes heavy work, as much as an able healthy woman can do. So you see –' He stopped, wishing her to understand his meaning without words. But she would not. She fixed her dark eyes on him, as if reading his soul, till he flinched under her gaze.

'Well,' said she, at length, 'say on. Remember I've a deal of work in me yet, and what strength is mine is my daughter's.'

'You're very good. But, altogether, you must be aware, Nest will never be the same as she was.'

'And you've not yet sworn in the face of God to take her for better, for worse; and, as she is worse' – she looked in his face, caught her breath, and went on – 'as she is worse, why, you cast her off, not being church-tied to her. Though her body may be crippled, her poor heart is the same – alas! – and full of love for you. Edward, you don't mean to break it off because of our sorrows. You're only trying me, I know,' said she, as if begging him to assure her that her fears were false. 'But, you see, I'm a foolish woman – a poor foolish woman – and ready to take fright at a few words.' She smiled up in his face; but it was a forced doubting smile, and his face still retained its sullen dogged aspect.

'Nay, Mrs Gwynn,' said he, 'you spoke truth at first. Your own good sense told you Nest would never be fit to be any man's wife – unless indeed, she could catch Mr Griffiths of Tynwntyrybwlch; he might keep her a carriage, may-be.' Edward really did not mean to be unfeeling; but he was obtuse, and wished to carry off his embarrassment by a kind of friendly joke, which he had no idea would sting the poor mother as it did. He was startled at her manner.

'Put it in words like a man. Whatever you mean by my child, say it for yourself, and don't speak as if my good sense had told me any thing. I stand here, doubting my own thoughts, cursing my own fears. Don't be a coward. I ask you whether you, and Nest are troth-plight?'

'I am not a coward. Since you ask me, I answer, Nest, and I *were* troth-plight; but we *are* not. I cannot – no one would expect me to wed a cripple. It's your own doing I've told you now; I had made up my mind, but I should have waited a bit before telling you.'

'Very well,' said she, and she turned to go away; but her wrath burst the flood-gates, and swept away discretion and forethought. She moved, and stood in the gateway. Her lips parted, but no sound came; with an hysterical motion she threw her arms suddenly up to heaven, as if bringing down lightning towards the grey old house to which she pointed as they fell, and then she spoke: –

'The widow's child is unfriended. As surely as the Saviour brought the son of a widow from death to life, for her tears and cries, so surely will God and His angels watch over my Nest, and avenge her cruel wrongs.' She turned away weeping, and wringing her hands.

Edward went in-doors: he had no more desire to reckon his stores; he sat by the fire, looking gloomily at the red ashes. He might have been there half-an-hour or more, when some one knocked at the door. He would not speak. He wanted no one's company. Another knock sharp and loud. He did not speak. Then the visitor opened the door; and, to his surprise – almost to his affright – Eleanor Gwynn came in.

'I knew you were here. I knew you could not go out into the clear holy night, as if nothing had happened. Oh! did I curse you? If I did, I beg you to forgive me; and I will try and ask the Almighty to bless you, if you will but have a little mercy – a very little. It will kill my Nest if she knows the truth now – she is so very weak. Why, she cannot feed herself, she is so low and feeble. You would not wish to kill her, I think, Edward!' She looked at him as if expecting an answer; but he did not speak. She went down on her knees on the flags by him.

'You will give me a little time, Edward, to get her strong, won't you, now? I ask it on my bended knees! Perhaps, if I promise never to curse you again, you will come sometimes to see her, till she is well enough to know how all is over, and her heart's hopes crushed. Only say you'll come for a month, or so, as if you still loved her – the poor cripple – forlorn of the world. I'll get her strong, and not tax you long.' Her tears fell too fast for her to go on.

'Get up, Mrs Gwynn,' Edward said. 'Don't kneel to me. I have no objection to come and see Nest, now and then, so that all is clear between you and me. Poor thing! I'm sorry, as it happens, she's so taken up with the thought of me.'

'It was likely, was not it? and you to have been her husband before this time, if – Oh, miserable me! to let my child go and dim her bright life! But you'll forgive me, and come sometimes, just for a little quarter of an hour, once or twice a-week. Perhaps she'll be asleep sometimes when you call, and then, you know, you need not come in. If she were not so ill, I'd never ask you.'

So low and humble was the poor widow brought, through her exceeding love for her daughter.

ELIZABETH GASKELL

from Contemplative Nuns Speak

YES and no. Sometimes it has driven me to rebellion . . . and many a time it has made me weep. When one knows that God exists, one is pursued and tormented until one surrenders, vanquished and defeated. Oh, my pride and ingratitude! You stiff-necked people, what is your reply? You cannot escape from that certitude which dazzles and confounds you, and shows you the state you are in. I have often had this atrocious thought: Better not discover anything of God, then one would not have to give up anything. I felt with some reason that if I had not yielded, I would have gone to perdition.

Visitation nun, aged 37, in religion 9 years

from West–Eastern Divan

Zuleika

How I envy thee, O West,
For thy damp and humid wing;
How I suffer when we part,
Thou canst him the tidings bring.

With the stirring of thy wings
Longing in my breast appears:
Flowers, meadows, wood and hillock
At thy breath dissolve in tears.

Yet thy mild and gentle movements
Of my eyelids cool the pain:
With grief, alas! I soon should perish,
Hoped I not him to meet again.

Haste thee, then, to my belovèd,
Speak so gently to his heart,

Yet forbear to make him sorrow,
Nor my heavy grief impart.

Tell him, aye, but so discreetly,
That I live but in his love;
For us both a sweet sensation
Would his nearness to me prove.

MARIANNE WILLEMER

from Journey into Burmese Silence

EVERYONE is constituted differently, and I can of course speak only from my own experience. But the question was of particular interest to me, because about fourteen years before the first visit to a Vipassana centre I had started writing down dreams and visions consequent on reading some of Jung's books. (See especially his *Modern Man in Search of a Soul, Psychology and Religion West and East* and *The Secret of the Golden Flower.*) The practice was undertaken purely out of idle curiosity. But after about six months there was a sudden flash of understanding on a whole series of dreams. The result was most humiliating, for it revealed the shadow-side of the psyche. However, there was no alternative to accepting it. Within twenty-four hours nervous dyspepsia and nausea, which had made life nearly unbearable, disappeared completely. The festering sore of egoism and discord between conscious and subconscious had been lanced and there was relief physical as well as mental. A considerable time after this there was a startling vision of the archetypal kind which I interpreted as the cross of suffering from which sprang the wings of victory. According to Jung's theories, this should have brought a marvellous mental healing power. But I cannot remember anything of the kind. It certainly did not end the darkness of the spirit, nor did it obviate the need for ceaseless training afterwards. After the return from the second visit to the Vipassana centre, I again started noting dreams and visions. They were interesting,

especially the one which showed the development of the first
vision seen on the first visit; and it was gratifying to observe that
the previously empty candlestick now held a brightly burning
candle against a background of pure white. But so far as I could
see, observing these dreams and visions was now merely a distraction and a waste of time.

MARIE BEUZEVILLE BYLES

from The Coming of God

WE have to pray from a position of chaos, because that is where
we are, and that is the material on which the Spirit delights to
work. The implications of this for personal prayer will be suggested in a moment, but it is worth noting first that the psalms
can make great sense as chaotic prayer. They are full of darkness
and conflict as well as joy in God's presence; they are not always
pure praise but often ugly with vengeance, hatred and smugness.
In the psalms people cry out in joy and pain, bewilderment and
wonder, fear, shame and rebellion; and they go on tediously
telling God about their tedious lives. This is the human condition
as familiar to us. The psalms are about human experience, and no
part of it is hidden from God or felt to be unmentionable in his
presence. They were waiting for Christ, waiting to be taken up
and transformed by him, waiting to be Christified, like all human
experience. They were the raw material of his prayer, as the flesh
of Israel was the raw material that would make his body, the stuff
of his sacrifice. They were like unconsecrated hosts, destined for
a fulfilment beyond themselves. His cry from the cross in the
words of a psalm, 'My God, my God, why have you forsaken
me?' gathered up all the inarticulate, chaotic cries of the poor
and sinful in every generation of the world's history, and the cries
of our own lives. Much in us is still pre-Christian and waits to be
gathered into Christ's Easter.

Prayer is a listening to the creative, life-giving word that loves
us into being. Yet prayer of a simple, contemplative kind, in

which we try to stand before God and let him know us, not much preoccupied with particular thoughts but just loving, invariably produces a sense of our own sinfulness. There seem to be two distinct kinds of sin. One is a deliberate 'No' to God in any area whatever; this automatically cancels the simple kind of prayer, until it is repented of and a 'Yes' substituted. It is obvious why this must be so: life and prayer cannot be compartmentalized. The other kind of sinfulness makes itself felt in a global sense of being weak and shabby and in need of God's mercy, an awareness of the general slum-situation within. This kind is not an act but a state, and it almost seems to help; or at least the experience of it is part of prayer. You know that you are an undeserving beggar, that you have not a leg to stand on; yet somehow it is good to be there, because it is real, and to avoid this confrontation would be to escape into untruth. The strange thing is that although prayer is often completely unsatisfying and very humbling, although you seem to fail and fail again in prayer, you dimly know that it is all-important to stay there in that emptiness, refusing to fill the void with anything that is not God.

If this is your experience, you have attained a fellowship with the tax-collector in the Gospel. He had no achievements and no claim; he could only pray from his chaos, 'O God, be merciful to me, a sinner' (cf. Luke 18.13). All he could do was to make a space for God to be merciful, for God to be God for him. You have to make a space for God to be God for you, so that he can draw you into that truth-relationship with himself. This means space in the practical sense: you need a measure of time and silence to let him do it. It also means space in the sense of personal emptiness, not clinging to any righteousness of your own, letting go of any kind of inner defence against the living God. Then just abide there under his judgement and let him love you. He is a God who delights to give himself where there is hunger and thirst of spirit.

There are times in our lives when we are led deeply into the experience of inner poverty. You know that you have no prayer, no feeling of love or power to care, no words to speak when it is your duty to speak, nothing to give. Why does it happen? The obvious answer is, Because we have sinned. Certainly this is true; were it not, the experience would not be one of genuine personal poverty, but would be something that remained outside our real life with God, something that did not bite deeply. Nevertheless, God means it to happen; he does lead us into it, because he wants to open us wider to the reality of his salvation. Joseph was told, 'You shall call his name Jesus, for he will save his people from their sins' (Matt. 1.21). Until you know him as Jesus for you, you scarcely know him at all.

MARIA BOULDING

Of the Theam of Love

> O Love, how thou art tired out with rhyme!
> Thou art a tree whereon all poets climb;
> And from thy branches every one takes some
> Of thy sweet fruit, which fancy feeds upon.
> But now thy tree is left so bare, and poor,
> That they can hardly gather one plum more.

MARGARET CAVENDISH, Duchess of Newcastle

from The Journey

PRAYER . . . . I knew that I did not understand it. I recognized its great power but I did not understand how a human being relates himself on so deep a level with God. It might be a wordless relationship, as I felt in the singing of the women. It could be made with words. I am sure it is no easier to pray than it is to create music or write a poem; it must be as hard to do as it is to build a bridge, or to discover a great scientific principle, or to heal the sick, or to understand another human being. It is surely as important as these to man in his search for his role in the universal scheme of things. That role? I hoped to understand it better on this journey, somewhere.

To pray . . . . It is so necessary and so hard. Hard not because it requires intellect or knowledge or a big vocabulary or special technics but because it requires of us humility. And that comes, I think, from a profound sense of one's brokenness, and one's need. Not the need that causes us to cry, 'Get me out of this trouble, quick!' but the need that one feels every day of one's life – even though one does not acknowledge it – to be related to something bigger than one's self, something more alive than one's self, something older and something not yet born, that will endure through time.

LILLIAN SMITH

from Letters from Dorothy Osborne to Sir William Temple

SIR, – I can say little more than I did, – I am convinced of the vileness of the world and all that's in it, and that I deceived myself extremely when I expected anything of comfort from it. No, I have no more to do in't but to grow every day more and more weary of it, if it be possible that I have not yet reached the highest degree of hatred for it. But I thank God I hate nothing else but the base world, and the vices that make a part of it. I am in perfect charity with my enemies, and have compassion for all people's misfortunes as well as for my own, especially for those I may have caused; and I may truly say I bear my share of such. But as nothing obliges me to relieve a person that is in extreme want till I change conditions with him and come to be where he began, and that I may be thought compassionate if I do all that I can without prejudicing myself too much, so let me tell you, that if I could help it, I would not love you, and that as long as I live I shall strive against it as against that which had been my ruin, and was certainly sent me as a punishment for my sin. But I shall always have a sense of your misfortunes, equal, if not above, my own. I shall pray that you may obtain a quiet I never hope for but in my grave, and I shall never change my condition but with my life. Yet let not this give you a hope. Nothing ever can persuade me to enter the world again. I shall, in a short time, have disengaged myself of all my little affairs in it, and settled myself in a condition to apprehend nothing but too long a life, therefore I wish you would forget me; and to induce you to it, let me tell you freely that I deserve you should. If I remember anybody, 'tis against my will. I am possessed with that strange insensibility that my nearest relations have no tie upon me, and I find myself no more concerned in those that I have heretofore had great tenderness of affection for, than in my kindred that died long before I was born. Leave me to this, and seek a better fortune. I beg it of you as heartily as I forgive you all those strange thoughts you have had of me. Think me so still if that will do anything towards it. For God's sake do take any course that may make you happy; or, if that cannot be, less unfortunate at least than

Your friend and humble servant,

D. OSBORNE

The Gardens of Pleasure

SHE walked upon the beds, and the sweet, rich scent arose; and she gathered her hands full of flowers. Then Duty, with his white clear features, came and looked at her. Then she ceased from gathering, but she walked away among the flowers, smiling, and with her hands full.

Then Duty, with his still white face, came again, and looked at her; but she, she turned her head away from him. At last she saw his face, and she dropped the fairest of the flowers she had held, and walked silently away.

Then again he came to her. And she moaned, and bent her head low, and turned to the gate. But as she went out she looked back at the sunlight on the faces of the flowers, and wept in anguish. Then she went out, and it shut behind her for ever; but still in her hand she held of the buds she had gathered, and the scent was very sweet in the lonely desert.

But he followed her. Once more he stood before her with his still, white, death-like face. And she knew what he had come for: she unbent the fingers, and let the flowers drop out, the flowers she had loved so, and walked on without them, with dry, aching eyes. Then for the last time he came. And she showed him her empty hands, the hands that held nothing now. But still he looked. Then at length she opened her bosom and took out of it one small flower she had hidden there, and laid it on the sand. She had nothing more to give now, and she wandered away, and the grey sand whirled about her.

OLIVE SCHREINER, from *Dreams*

from Adam Bede

'YOU believe in my love and pity for you, Hetty; but if you had not let me come near you, if you wouldn't have looked at me or spoken to me, you'd have shut me out from helping you: I couldn't have made you feel my love; I couldn't have told you what I felt for you. Don't shut God's love out in that way, by clinging to sin. . . . He can't bless you while you have one false-hood in your soul; his pardoning mercy can't reach you until you open your heart to him, and say, "I have done this great wicked-ness; O God, save me, make me pure from sin." While you cling to one sin and will not part with it, it must drag you down to misery after death, as it has dragged you to misery here in this world, my poor, poor Hetty. It is sin that brings dread, and dark-ness, and despair: there is light and blessedness for us as soon as we cast it off: God enters our souls then, and teaches us, and brings us strength and peace. Cast it off now, Hetty – now: con-fess the wickedness you have done – the sin you have been guilty of against your heavenly Father. Let us kneel down together, for we are in the presence of God.'

Hetty obeyed Dinah's movement, and sank on her knees. They still held each other's hands, and there was long silence. Then Dinah said,

'Hetty, we are before God: he is waiting for you to tell the truth.'

Still there was silence. At last Hetty spoke, in a tone of beseeching,

'Dinah . . . help me . . . I can't feel anything like you . . . my heart is hard.'

Dinah held the clinging hand, and all her soul went forth in her voice:

'Jesus, thou present Saviour! Thou hast known the depths of all sorrow: thou hast entered that black darkness where God is not, and hast uttered the cry of the foresaken. Come, Lord, and gather of the fruits of thy travail and thy pleading: stretch forth thy hand, thou who art mighty to save to the uttermost, and rescue this lost one. She is clothed round with thick darkness: the fetters of her sin are upon her, and she cannot stir to come to thee: she can only feel her heart is hard, and she is helpless. She cries to me, thy weak creature. . . . Saviour! it is a blind cry to thee. Hear it! Pierce the darkness! Look upon her with thy face of love and sorrow that thou didst turn on him who denied thee; and melt her hard heart.

'See, Lord, – I bring her, as they of old brought the sick and helpless, and thou didst heal them: I bear her on my arms and carry her before thee. Fear and trembling have taken hold on her; but she trembles only at the pain and death of the body: breathe upon her thy life-giving Spirit, and put a new fear within her – the fear of her sin. Make her dread to keep the accursed thing within her soul: make her feel the presence of the living God, who beholds all the past, to whom the darkness is as noonday; who is waiting now, at the eleventh hour, for her to turn to him, and confess her sin, and cry for mercy – now, before the night of death comes, and the moment of pardon is for ever fled, like yesterday that returneth not.

'Saviour! it is yet time – time to snatch this poor soul from everlasting darkness. I believe – I believe in thy infinite love. What is *my* love or *my* pleading? It is quenched in thine. I can only clasp her in my weak arms, and urge her with my weak pity.

Thou – thou wilt breathe on the dead soul, and it shall arise from the unanswering sleep of death.

'Yea, Lord, I see thee, coming through the darkness, coming, like the morning, with healing on thy wings. The marks of thy agony are upon thee – I see, I see thou art able and willing to save – thou wilt not let her perish for ever.

'Come, mighty Saviour! let the dead hear thy voice; let the eyes of the blind be opened: let her see that God encompasses her; let her tremble at nothing but at the sin that cuts her off from him. Melt the hard heart; unseal the closed lips: make her cry with her whole soul, "Father, I have sinned." . . .'

'Dinah,' Hetty sobbed out, throwing her arms round Dinah's neck, 'I will speak . . . I will tell . . . I won't hide it any more.'

But the tears and sobs were too violent. Dinah raised her gently from her knees, and seated her on the pallet again, sitting down by her side. It was a long time before the convulsed throat was quiet, and even then they sat some time in stillness and darkness, holding each other's hands. At last Hetty whispered,

'I did do it, Dinah . . . I buried it in the wood . . . the little baby . . . and it cried . . . I heard it cry . . . ever such a way off . . . all night . . . and I went back because it cried.'

GEORGE ELIOT

Sonnet II

O sweet brown eyes, O shy averted glances,
O red-hot sighs, O wanton streams of tears,
O black insomniac nights long as the years,
O glittering days of sunlight's mocking dances:
O lovesick songs, O stubborn heart's desire,
O misspent youth, O heavy-hanging cares,
O thousand deaths died in a thousand snares,
O horrors that against my health conspire!
O smile, O forehead, hair, arms, hands and fingers!

O lute, O viol, O voice that sweetly lingers:
So many flames to set a girl alight!
Pity me, love, that with so many fires
Inflaming my poor heart's inmost desires,
Not one small spark has warmed your dark midnight.

LOUISE LABÉ

DEAREST daughter in Christ sweet Jesus: I Catherine, servant and slave of the servants of Jesus Christ, write to you in His Precious Blood, with the desire to see you established in true patience, since I consider that without patience we cannot please God. For just as impatience gives much pleasure to the devil and to one's own lower nature, and revels in nothing but anger when it misses what the lower nature wants, so it is very displeasing to God. It is because anger and impatience are the very pith and sap of pride that they please the devil so much. Impatience loses the fruit of its labour, deprives the soul of God; it begins by knowing a foretaste of hell, and later it brings men to eternal damnation: for in hell the evil perverted will burns with anger, hate and impatience. It burns and does not consume, but is evermore renewed – that is, it never grows less, and therefore I say, it does not consume. It has indeed parched and consumed grace in the souls of the lost, but as I said it has not consumed their being, and so their punishment lasts eternally. The saints say that the damned ask for death and cannot have it, because the soul never dies. It dies to be sure to grace, by mortal sin; but it does not die to existence. There is no sin nor wrong that gives a man such a foretaste of hell in this life as anger and impatience. It is hated by God, it holds its neighbour in aversion, and has neither knowledge nor desire to bear and forbear with its faults. And whatever is said or done to it, it at once empoisons, and its impulses blow about like a leaf in the wind. It becomes unendurable to itself, for perverted will is always gnawing at it, and it craves what it cannot have; it is discordant with the will of God and with the rational part of its own soul. And all this comes from the tree of Pride, from which oozes out the sap of anger and impatience. The man becomes an incarnate demon, and it is much worse to fight with these visible demons than with the invisible. Surely, then, every reasonable being ought to flee this sin.

But note, that there are two sources of impatience. There is a common kind of impatience, felt by ordinary men in the world, which befalls them on account of the inordinate love they have for themselves and for temporal things, which they love apart from God; so that to have them they do not mind losing their soul, and putting it into the hands of the devils. This is beyond help, unless a man recognizes himself, how he has wronged God, and cuts down that tree of Pride with the sword of true humility, which produces charity in the soul. For there is a tree of Love, whose pith is patience and good-will toward one's neighbour. For, just as impatience shows more clearly than any other sin that the soul is deprived of God – because it is at once evident that since the pith is there, the tree of Pride must be there – so patience shows better and more perfectly than any other virtue, that God is in the soul by grace. Patience, I say, deep within the tree of Love, that for love of its Creator disdains the world, and loves insults whence-soever they come.

I was saying that anger and impatience were of two kinds, one general and one special. We have spoken of the common kind. Now I talk of the more particular, of the impatience of those who have already despised the world, and who wish to be servants of Christ crucified in their own way; that is, in so far as they shall find joy and consolation in Him. This is because spiritual self-will is not dead in them: therefore they imperiously demand from God that He should give them consolations and tribulations in their own way, and not in His; and so they become impatient, when they get the contrary of what their spiritual self-will wants. This is a little offshoot from Pride, sprouting from real Pride, as a tree sends out a little tree by its side, which looks separated from it, but nevertheless it gets the substance from which it springs

from the same tree. So is self-will in the soul which chooses to
serve God in its own way; and when that way fails it suffers, and
its suffering makes it impatient, and it is unendurable to itself,
and takes no pleasure in serving God or its neighbour. Nay, if any
one came to it for comfort or help it would give him nothing but
reproaches, and would not know how to be tolerant to his need.
All this results from the sensitive spiritual self-will that grows
from the tree of Pride which was cut down, but not uprooted. It
is cut down when the soul uplifts its desire above the world, and
fastens it on God, but has fastened there imperfectly; the root of
Pride was left, and therefore it sent up an offshoot by its side, and
shows itself in spiritual things. So, if it misses consolations from
God, and its mind stays dry and sterile, it at once becomes disturbed and depressed, and, under colour of virtue – because it
thinks itself deprived of God – it begins to complain, and lays
down the law to God. But were it truly humble and had true hate
and knowledge of itself, it would deem itself unworthy of the
visitation of God to its soul, and worthy of the pain that it suffers,
in being deprived, not of God's grace in the soul, but of its consolations. It suffers, then, because it has to work in its chains; yes,
spiritual self-will suffers under the delusion that it is wronging
God, while the trouble is really with its own lower nature.

ST CATHERINE OF SIENA

Face to Face with God

From the prison confines of darkness
From the turbid cesspool of the world
Hear my needful clamor,
O able, unique God.

Rend this veil of blackness, and
Perhaps you'll see within my breast
The source and substance
Of sin and corruption.

The heart you gave me, it isn't a heart
Beating in blood; free it, or
Keep it empty of carnal desires,
Or encumber it with affection and fidelity.

Only you are aware and only you know
The secrets of that first sin;
Only you are capable of granting
To my soul the original bliss.

O Lord, O Lord, how can I tell you
Of my weariness with my own body and my vexation?
Every night on the threshold, as it were, of your glory
I have the hope of another body.

From my eyes snatch
The eagerness to run to another;
O God, have mercy, and teach my eyes
To shy away from the shining eyes of others.

Give me a love that will shape me
Like the angels in your heaven,
Give me a friend, a lover in whom I might see
A glimpse of the bliss of your being.

Some night rub from the state of my mind
The image of love and the picture of its treachery;
In avenging faithlessness
I want victory over its rival in a fresh love.

O Lord, O Lord, whose powerful hand
Established the foundation of existence,
Show your face and pluck from my heart
The zest for sin and lust.

Don't be satisfied with an insignificant slave's

Rebelliousness and seeking of refuge in another;
Don't be satisfied with the flood of her tears
At the foot of a wine cup.

From the prison confines of darkness
From the turbid cesspool of the world
Hear my needful clamor,
O able, unique God.

FURUGH FARRUKHZAD

from Journey into Burmese Silence

MEDITATION was beginning to settle into an even rhythm when, according to arrangement, U Sein Maung came to take me to see whether the Bank had at last got some money for me. It had not. The money shortage did not worry me very much, for I had a few travellers' cheques not yet cashed. But the goddess of efficiency raised her ugly head and because of living in complete solitude the mood of irritation was irrationally heightened. That appears to be a characteristic of a period of isolation. I had often noticed the same thing during the annual week spent camping alone in Australia. There is no distraction to prevent moods of depression and moods of elation from having full sway. It gives the naturally solitary person some inkling of the terrors that must assail the naturally gregarious person when forced into solitary confinement; for such a one, physical torture would be far preferable. On re-reading my journal it seems incredible that this and other moods should have caused such disturbances. Meditation at such times, as the Buddha said, is like trying to light a fire with damp wood. The ceaseless repetition of *Lead Kindly Light* will ultimately take effect, but in the meantime the only sane thing to do is to remember that mankind has always been able to endure, and that this particular specimen can do as others have done. Always these black moods are succeeded by moods of peacefulness and joy, and in this case there were three hours of blissful absorption with the phyit-pyet flowing like a gentle stream and mind and body merged and one with it, and two visions at intervals. But these blissful experiences are far more dangerous, because it is more difficult to stand aside and be detached from joy than from pain. Both are only moods and must be transcended. Possibly U Thein's wisdom might have shortened the period it took to learn these things, but he was away, and before he returned things were well into focus again. One more complex or 'self' had been slain. That is the reason why the Buddha emphasized the need for solitude. If there are outward distractions the black mood disappears fairly quickly, but the complex that gave rise to it is still there, and the pain to which it gives birth will return again and again each time there is the appropriate stimulous. In solitude, however, the complex has a chance of being rooted out completely, and then the pain arising from it will never return.

MARIE BEUZEVILLE BYLES

Eudaimon

Bound and free,
I to you, you to me,
We parted at the gate
Of childhood's house, I bound,
You free to ebb and flow
In that life-giving sea
In whose dark womb
I drowned.

In a dark night
In flight unbounded
You bore me bound
To my prison-house,
Whose window invisible bars
From mine your world.

Your life my death
Weeps in the night
Your freedom bound
To me, though bound still free
To leave my tomb,

On wings invisible
To span the night and all the stars,
Pure liquid and serene,
I you, you me,
There one; on earth alone
I lie, you free.

KATHLEEN RAINE

from Speculum of the Other Woman

A One-way Passage

YET a *path* would seek to bring you there: the philosophical *paideia*. A steep and arduous path, full of difficulties, which the child will not follow without pain and which he would not risk taking if someone – some master, of the male sex – did not draw him along, constantly pushing him forward to the 'day,' toward the 'natural light.' Despite his resistance, his nostalgia, his longing to go back to his former home. His pain, his blindness, his dizziness. This journey culminates in the solar glare and the ecstasy in God. But a *cut* separates these two 'visions of the world,' these two modes of representation. A transition is lacking – or lost? – between inside and outside, but also between outside and inside. Access, and egress, from one to the other, from the other with relation to the one, is, in essence, relegated to a different life. Progress flags at the limit of this existence, it ends on the border of death, in the expectation of entering or exiting on the other side. Where there will be no more walking – *khōrein*. The distance to be covered is limited to this universe. But, to get past it, to go beyond it, there remains a *leap* that one will not simply make in one's lifetime and that one cannot make in reverse – or at any rate not the same as one is – after death. And if they promise you the sublimation of that threshold, in the form of immortality, it is on the condition of trans-forming your 'body' into 'soul.' And if you sublimate a body it is nothing but airs and phantoms. Fantasies? Ideas? From now on nothing stops it. At least no division, separation, or even opposition. Things like that are rather what makes it a body. So, without the 'other,' would the soul have to constitute itself as the place where the like is duplicated, the same is remembered? Without the other, does man need this retreat of/into the 'interior' of the *psychē*? Does God need a soul? But if in the soul the purest, most divine and intelligible principle is to be distinguished from the impure, the earthly, the sensible, then it is essential that both be represented, isolated as far as possible by 'isthmuses' and 'partitions.' Just as the 'parts' attributed to men are isolated from the 'chambers' reserved for women by corridors, walls, and so on.

LUCE IRIGARAY

On Not Being Able to Look at the Moon

There may be a moon.
Look at the masklike complexion of the roof,
recognizable but relieved of familiarity.
The street, too. How weakened, unstable.
Shadows have more substance than the walls
they lean from. Thick phosphorescence
gathers in the spaces between window
and black window. Something subtle, like a moon,
has been creeping under surfaces,
giving them queer powers of illumination.

In this centreless light
my life might really have happened.

It rises, showing its wounds, longing for
abrasive penances. It touches me with a mania for
stealing moonlight and transforming it into my own pain.
I can feel myself closing like an eye.
I'm unable to look at the moon
or at anything pitted and white that is up there
painted on the sky.

ANNE STEVENSON

from My Ascent of Mont Blanc

IF I caught sight of the top of Mont Blanc towering over this
snowy landscape, I was thrown into a condition that I now find
hard to comprehend or to explain: my heart beat furiously, my
breathing was impeded, and deep sighs burst from my breast. I
felt such a burning desire to climb that an allied impulsion
throbbed in my feet, and the mere thought of delaying the ascent
to the following year plunged me into an inexpressible physical
and moral distress . . . When, on my return from these walks, I
met friends or acquaintances who said triumphantly: 'Well! Is
that the end of your great plans? You cannot go up this year
now!', these words caused me a deep and private pain. I came
home fatigued and agitated, could neither eat nor sleep, and spent
a night of agony, listening to the rain lashing the shutters. But,
not before time, my torments came to an end: the sun shone
again at last, and with it hope revived.

HENRIETTE D'ANGEVILLE

TO A relation of mine who had become a nun in Shugaku Temple
I sent the following poem in Winter,

> My thoughts go out to you
> In your wintry mountain home,
> And, picturing the storms that rage about your head,
> I find myself in tears.

This was her reply,

> How good you are to send those thoughts to one
> Who wanders in a state of mind as drear
> As the dense, dark groves of summer trees!
>
> LADY SARASHINA

from The Coming of God

GOD brings us to these winters, these dreary times of deadness
and emptiness of spirit, as truly as he brings winter after
autumn, as a necessary step towards next spring. But while we
are in them they feel like a real absence of God, or our absence
from him:

> How like a winter hath my absence been
> From thee, the pleasure of the fleeting year!
> What freezings have I felt, what dark days seen!
> What old December's bareness everywhere!

Or, as Shakespeare has it even more poignantly in another sonnet:

> Yet seemed it winter still, and you away.

Looking back, you know that these times brought you closer
to the Lord of the winter, that it was necessary for you to go
through them. In the winters of your prayer, when there seems to

be nothing but darkness and a situation of general frozenness, hold on, wait for God. He will come.

Meanwhile, it is not all dead loss, any more than the winter of the fields is wasted. It is a creative time, even if we do not perceive it so. Our strength can sometimes be a greater obstacle to God's work than our weakness. The key moments in the history of salvation, the vital moments remembered in the Christian creeds, were moments not of action but of freely accepted passivity: Mary's consent to the Word becoming flesh, Jesus's crucifixion and his being raised from the dead. When people are making demands on you and you feel drained and empty; when you have to speak and you have not had the time you wanted to prepare; when God calls you to a task for which you know yourself inadequate; when you feel humiliated and foolish because some undertaking in which you did your honest best has turned out disastrously – then, it may be, to your astonishment, someone will tell you that you helped most, did your most fruitful work. When our ego is humbled and not obstructing, God's creative Spirit can often have freer play. Like the bare trees, it may be that we allow the glory to shine through at these times more purely than in our summer prosperity.

MARIA BOULDING

Last Thoughts

26th May, 1942
(From Casablanca)

Father,

It was a very kind act on your part, to write to me all the same.

I valued having a few affectionate words from you at the moment of leaving.

You quoted some glorious words of St. Paul. I hope though that in owning my wretchedness to you I did not give you the impression of misunderstanding God's mercy. I hope I have never fallen, and never shall fall, to such a depth of cowardice and ingratitude. I do not need any hope or any promise in order to believe that God is rich in mercy. I know this wealth of his with the certainty of experience, I have touched it. What I know of it through actual contact is so far beyond my capacity of understanding and gratitude that even the promise of future bliss could add nothing to it for me; since for human intelligence the addition of two infinites is not an addition.

God's mercy is manifest in affliction as in joy, by the same right; more perhaps, because under this form it has no human analogy. Man's mercy is only shown in giving joy, or maybe in inflicting pain with a view to outward results, bodily healing or education. But it is not the outward results of affliction which bear witness to divine mercy. The outward results of true affliction are nearly always bad. We lie when we try to disguise this. It is an affliction itself that the splendour of God's mercy shines; from its very depths, in the heart of its inconsolable bitterness. If still persevering in our love, we fall to the point where the soul cannot keep back the cry 'My God, why hast thou forsaken me?' if we remain at this point without ceasing to love, we end by touching something which is not affliction, which is not joy; something which is the central essence, necessary and pure; something not of the senses, common to joy and sorrow; something which is the very love of God.

We know then that joy is the sweetness of contact with the love of God, that affliction is the wound of this same contact when it is painful, and that only the contact matters, not the manner of it.

It is the same as when we see someone very dear to us after a long absence, the words we exchange with him do not matter, but only the sound of his voice, which assures us of his presence.

SIMONE WEIL, from Waiting on God

Keep Hidden from Me

Keep from me all that I might comprehend!
O God, I ripen toward you in my unknowing.

The barely burgeoning leaf on the roadside tree
Limns innocence: here endeth the first lesson.

Keep from me, God, all forms of certainty:
The steady tread that paces off the self

And forms it, seamless, ignorant of doubt
Or failure, hell-bent for fulfilment.

To know myself: is not that the supreme disaster?
To know Thee, one must sink on trembling knees.

To hear Thee, only the terrified heart may truly listen;
To see Thee, only the gaze half-blind with dread.

Though the day darken, preserve my memory
From Your bright oblivion. Erase not my faulty traces.

If I aspire again to make four poor walls my house,
Let me pillow myself on the book of my peregrinations.

God, grant me strength to give over false happiness,
And the sense that suffering has earned us Your regard.

Elohim! Though sorrow fill me to the brim,
Let me carefully bear the cup of myself to Thee.

RACHEL KORN

from The Joy of the Snow

IN this world where we live now no single man or woman can come to the end of their life without suffering, some not more than can reasonably be borne, some more than that, some intolerably and hideously. If we all suffered equally there would be no problem, but we do not suffer equally, and it is the inequality that creates the heart-searching for those among us who believe in the love of God. My father would say austerely, 'It does not matter what we suffer as long as we suffer enough.' He believed whole-heartedly in the cleansing and redemptive power of pain and its value when offered as intercession, but he acknowledged the problem and staggered under it because of the fact that unbearable suffering can corrupt as well as redeem.

'I am tormented by the suffering of so many good and innocent people,' someone said to Archbishop Temple during the last war. 'Yes,' he replied, 'but what bothers me even more is the suffering of the wicked.'

That would suggest that how an individual takes his pain, what he allows it to do in him and through him, is much more important than the pain itself. The scene of suffering in each person seems to be a battleground where a thing evil in its origin comes up against the battling love of God that would transform it into an instrument of victory; not victory for the individual alone but also for God himself in the cosmic battle between good and evil . . .

But the deepest mystery of all, for me, is this one. Suffering, we believe, stems from evil, and evil has no part in the will of God. Yet God allowed the cruelty, jealousy and cowardice of man to put his son upon the cross and when he was there made no move to end his torture; God himself in man had to stick it out until the end. And so God and the suffering caused by sin are inseparably united, and will be so until sin ends. The mind boggles but there is enormous comfort here. For one thing it is hard to doubt the love of a God who is ready to suffer and die for us. For another thing, when we suffer we must be as close to God as we are to the pain. At the worst of it we may feel, as Christ did, that God forsakes when unbearable pain takes over. But the truth must be the reverse. Devout people used to say of pain or grief, 'God touched me.' Gerard Manley Hopkins says, 'And dost thou touch me afresh? Over again I feel thy finger and find thee.'

ELIZABETH GOUDGE

IT is related that Rabi'a engaged in constant crying and lamentations.

People would say to her 'Outwardly, this weeping seems senseless, why should you weep?' She would reply 'Deep within my breast lies the reason for my bereavement and pain. This malady no doctor can remedy. The sole cure of this pain is Union with the Friend, and by this mourning I hope that perhaps hereafter I will reach what I seek. Though I was not originally conceived in that Divine Grief, I attempt to simulate the state of those who are truly afflicted with Divine Love, that I may be deemed no less than they . . .'

RABI'A THE MYSTIC

from You Looked at Me

Intense desires

I HAD such great desires to suffer that, with St Teresa, I could say not only, 'Either to suffer or to die', but also add, 'To suffer is preferable even to Paradise!' These desires and affections I had only in my heart, but they were so violent that I suffered like a martyr because of them; and I would indeed have acted badly if I had practised the precept which requires that we do to others what we would like others to do to us, since I would certainly have wished that they despise me, scoff at me and do all the out-

rages possible to me. Those thoughts were the only ones I entertained and I conceived of nothing but those longings, but with a
fondness of feeling I would be unable to describe. And whenever
this happened to me, I was overwhelmed with inexplicable joy.
Burdened with insults and shame, I would have wished to be
dragged through the streets with all the ignominies possible. Such
great desires I had for penance, and to make satisfaction to God
for sins I had committed, that considering in myself the things on
account of which I offended him, I tore out my hair with violence,
twisted my arms, and caused myself thus other pains in my body
which I almost wished to pull to pieces. But my confessor pro-
hibited me from following these movements and ordered me to
resist them; which I did, having always preferred to obey more
than anything else. I greatly desired to live by begging from door
to door, or by the door of the church, and to see myself confined
to the corner of a street on a piece of straw. It would have been the
joy of my soul; but my sins rendered me unworthy of following so
closely the poor Jesus.

When my sister and I came to Paris, the Ursuline sisters at
[Langres], where I had stayed, had given us many letters of introduction, recommending us with affection to the persons who
knew them in Paris. We were known in this way by some people
of means and piety who helped us in our needs. It was even
arranged that something would be given to us monthly. When
my sister was no longer with me, a part of it was continued for
me. However, since the time when our Lord touched me so
strongly, I was never troubled about having anything secure in
this world. Only mindful of taking the things which his divine
Providence had provided me with, I regarded this as one of the
many means by which Providence wished to help. This is why I
went to accept what was given to me. It was customary there to
receive us with great civility, on account of the report which had
been given them about us, as I believe. But holding on to the
honour of rendering myself as conformable as was possible for me
to the poor Jesus, I now stayed at the door with the other people,
not wishing to enter any more the way I was accustomed to do;

and I received willingly the charity that was given to me in the presence of everyone.

When my daily meal was given to me by Monsieur, I went sometimes to fetch it myself. It is true that this was not very often, because I was too clumsy to carry it. But frequently I would take back the jug and the dish in which it had been brought to me. I had a certain repugnance for this. But these were things which I had a fondness in doing, more particularly when I felt profoundly some natural revulsion for them, my mind laying claim to such an absolute authority that it never relished being opposed in anything whatsoever.

I made my poverty well enough known when I saw that all I received from it was shame and contempt, taking pleasure in swallowing all this in its natural state; but I had only just discovered this when I realised that it was having other effects.

To suffer in secret

I adored with great respect all the designs of divine Providence for me, and I accepted and embraced with feelings of love and gratitude that were very special those designs which succeeded further in destroying nature in me, thus rendering me more conformable to Jesus Christ, who was poor, despised, unknown and suffering. Since then, our Lord in his goodness has always conserved these affections in me. In order to be able to suffer as he did, and to have a human body in which I suffer pains continually for love of him, how often have I thanked him for having created me from human nature instead of that of the angels. However, I complained about it once to our Lord. For seeing that sickness often never shows itself outwardly, nature would indeed prefer a great sickness, and then to have health, than to be the way I am. But inwardly he let me understand that he is more pleased with secret sufferings than with those that are known, something which made me since love my own sufferings for this reason. In this he taught me not to speak about my sufferings. It is by no means a small mortification for nature not to say a word, make a gesture, or utter a sigh in order to complain and have some relief.

I ask pardon of you, my God, that often, seduced by self-love, I made known my little pains more than was necessary. Aid me with your grace that, correcting myself of that fault and of all those of my life, I may do and suffer all things in the way that will be more agreeable to you.

Claudine Moine

244

It is easy to work when the soul is at play –
But when the soul is in pain –
The hearing him put his playthings up
Makes work difficult – then –

It is simple, to ache in the Bone, or the Rind –
But Gimlets – among the nerve –
Mangle daintier – terribler –
Like a Panther in the Glove –

Emily Dickinson

from The Letters of Abelard and Héloïse

You know, beloved, as the whole world knows, how much I have lost in you, how at one wretched stroke of fortune that supreme act of flagrant treachery robbed me of my very self in robbing me of you; and how my sorrow for my loss is nothing compared with what I feel for the manner in which I lost you. Surely the greater the cause for grief the greater the need for the help of consolation, and this no one can bring but you; you are the sole cause of my sorrow, and you alone can grant me the grace of consolation. You alone have the power to make me sad, to bring me happiness or comfort; you alone have so great a debt to repay me, particularly now when I have carried out all your orders so implicitly that when I was powerless to oppose you in anything, I found strength

at your command to destroy myself. I did more, strange to say –
my love rose to such heights of madness that it robbed itself of
what it most desired beyond hope of recovery, when immediately at your bidding I changed my clothing along with my mind,
in order to prove you the sole possessor of my body and my will
alike. God knows I never sought anything in you except yourself;
I wanted simply you, nothing of yours. I looked for no marriage-
bond, no marriage portion, and it was not my own pleasures and
wishes I sought to gratify, as you well know, but yours. The name
of wife may seem more sacred or more binding, but sweeter for
me will always be the word mistress, or, if you will permit me,
that of concubine or whore. I believed that the more I humbled
myself on your account, the more gratitude I should win from
you, and also the less damage I should do to the brightness of
your reputation.

Spell Against Sorrow

Who will take away
Carry away sorrow,
Bear away grief?

Stream wash away
Float away sorrow,
Flow away, bear away
Wear away sorrow,
Carry away grief.

Mists hide away
Shroud my sorrow,
Cover the mountains,
Overcloud remembrance,
Hide away grief.
Earth take away

Make away sorrow,
Bury the lark's bones
Under the turf.
Bury my grief.

Black crow tear away
Rend away sorrow,
Talon and beak
Pluck out the heart
And the nerves of pain,
Tear away grief.

KATHLEEN RAINE

from Earthen Pitchers

THE sun is heat to her now, and the sea, water.

Presently, when evening begins to gather, and the sunset colors the sky and the pools in the marshes behind them blood-red, and the sea washes into their feet, dark and heavy, with subdued cries and moans as though all the love and unappeased longing of the world had gone down into it, and sought to find speech in it, Audrey takes up the child, and begins to hush it on her breast, singing a little cradle song, a simple chant with which she was always crooning it to sleep. It is so hopeful, so joyful, so full of the unutterable brooding tenderness of mother's love, that Kit, who cares little for music, finds his heart swell and his eyes dim.

'Your uncle and that Goddard,' he observes, 'used to think you had a pretty talent for music Audrey. You were going to teach the whole world by your songs, I remember. But that little tune is all you ever made, eh? . . . And nobody ever heard it but Baby and me. However, it's very pretty, very pretty. And it was lucky your uncle taught you as thoroughly as he did. Your scales and notes helped us over a rough place. They served their purpose very well, though your voice is quite gone with teaching.'

He strolls on up the beach.

When he was out of sight, a flock of kingbirds fly up from the hedges of bay bushes, and light near her, turning on her their bright black eyes with a curious look of inquiry. When was it they had looked at her so before?

For one brief moment the tossing waves, the sand dunes, the marshes put on their dear old familiar faces. Old meanings, old voices came close to her as ghosts in the sunlight. The blood rushed to her face, her blue eyes lighted. She buried her hands in the warm white sand. She held the long salt grass to her cheeks. She seemed to have come home to them again. 'Child,' they said to her, as the statues to Mignon, 'where hast thou stayed so long?'

It seemed to her that she must answer them. She began to sing, she knew not what. But the tones were discordant, the voice was cracked. Then she knew that whatever power she might have had was . . . wasted and gone. She would never hear again the voice that once had called to her.

She rose then, and, taking up her child, went to the house, still looking in its face. Kit joined her, and was dully conscious that she had been troubled. 'You're not vexed at what I said down there, eh?' he asked. 'You're not really sorry, that you leave nothing to the world but that little song?'

'I leave my child,' said Audrey; repeating after a while, 'I leave my child.'

Her husband, at least, was sure that she made no moan over that which might have been and was not.

REBECCA HARDING DAVIS

To J. M. Murry

[Le Prieuré, Fontainebleau] Tuesday.
[25 October 1922]

My Darling Bogey

I was so glad to get your second letter today. Don't feel we are silently & swiftly moving away from each other. Do you *really*? And what do you mean by us meeting 'on the othe side'? Where, Boge? You are much more mysterious than I!

I have managed this badly for this reason. Ive never let you know how much I have suffered in these five years. But that wasn't my fault. I could not. You would not receive it, either. And all I [am] doing now is trying to put into practice the 'ideas' I have had for so long of another, and a *far more truthful* existence. I want to learn something that no books can teach me, and I want to try & escape from my terrible illness. That again you cant be expected to understand. You think I am like other people – I mean – *normal*. I'm not. I don't know which is the ill me or the well me. I am simply one pretence after another – only now I recognise it.

I believe Mr Gurdjieff is the only person who can help me. It is great happiness to be here. Some people are stranger than ever but the strangers I am at last feeling near & they are my own people at last. So I feel. Such beautiful understanding & sympathy I have never known in the outside world.

As for writing stories & being true to one's gift. I couldn't write them if I were not here, even. I am at the end of my source for the time. Life has brought me no <u>flow</u>. I want to write but differently – far more steadily. I am writing this on a corner of the table against orders for the sun shines & I am supposed to be in the garden. Ill write again, my darling precious.

Ever your own
Wig.
from *Katherine Mansfield: Selected Letters*

6

GRACE UNDER PRESSURE

There can never be peace between nations until there is first
known that true peace which . . . is within the souls of men

ELIZABETH KÜBLER-ROSS

from The Opening Keynote Address at the NGO
Forum on Women, Beijing '95

THIS year is the International Year for Tolerance. The United Nations has recognized that 'tolerance, human rights, democracy and peace are closely related. Without tolerance, the foundations for democracy and respect for human rights cannot be strengthened, and the achievement of peace will remain elusive.' My own experience during the years I have been engaged in the democracy movement of Burma has convinced me of the need to emphasize the positive aspect of tolerance. It is not enough simply to 'live and let live': genuine tolerance requires an active effort to try to understand the point of view of others; it implies broad-mindedness and vision, as well as confidence in one's own ability to meet new challenges without resorting to intransigence or violence. In societies where men are truly confident of their own worth women are not merely 'tolerated,' they are valued. Their opinions are listened to with respect, they are given their rightful place in shaping the society in which they live.

There is an outmoded Burmese proverb still recited by men who wish to deny that women too can play a part in bringing necessary change and progress to their society: 'The dawn rises only when the rooster crows.' But Burmese people today are well aware of the scientific reasons behind the rising of dawn and the falling of dusk. And the intelligent rooster surely realizes that it is because dawn comes that it crows and not the other way round. It crows to welcome the light that has come to relieve the darkness of night. It is not the prerogative of men alone to bring light to this world: women with their capacity for compassion and self-sacrifice, their courage and perseverance, have done much to dissipate the darkness of intolerance and hate, suffering and despair.

AUNG SAN SUU KYI

from Elemental Passions

YOU want to make me into a flower? I also have roots and from them I could flower. Earth, water, air, and fire are my birthright too. Why abandon them to let you appropriate them and give them back to me. Why seek ecstasy in your world when I already live elsewhere. Why spread my wings only in your sunlight, your sky, only as your air and your light permit? Before I knew you, already I was a flower. Must I forget that, to become your flower? The one which is your destiny for me. Which you draw in me or around me. The one which you would produce, keeping it within your horizon?

Let me flower outwards too. Free, in the air. Come out of the earth and blossom, following the rhythm of my growth. Cut off from the soil which gives me birth, my efflorescence is supported by the strength of your desire, but is deprived of sap. My petals swell with your vigour, itself nourished by my blood, but thus separated from their life's source, they appear or disappear with the care which you bestow on them. With the attention you give them. Or else they are held open in an ideal permanence so that, eternally fixed, I guarantee the concept of the flower for you.

Are you aware that in this way you keep repeating, in me also, the flower which I have already given you. Which has already appeared to you but without ever becoming visible. Which is buried in the depths of your memory, where you constantly try to grasp it again. To draw it again. But you reimplant that remembrance of me, which is yours alone, in between my earth and its flower. And so the earth is left fallow, a mere support for your marks and imprints, and the flower has no reason other than your desire to bloom again and again for you. You have forced it into a reproduction, your production, and, when you want to reach it, it is no more than a dream retreating ever further into immemorial oblivion. Or inert matter.

What prevents my spreading my wings again? Is it not your appropriation of my *jouissance*? You cannot bear the mystery of my flowering, you cannot make this secret wholly yours though in some dark sense you are part of it – you therefore seek to go or return ever deeper to make the flower bloom.

LUCE IRIGARAY

A Prayer

O God,
In my deeds,
In my words,
In my wishes,
In my reason,
And in the fulfilling of my desires,
In my sleep,
In my dreams,
In my repose,
In my thoughts,
In my heart and soul always,
May the blessed Virgin Mary,
And the promised Branch of Glory dwell,
Oh! in my heart and soul always,
May the blessed Virgin Mary,
And the fragrant Branch of Glory dwell.

ANN MACDONALD

from A Touch of God

IN the second retreat I heard from Abbot Hume, as he was then, he said jokingly but truly that in community we were all either 'crooks or crocks', to which we added 'cranks and creeps'. This means, of course, that it is not easy to live in community. So I have come to value increasingly St Benedict's injunction that the

'Our Father', is to be said aloud twice a day in the Office, because of 'the thorns of scandal which may arise'. This is by no means a new idea for me, because I needed forgiveness before I could come to accept myself and I still stand in constant need of it.

The gift of friendship is the greatest gift any human being can bestow on another, because it is the loving sharing of the most personal and intimate in one's being. But it can never be a total communion, as God alone has the key to the incommunicable in us; so in one sense we shall never be known by anyone except God. Yet love is a stimulus to growth and love freely given and freely received is the only incentive to constant reaching out; and we need human love to become ourselves. It is very freeing to be able to admit one's faults and failings without being judged, knowing that one is perhaps loved even more because one is vulnerable. With this acceptance comes the desire to respond more fully, to become more human with a heart of flesh and so perhaps a little less unworthy of love, human and divine.

Yet we need to learn what love is really all about. I found a key in the reverential awe in which Moses stood before the burning bush and I sympathized with Peter when he stepped back from the Lord, saying, 'Depart from me, for I am a sinful man'. There is much to reverence in human beings, as well as in God, so we need to become aware of the respect others deserve in their own right. This is what attracts me to the Rule of St Benedict, although most of the time I lack this reverence towards people and created things. Yet it is only through standing back and worshipping that we gain the gift of unpossessive love.

Through the small moments of awareness in my life I have come to appreciate the phrase 'the fear of the Lord'. I understand this as love and awe which want to serve and whose greatest joy is having the service accepted. During my monastic life I have often prayed for this gift of the Holy Spirit, as I also pray for wisdom. I can identify readily with the young Solomon as he dedicated the new temple, since I have now learned what he already knew. He knew that the greatest gift God can give us is forgiveness, because only when we have been forgiven and accepted in love can we turn outwards in love and acceptance of others. This was the basis of my key experience, surely a fore-shadowing of the day when I shall finally stand before the face of God.

Since there is a wholeness about my present life and a constant awareness of being in God's presence, the fact that my periods of personal prayer are often far from inspiring does not seem to matter. I have long accepted my helplessness in this area and most of my moments of deepest peace come outside the time of 'prayer'. While grappling with the question of God's indwelling and our efforts at praying, I wrote the following:

> ' . . . and let the questing mind be still . . .'
> In the ground of your being I have my home,
> so do not seek me in the world apart.
> Within your spirit true communion lies.
> You are no homeless stranger in a land afar,
> no alien on a foreign shore,
> for I am with you.
> Do but be still and know that I am God.
> I look upon the world with your dark eyes;
> I feel the flowing air on your cool cheek.
> I hear the twittering in the moving trees,
> for with your senses I perceive.
> I am with you, I am within you.
> So do not turn away but come to rest in me.
> Within you is our meeting place.
> Be but still, and I will speak in silence
> to your loving, wayward heart.

PAULA FAIRLIE

from Pride and Prejudice

UPON the whole, therefore, she found, what has been sometimes found before, that an event to which she had looked forward with impatient desire did not, in taking place, bring all the satisfaction she had promised herself. It was consequently necessary to name some other period for the commencement of actual felicity – to have some other point on which her wishes and hopes might be fixed, and by again enjoying the pleasure of anticipation, console herself for the present, and prepare for another disappointment. Her tour to the Lakes was now the object of her happiest thoughts; it was her best consolation for all the uncomfortable hours which the discontentedness of her mother and Kitty made inevitable; and could she have included Jane in the scheme, every part of it would have been perfect.

'But it is fortunate,' thought she, 'that I have something to wish for. Were the whole arrangement complete, my disappointment would be certain. But here, by carrying with me one ceaseless source of regret in my sister's absence, I may reasonably hope to have all my expectations of pleasure realized. A scheme of which every part promises delight can never be successful; and general disappointment is only warded off by the defence of some little peculiar vexation.'

JANE AUSTEN

from The Chasm of Fire

20 July

'What is this stillness? Could it really be peace? Isn't love the most peaceless state? I don't remember having experienced such deep, uniform state of stillness and lasting so long.'

'I call it the natural state,' he answered. 'Why should I say that I am giving it to you? It is given; that's all. And it is the natural state. But one does not always realize it. The soul is covered with so many sheaths, veiled by many curtains.'

'One curtain has been withdrawn?' I suggested. He nodded. 'But there is so little understanding left, I am puzzled . . .'

But he was in samadhi.

21 July

This morning I realized in a flash that love cannot increase in quantity. It is given from the beginning in the exact measure the Master wants to give, according to the size of the cup the shishya brings with him. If the cup is large, more love can be poured into it; some containers are larger, some smaller. The shishya learns to respond to it better and better, so it seems to him as if it is growing. Love at the beginning and at the end is *the same*. I was astonished at this piece of knowledge, for the mind cannot even think clearly.

The beginning and the end from the point of view of God is the same always; it is a complete circle. I know it from books. But now I experienced it as my very own flash of knowledge into a mind which is sterile . . . Strange, and wonderful. And my work will be the same as before. I had to work with people, trying to help them to come one step nearer to the Truth. When I leave this place, (may the day never come!) I will continue on the same lines as before, though the conditions will necessarily be different (or perhaps not). But the work itself will remain the same. We are given work according to our capacities.

He smiled when I was relating all this to him and when I asked how is it possible that any glimpse of knowledge can come to a brain that can hardly function and with the greatest difficulty can put thoughts together, he said:

'If the cup is empty it can be filled. It is the knowledge of the soul which comes through. It comes to the physical mind and then it becomes the real knowledge, the integral part of you. If I would tell you, and you would have faith enough and believe me, then the faith and the knowledge would be two things, is it not so? But like this nothing is told. You will realize it yourself. It becomes part of you. There is no duality. You see how it is done, how easy?'

Then he began to tell me how men and women are trained; the difference in the practices; the approach to the psychological make-up of the trainee. How forces from the depth of the unconscious are gathered and chanelled. And this is the work of the Teacher and each individual is treated differently. I listened, fascinated, hoping fervently to remember it all.

'From what you have told me just now I have to conclude that you wish me to guide people?' I asked, feeling disturbed. 'It is a great responsibility! Do you realize to what kind of life you are sending me out?'

He did not answer but gently looked down at his feet as if examining his sandals.

'I hope, I hope that I will not go wrong; to have power is a terrible thing,' I said, fear creeping from the very depth of my being into my heart.

'I know,' he said, half-audibly, with a still and serious expression.

'Is it not too heavy a burden for the shoulders of an elderly woman? I will be accused of contradictions. If I have to live like you, I will have no habits. I am bound to do and say things which people cannot or will not understand. My words will be twisted, misinterpreted. There might be lawyers in the audience who will twist my words, accuse me of contradictions!'

He suddenly laughed. 'Lawyers know of one thing; the transfer of property! The property, the power, the knowledge will be transferred; there is no question of being a woman or not. It makes no difference.'

IRINA TWEEDIE

from A Map of the World

[*Towards the end of the book, the narrator Alice, who had spent time in jail, reflects on the nature of God and forgiveness.*]

THAT morning, walking in our woods, it seemed as if everything had been out of focus all year and gradually, very slowly, the lens was being turned, the picture coming clear. For Theresa, God was something that was outside of her, some unfathomable being who made the highway radiant. `I thought in the harsh December wind that for me God was something within that allowed me, occasionally, to see. Theresa had forgiven us, forgiven me – she had done so not long after Lizzy's death. I hadn't known that a person could so willingly forgive, didn't know what it meant, how it could be, what it was made of, the strange stuff called forgiveness. She had forgiven me nearly as soon as she thought to blame, so that her forgiveness was allied with what seemed a holy sort of understanding and love.

They had looked as if they belonged, Howard and Theresa, when they walked out of the courtroom together, side by side, shoulder to shoulder, as if they were the ones who lived together and were going home to their supper. And I thought how much easier it would be for Howard to love someone like Theresa, someone whose trouble is clear. My misfortunes were messy, hard to pin down, brought upon me by my own hand. In the woods it seemed to me that Theresa represented the world as a wholesome, good place, and that she must seem so for Howard too. I walked around the marsh, scaring up some ducks and a few geese that had not yet gone south. I would someday soon try to tell Howard more about it, all of it, I said to myself. I didn't know who else I would live with if it wasn't Howard, who else would understand the strangeness of our life. But I also knew that we might go along and along, that we might come to a point where we'd look back to find that the relationship had disappeared.

I had walked out into the old orchard, looking at the brown, hard, rotten apples still hanging on the trees. I remembered the night, after the funeral, when I'd run into Theresa and we had stood against the trees, talking. I was grateful for that accidental meeting. As much as it pained me to think of it, I loved that night, too. We hadn't realized it at the time but the conversation had been our chance to make an ending. It had been a suitable and good end.

JANE HAMILTON

What are you, my soul, you lean and bloodless thing
Like a withered fig that has survived the winter?
In youth it was so different: then the blood
Sang along the veins and it was easy both to love and welcome
    love.
But when you are old grace conquers only by hard victories;
You are stiffened, crusted by the salt spray
After the long sea voyage.

The lanes of memory may be as green
As in the year's paradise of spring.
It is the immediate present that slips unremembered,
Yet in love's presence there is only this one moment –
A question not of time but of understanding,
As when beauty seeps through the crevices of the soul
Burning the dead wood and illuming the self's verities. –
This, only after a long journey.

So limping, my soul, we will together go
Into the city of the shining ones,
Of those whose crutches have been cast into the sea,
Whose love is garlanded across the festal stars;
And we with them will bow before the sceptred wisdom of a
    child.

The trembling broken years shall be restored
And these shall be our offering; for by them we shall know
Love has travailed with us all the way.

M.L., a nun of Burnham Abbey

from The Swan in the Evening

SUDDENLY, a clear high-pitched vibration, like the twang of a harp-string, crossed my ears. I thought: 'This again . . . what is it?' – remembering that I had heard it before, very soon after the news came: in fact, that it had preceded that sensation of being 'lifted by the Breath', But this time, instead of being transitory, the sound settled into a strong, rising and sinking hum like the sound of a spinning top. At the same time a sort of convulsion or alarum struck me in the heart centre, followed by a violent tugging sensation in this region. As if attached to an invisible kite string that was pulling me out, out, upwards, upwards, I began to be forcibly ejected from the centre of my body. I heard myself moan, felt a torrent of tears pour down my face, distinctly remarked to myself that this was like some very peculiar birth process; registered phenomenal occurrences deep inside my head: it seemed that my eardrums were being plucked – literally plucked and shaken – as if they were closed doors that must be shaken loose: my hearing was being freed, I suppose, and it was a difficult yet painless process. Then the humming faded out, and the song of the blackbird, swelled, swelled, as if it was being stepped up a hundredfold. Never could I have imagined notes of such wild, piercing purity and sweetness. For a while I did hear that bird – I must have heard him – with liberated ears.

I was drifting and floating now . . . but where, and for how long? There is no way of telling. Perhaps for only a few seconds of earth time. A passage of symphonic music, jubilant, penetrating, vigorous, crossed and receded from me like a wave. Was I picking up, suprasensibly, from the ether, an actual performance going on somewhere at that moment? There was certainly no gramophone or radio switched on in the house: I was entirely alone in it, and it stood by itself, surrounded by barns and garden, the building nearest to it being the small, ancient village church. Whatever I heard seemed at once familiar and unknown. As I write, I can recall its melodic outline, but I cannot recognize it.

Now I was with Sally. She was behind my left shoulder, leaning on it. Together we were watching Patrick. His face, only his face, confronted us: it was clearly recognizable but the whole scale of it was altered, expanded; and it was self-luminous, and transformed by an expression of dreaming beatitude. He was (we both knew) starting on a journey. I said: 'Aren't you going with him?' 'No,' she said, 'he's got to go alone.' I said: 'I expect he's going to D.' – (one of his closest friends, at that time a novitiate in the Dominican Order.) Again she said: 'No'; and added: 'He'll go to Auntie Peg.' This is the name by which my sister Beatrix, the actress, is known to all her nephews and nieces. I am anxious not to make hard and fast interpretations. All I want to say is that, in those early days, I held to the entirely erroneous supposition that Patrick might decide to retire from a world become intolerable. It never occurred to me that he might choose to become an actor, as well as a writer. Although he had been prominent and successful in various amateur productions at Oxford he had rejected the idea of the theatre as his profession. However, two years after his return from Java, he suddenly decided to throw up his job in a publisher's office and joined the Salisbury Repertory Theatre: thus, as one might say, 'going to Auntie Peg!'

Patrick's lit face vanished, but Sally and I remained together, wordlessly communicating. More than anything, it was like laughing together, as we always did laugh; like sharing the humour of a situation: his going off without her in some sort of state of disarray and unpreparedness . . . She made some characteristic joke (I can't define it) about the muddle of his packing. I did not see her. I had the unaccountable impression that she was hiding her face, that I was forbidden to look round. There was no light, no colour, no external scenic feature: only close embrace, profound and happy communion; also the strongest possible impression of her individuality.

Then, with no shock or sense of travelling, I was back in my body, awake, cheerful as if I had just replaced the receiver after one of our long gossiping joking conversations. I lay drowsily, trying to piece my 'dream' together . . . then in a flash remembered. Now for the bite of the steel-toothed trap. . . . Prepare, accept, understand . . . But it did not spring. Memory stayed in sweet tranquillity on the fringes of consciousness. If I was conscious of anything that I ought to scrutinize or question, it was my glimpse of Patrick. He looked so very splendid, so handsome and happy; why on earth had I thought him so shocked, so ground into the dust, that I had hardly dared to leave him in London and come away for two nights?

I looked at my watch and found that over an hour had passed. I sprang up, went to the window and looked out . . . and beheld a visionary world. Everything around, above, below me was shimmering and vibrating. The tree foliage, the strip of lawn, the flower-beds – all had become incandescent. I seemed to be looking through the surfaces of all things into the manifold iridescent rays which, I could now see, composed the substances of all things. Most dramatic phenomenon of all, the climbing roses round the window-frame had 'come alive' – the red, the white. The beauty of each one of them was fathomless, – a world of love. I leaned out, they leaned towards me, as if we were exchanging love. I saw, I *saw* their intensity of meaning, feeling.

I came downstairs to join the others. I couldn't think of anything to say except: 'I've had a wonderful rest.' L. glanced at me and said: 'You look as if you had.' Later she told me that she wondered if it was an hallucination that I suddenly looked about thirty years younger.

After tea, J. took me for a drive through the midsummer countryside. What a drive! The sun shone powerfully among full-sailed somnolent cloud-galleons; but the light suffusing earth and sky was not the sun's: it was a universal, softly gold effulgence. Hills, woods, groves, clouds, cornfields, streams and meadows – all were moving and inter-lacing buoyantly, majestically, as if in the ineffable rhythm and pattern of a cosmic dance. I was outside, watching the animating, moulding eternal principle at work, at play, in the natural world; and at the same time I seemed to be inside it, united with and freely partaking in its creativity.

Astounded; awestruck. . . . Awestruck, astounded. What words are possible? *And yet*, the sense of recognition, recollection, was predominant. Again and again I told myself: 'Yes. Yes. This is reality. I had *forgotten*.'

ROSAMOND LEHMANN

WHEN asked by a rich man to marry him:

'Just as abstinence (zuhd) in this world is a source of bodily comfort, likewise attention to the world results in worry and grief. Lay aside your excess wealth, dedicate your riches here to the life hereafter. Be trustee of your own soul now; do not let men administer and divide your wealth later on. Fast from life; let death break your fast. As for me, even if God were to place at my disposal as much as you offer, or even much more, it would not be possible for me to heed ought beside Him for as much as the wink of an eye.'

RABI'A THE MYSTIC

Finding Inner Peace

FROM the teachings of Black Elk comes the following about finding inner peace:

The first peace, which is the most important, is that which comes within the soul of men when they realize their relationship, their oneness with the universe and all its powers, and when they realize that at the center of the universe dwells Wakan-Tanka (God) and that this center is really everywhere; it is within each of us.

This is the real peace, and the others are but reflections of this. The second peace is that which is made between two individuals, and the third is that which is made between two nations. But above all you should understand that there can never be peace between nations until there is first known that true peace which . . . is within the souls of men.

The only way I know how to find the inner peace referred to above is through an honest, ongoing observation of our own behavior. Each time we notice ourselves being judgmental or resentful, we have to ask ourselves: 'What is it that I react to?' If our angers and bad moods last hours or days, we have to become honest with ourselves and acknowledge that all bad moods serve only one purpose – consciously or not – and that is to punish. Whom do we want to punish and whom do we punish? It can be anyone or anything, but it puts the responsibility for our pain onto others, or sometimes just back on ourselves. We punish our children with silence or avoidance; we do the same thing with our mates, neighbors, or in-laws. The implicit message is always: I don't want to have anything to do with you.

Our anger can be directed at our destiny, at God, at the world. We will always find enough negative situations to enable ourselves to dwell in a pool of anguish and self-pity, blaming the economic situation of the country, the increased violence, the unemployment rate, the wars – but in reality, all these things are just good for our dissatisfaction and give us 'permission' to be unhappy.

If, from time to time, we look at the blessings in our lives, at the warmth and care and love so many people respond with when there is a tragedy, at the fact that we can walk and talk, eat and breathe, then maybe we would reevaluate our bad moods and become aware that all negative thoughts bring with them more negativity, but all love shared returns a thousandfold.

'As a man thinketh' perhaps describes best how we are the creators of our own worlds.

ELISABETH KÜBLER-ROSS, from *On Children and Death*

IT is only necessary to know that love is a direction and not a state of the soul. If one is unaware of this, one falls into despair at the first onslaught of affliction.

SIMONE WEIL, *Waiting on God*

from A Woman of Genius

AFTER the evening of the storm we talked no more of marriage for a while, and about a week later I went over to Paris ostensibly to shop, and was joined there by Mr. Garrett on the way to Italy. I suppose that Italy must always lie like some lovely sunken island at the bottom of all passionate dreams, from which at the flood it may arise; the air of it is charged with subtle essences of romance. One supposes Italy must be organized for the need of lovers. Nothing occurred there to break the film of our enchanted bubble. For a month we kept to the hill towns and to Venice, where we could go about in the conspicuous privacy of a gondola, and all that time we met nobody we had ever known.

It was all so easily managed – we had to think of the girls, of course – no one seeing our registered names side by side, Mrs. Thomas Bettersworth, New York, and Helmeth Garrett, Chilicojote, Mexico, would have thought of connecting them. Helmeth attended to all his business correspondence as though he were still in London, and nobody expected to hear from me in any case.

It is strange how little history there is to happiness. We had come together past incredible struggles, anxieties, triumphs, defeats; we had been buffeted and stricken, and now suddenly we were stilled. If at any time the ghosts of the uneasy past rose upon us, we kissed and they were laid. So long as we kept in touch, there ran a river of fire between our blessed isolation and the world. And for the first time we looked upon the world free of the obligations of our being in it. We looked, and exchanged our separate knowledges as precious treasure. My exploration of life had been from within – I knew what Raphael was thinking about when he painted that fine blue vein on his Madonna's wrist. But Helmeth had looked on the movement of history; what he saw in Italy was the path of armies, lines of aqueducts, old Roman roads to and from mines. Everything began or ended for him in a mine, in Gaul or Austria or Ophir; dynasties were marked for him by change in the ownership of mines. So he drew me the white roads out of Italy as one draws fibre from a palm, and strung on them the world's great adventures. There were hours also when we let all this great fabric of art and history float from us, sure that by the vitalizing thread of understanding which ran between us like a new, live sense, we could pull it back again . . . but we loved . . . we loved.

Nothing that happened to us there, came with a more revealing touch than the attitude in which I caught myself, looking out for and being surprised at not discovering in myself any qualms of conscience. All that I had known of such relations in other people, had made itself known by a subtle, penetrating, fetid savour, against which some instinct, as sure as a hound, threw up its head and bayed the tainted air.

But in my own affair, the first compulsion that irked me was the necessity I was under of not telling anybody. I wasn't conscious at any time of any feeling that wouldn't have gone suitably with the outward form of marriage; there were times even when I failed to see why one should take exception to the neglect of such form. I was remade every pulse and fibre of me, my beloved's . . . and so obviously, that the necessity of tagging my estate with a ceremony struck me as an impertinence. Marriage I think must be a fact, capable of going on independently of the prayer book and the county clerk. Whatever *you* may think, no god could have escaped the certainty of my being duly married.

There were days though, just at first, when I suffered the need of completing my condition by an outward bond. I knew very well where the custom of wedding rings came from; I should have worn anklets and armlets as well, if only they could have been taken as the advertisement of my belonging wholly to my man. Depend upon it, the subjugation of woman will be found finally to rest in the attempt visibly to establish, what the woman herself concurs in, the inward conviction of possession.

MARY AUSTIN

Maulana's Last Letter to Shams

Sometimes I wonder, sweetest love, if you
Were a mere dream in a long winter light,
A dream of spring-days, and of golden night
Which sheds its rays upon a frozen heart;
A dream of wine that fills the drunken eye.
And so I wonder, sweetest love, if I
Should drink this ruby wine, or rather weep;
Each tear a bezel with your face engraved,
A rosary to memorize your name . . .
There are so many ways to call you back –
Yes, even if you only were a dream.

ANNE MARIE SCHIMMEL, from *Mirror of an Eastern Moon*

from Contemplative Nuns Speak

'LET the mountains be moved, the hills shake; my compassion towards thee stands immovable' (Is. 54.10). 'If we play him false, he remains true to his word; he cannot disown himself' (2 Tim. 2.13). '*Ipse prior dilexi* . . .' In hours of weariness and discouragement, when the road seems long and one feels weighed down by one's misery, inadequacy and weakness, it is good to think of our Lord's immutable love, which nothing can discourage and which remains always ready to receive us . . . And we know that the future is in the hands of him who loves us, and that he will be there always; that in the midst of the desert, all through the night, his hand will hold ours. Then our fears grow less.

DOMINICAN, aged 37, in religion 14 years

from Experiences Facing Death

IT has been the weakness of Occidental man always to believe too much. It was the weakness of Christian mystics to limit their exploration of the inner consciousness by the tight but not restrictively narrow doctrines of a patristic and medieval Christianity. This gives to their interpretations often the effect of being narrower than they actually are. If, with a modern intelligence, you set about reexperiencing these doctrines, you discover that they are of a more extensive content than has been popularly believed.

Going back to the list of concepts and mental attitudes of our Occidental religious inheritance, we discover in the mystic approach certain essentials. First, we find 'a clear conviction of a living God as a primary interest of consciousness; and of a personal self capable of communion with him.' [Evelyn Underhill, *The Essentials of Mysticism*] It is not necessary, however, that the God envisaged should correspond in any particular to Jehovah.

The second essential to the successful practise of mysticism is a realization that it is impossible by intelligence alone to sort out man's various experiences of the universe and coördinate all their aspects with a felt reality. To reduce his experience to order, man must call into play all his higher and deeper subjectivity, and by intelligent criticism of his mystical activity, make a closer approach to the truth.

Starting with these essential motions of the mind, there is a considerable latitude of method, which may have its roots in the sex of the postulant, in his racial temperament, in his social environment, in his religious inheritance. The absolute test of the validity of a mystical experience is that it is a genuine motion of the mind. It is not essentially, nor inescapably, an *emotion*, although, in mobile temperaments, mystical experience may react emotionally in such a way as to over-fill the vessel of personality almost to the point of hysteria. One has to make these distinctions between the experience of mysticism and the individual reaction to its revelations. Especially one has to make them in respect to the technique of seeking and attaining such experience.

Very early in the history of man's discovery that by the motions of his psyche he could acquire knowledge important to his continued personal existence, he also discovered that every mystical state had a definite relation to at least two other states. All these states occur in an orderly sequence, one leading to another which may not be successfully reached without the first. When intertribal communication began, it was discovered that under whatever name these states were described, their consecutive order was the same, and that experience acquired in one tribal or racial mode matched with experience in every other. Medicine men could exchange experiences profitably, and methods invented or acquired by instruction became recognizable items of such exchange.

It was discovered, for example, that the first motion was to clear the self of prepossessing interests and emotions, to withdraw the least, remotest filament of attention from the not-self, in a state known as Recollection. Once this state of complete Detachment is attained, it is practised until it can be held without too much effort as Concentration. After this, at longer or shorter periods, according to the individual, normally occurs a state known as Dilation of Consciousness, in which the whole boundary of spiritual capacity moves outward to give the spirit room. From this point there is an orderly succession of other states of consciousness, culminating in complete Union with the Source; and this whole range of spiritual activities taken in their natural order, is known as the Mystic Way. It is traveled according to individual capacity and probably follows the same law of personal instrumentation that is observed in intellectual capacities.

In general, after one passes the first stage of the Mystic Way, in which detachment from the objective life is secured, it is important to realize that mystical technique is in every case *an activity of the subconscious*, phases of it taking place at deeper and deeper levels successively. In talking with the uninitiate, I often have the greatest difficulty in making them understand that mystical experience is not an activity of the intelligence, which only comes into play afterward to explain and verify the experience. Meditation, to a mystic, is not the same thing as 'thinking things over,' nor is Concentration merely the state of not thinking about anything else. Mystical revelation is the farthest remove from an intellectual conclusion.

MARY AUSTIN

from The Opening Keynote Address at the NGO Forum on Women, Beijing '95

THERE is an age-old prejudice the world over to the effect that women talk too much. But is this really a weakness? Could it not in fact be a strength? Recent scientific research on the human brain has revealed that women are better at verbal skills while men tend towards physical action. Psychological research has shown on the other hand that disinformation engendered by men has a far more damaging effect on its victims than feminine gossip. Surely these discoveries indicate that women have a most valuable contribution to make in situations of conflict, by leading the way to solutions based on dialogue rather than on viciousness or violence?

The Buddhist *paravana* ceremony at the end of the rainy season retreat was instituted by the Lord Buddha, who did not want human beings to live in silence (I quote) 'like dumb animals.' This ceremony, during which monks ask forgiveness for any offense given during the retreat, can be said to be a council of truth and reconciliation. It might also be considered a forerunner of that most democratic of institutions, the parliament, a meeting of peoples gathered together to talk over their shared problems. All the world's great religions are dedicated to the generation of happiness and harmony. This demonstrates the fact that together with the combative instincts of man there co-exists a spiritual aspiration for mutual understanding and peace.

AUNG SAN SUU KYI

Serving God in Darkness

Letter to M.R., 1909

I AM so sorry you are 'left to yourself'. It is a cheerless experience but can be a fine piece of discipline if you choose to make it so. The causes I think are partly material – the inevitable fatigue of a spiritual sense which cannot live always on the stretch and is now resting. I think it helps one to go on if one remembers that one's true relation to God is not altered by the fact that one has ceased to be aware of it. Other things being equal, you are just where you were before, but are temporarily unable to see the Light. And the use of the disability, just like the use of any other sort of suffering, is to prevent you from identifying fullness of life with fullness of comfort. Your ideal of spiritual life must be right up above all the pleasure-and-pain oscillations of your finite, restless self: and you will not have any real peace till you have sur-rendered that self altogether, and tried to grasp nothing, not even love. When you absolutely and eagerly surrender yourself to the Will, you will cease to write under that sense of deprivation. You will take it all in the day's work and go on steadily. These are the sort of times when verbal prayer, if one has assimilated it and made it one's own in more genial seasons, becomes a help: and enables one to go doggedly on, praying *more* not less, because the light is withdrawn. To do otherwise would be a confession that

you have been living by sight and not really by faith at all. . . .
The true attitude is to rest with entire trustfulness on the Love of
God, and not care two straws what happens to one's self. If you
are *there* how little the question of whether you see you are there
can matter. It is rather an honour to be allowed to serve him in
the darkness instead of being given a night-light like a nervous
child.

EVELYN UNDERHILL

The Prisoner

Still my tyrants know, I am not doom'd to wear
Year after year in gloom and desolate despair;
A messenger of Hope comes every night to me,
And offers for short life, eternal liberty.

He comes with Western winds, with evening's wandering airs,
With that clear dusk of heaven that brings the thickest stars:
Winds take a pensive tone, and stars a tender fire,
And visions rise, and change, that kill me with desire.

Desire for nothing known in my maturer years,
When Joy grew mad with aw, at counting future tears;
When, if my spirit's sky was full of flashes warm,
I knew not whence they came, from sun or thunder-storm.

But first, a hush of peace – a soundless calm descends;
The struggle of distress and fierce impatience ends.
Mute music soothes my breast – unutter'd harmony
That I could never dream, till Earth was lost to me.

Then dawns the Invisible; the Unseen its truth reveals;
My outward sense is gone, my inward essence feels;
Its wings are most free – its home, its harbour found,
Measuring the gulf, it stoops, and dares the final bound.

O dreadful is the check – intense the agony –
When the ear begins to hear, and the eye begins to see;
When the pulse begins to throb – the brain to think again –
The soul to feel the flesh, and the flesh to feel the chain.

Yet I would lose no sting, and wish no torture less;
The more that anguish racks, the earlier it will bless;
And robed in fires of hell, or bright with heavenly shine,
If it but herald Death, the vision is divine.

EMILY BRONTË

from The Opening Keynote Address at the NGO Forum on Women, Beijing '95

THE last six years afforded me much time and food for thought. I came to the conclusion that the human race is not divided into two opposing camps of good and evil. It is made up of those who are capable of learning and those who are incapable of doing so. Here I am not talking of learning in the narrow sense of acquiring an academic education, but of learning as the process of absorbing those lessons of life that enable us to increase peace and happiness in our world. Women in their role as mothers have traditionally assumed the responsibility of teaching children values that will guide them throughout their lives. It is time we were given the full opportunity to use our natural teaching skills to contribute towards building a modern world that can withstand the tremendous challenges of the technological revolution which has in turn brought revolutionary changes in social values.

As we strive to teach others we must have the humility to acknowledge that we too still have much to learn. And we must have the flexibility to adapt to the changing needs of the world around us. Women who have been taught that modesty and pliancy are among the prized virtues of our gender are marvelously equipped for the learning process. But they must be given the opportunity to turn these often merely passive virtues into positive assets for the society in which they live.

AUNG SAN SUU KYI

from Experiences Facing Death

I perceive here that I have not said enough about the experience of prayer, the one spiritual exercise which is and has always been open to the humblest intelligence, the least flexible subconsciousness to use. Even in its least-evolved form as inarticulate but emotionally directed desire, prayer is not without effect. Made articulate, directed by the intelligence and gradually involving the whole range of consciousness, prayer becomes an incalculable power, whether measured by its effect on the user, or by its objective accomplishment. The average person, wholly uninstructed, begins usually with the emotionally driven petition: Lord, give! . . . give! . . . and keeps on until a new emotional equilibrium is reached, in the midst of which intellectual decision becomes possible. Most Protestant prayer stops there. If one goes on without instruction, one comes to a phase in which there is an answering *start* of consciousness. Intimations of the desired answer seem to arise on every side but do not eventuate. Most people who reach this stage, end by being disappointed, think of themselves as self-deluded, react from prayer in pronounced motions of disgust. In describing this phenomena to myself I have used the term 'mimicry' because it seems to me to be most akin to the thing that happens in protective mimicry of nature. Think of a bird, desiring a fat insect, hoping it is not a twig, deciding to chance it. The insect, made aware by that strange something in the lesser forms of life which is not intellect but is acted upon, the bird's mingled hope and doubt, assumes the appearance of a twig by an unpremeditated reaction, which by many repetitions becomes fixed in a habit of protective mimicry.

I have checked this over too many times not to feel certain of the mechanisms involved and since have learned that W.H. Hudson, whose opportunities for observing nature untainted were so much greater than mine, was of the same opinion. It was, for me, the first step in arriving at a fairly competent solution of the mystery of prayer being answered, as, if the practitioner will persist through the incident of protective mimicry to the next stage, he will discover it invariably is. From this on, there is an orderly progression of states, touching one step and then another of a winding stair, the end of which is never reached. How far you go in that practise depends, no doubt, upon your natural spiritual endowment and your persistence. But the unanticipated, the absolute, advantage in taking the first three steps is that, with each succeeding step, the necessary fluency between the two halves of man's mind, the intelligence and the subliminal, is augmented.

This is the best way I know to acquire that complete coordination, that wholeness which is indispensable to spiritual poise. The genius way, if you have ever so little genius, is almost equally profitable, unless you are one of those who have utilized your genius for purposes that have nothing to do with spirituality. The Mystic Way, if you have the courage to walk in it intelligently, not merely for the sake of enjoying mystical emotion, not, absolutely *not* as an escape from Here and Now, results naturally in establishing a superior control over the interactions of the immediate and the subliminal centers.

All these would seem to be serviceable to the self in an emergency – such as being thrust suddenly into the Hereafter – in which the submerged consciousness is likely to be forced sharply to the lead.

MARY AUSTIN

Rune before Prayer

I am bending my knee
In the eye of the Father who created me,
In the eye of the Son who purchased me,
In the eye of the Spirit who cleansed me ,
    In friendship and affection.
Through Thine own Anointed One, O God,
Bestow upon us fulness in our need,
        Love towards God,
        The affection of God,
        The smile of God,
        The wisdom of God,
        The grace of God,
        The fear of God,
        And the will of God
To do on the world of the Three,
As angels and saints
Do in heaven;
        Each shade and light,
        Each day and night,
        Each time in kindness,
        Give Thou as Thy Spirit.

ANN MACDONALD

from The Coming of God

IF you are to be able to respond to the invitation in prayer, 'Be still', you need a measure of silence in your life. In today's world silence is in short supply; this is a serious problem for our society, and anything we can do to help people recover a sense of silence as a necessary and positive element in human life is a contribution to the general sanity. Many people can, however, contrive some islands of silence in their lives, perhaps in holiday time. Without romantically ignoring our dependence on our environment it is also true to say that silence is partly an interior quality; you can learn to live from your own deep centre, rather than in the ego with its clamorous demands. You can make positive use of any period of silence that does occur, rather than looking on it as an empty stretch of time to be endured or filled up somehow. Silence like this is not a threat to us but an invitation to depth, to listening, to a loving communion in joy. It lays us open to the strong creativity of the Spirit, and he is the Spirit both of contemplation and of outgoing love. Contemplation, trust and reaching out to people go together. Mary's silent surrender to God at the Annunciation sent her swiftly out in the generous and practical love of the Visitation. Christ is in you, yours to give, a quiet light.

It may help us, when we are painfully conscious of turmoil, to remember that Christ's gifts are more than a spiritualized version of secular commodities. As the love he gives us is a love that has made itself vulnerable to all that hatred can do and has conquered hatred, as the life he gives is a life that has been through death and proved the stronger, so the peace he gives is something more than an absence of stress: 'Peace I leave with you; my peace I give to you; not as the world gives do I give to you' (John 14.27). The gift may sometimes be offered and received within the turmoil, in the eye of the storm.

Christian contemplation can never leave Jesus behind. However simplified and imageless prayer may become, however close the mystical union with God who is beyond all comprehension, it is Christ's incarnation and redemption that make them possible. St Teresa of Avila never gave up meditating on the Lord's passion to the end of her life. St John of the Cross, describing the mystical marriage at the summit of contemplative union, asserts that in this state the soul understands the mysteries of faith in a new way, for the Lord 'communicates to it the sweet mysteries of his incarnation and the ways and manners of human redemption'. Jesus is the revealer of the Father and the giver of the Spirit of prayer: 'No one comes to the Father but by me. If you had known me, you would have known my Father also. . . . He who has seen me has seen the Father. . . . Do you not believe that I am in the Father and the Father in me?' (John 14.6, 7, 9, 10). The Last Discourse reported by John is Jesus's 'intolerable wrestle with words and meanings', and here if anywhere language cracks under the strain. But he does truly reveal the Father, and we do really know amid all the bafflement and unknowing.

If you are called to contemplative prayer, which is not some esoteric adventure for the very few but by God's grace a normal flowering of baptismal life, you have to live in day-to-day fidelity to mysteries you do not fully understand, like Mary. This is what Advent is about, but it is also a general law of our lives, which are an Advent. You have to wait in hope, waiting for the mystery to unfold, going on doing ordinary things but all the time listening, learning, pondering, growing and energetically serving. You have to be silent before the mystery. In the Book of Job the 'comforters' are the ones who cannot be silent before it but must rush in with their explanations. You know your kinship with the mystery. By your closeness to Christ his mind is being formed in you, and he is leading you into his own experience, his own joy and longing, and his own knowledge of the Father. Whatever the renunciations, the inner poverty and the successive little deaths and lettings-go, this life of contemplation is a life of joy, because lived in Jesus it is a journey into God, an unfinished tale.

MARIA BOULDING

from Freedom from Fear

FEARLESSNESS may be a gift but perhaps more precious is the courage acquired through endeavour, courage that comes from cultivating the habit of refusing to let fear dictate one's actions, courage that could be described as 'grace under pressure' – grace which is renewed repeatedly in the face of harsh, unremitting pressure.

Within a system which denies the existence of basic human rights, fear tends to be the order of the day. Fear of imprisonment, fear of torture, fear of death, fear of losing friends, family, property or means of livelihood, fear of poverty, fear of isolation, fear of failure. A most insidious form of fear is that which masquerades as common sense or even wisdom, condemning as foolish, reckless, insignificant or futile the small, daily acts of courage which help to preserve man's self-respect and inherent human dignity. It is not easy for a people conditioned by the iron rule of the principle that might is right to free themselves from the enervating miasma of fear. Yet even under the most crushing state machinery courage rises up again and again, for fear is not the natural state of civilized man.

The wellspring of courage and endurance in the face of unbridled power is generally a firm belief in the sanctity of ethical principles combined with a historical sense that despite all setbacks the condition of man is set on an ultimate course for both spiritual and material advancement. It is his capacity for self-improvement and self-redemption which most distinguishes man from the mere brute. At the root of human responsibility is the concept of perfection, the urge to achieve it, the intelligence to find a path towards it, and the will to follow that path if not to the end at least the distance needed to rise above individual limitations and environmental impediments. It is man's vision of a world fit for rational, civilized humanity which leads him to dare and to suffer to build societies free from want and fear. Concepts such as truth, justice and compassion cannot be dismissed as trite when these are often the only bulwarks which stand against ruthless power.

AUNG SAN SUU KYI

IF you want peace of mind, do not find fault with others. Learn rather to see your own faults. Learn to make the whole world your own; no one is a stranger, my child, the whole world is your own.

SRĪ SĀRĀDA DEVĪ

from Collected Papers

WHAT, after all, is prayer? It is a mutual act, a communion of the created spirit with Uncreated Spirit: of the human self, immersed in contingency and succession, with the all-penetrating God who yet transcends contingency and succession – in whom, as St Augustine said, 'are all moments of time'. . . . Prayer, then, in the most general sense, is from the Divine side purposive. Its creative goal, however, may be concerned with almost any level or aspect of physical or spiritual life; for the prayer of a wide-open and surrendered human spirit appears to be a major channel for the free action of that Spirit of God with whom this soul is 'united in her ground'. Thus it seems certain that the energy of prayer can avail for the actual modifying of circumstance; and that its currents form an important constituent of that invisible web which moulds and conditions human life. It may open a channel along which power, healing or enlightenment goes to those who need it, as the watering-can provides the channel along which water goes to the thirsty plant. Or the object achieved may be, as we say, 'directly spiritual'; the gradual purifying and strengthening and final sublimation of the praying soul or of some other particular soul. In all such cases, though much remains mysterious, the connection between prayer and result appears as the connection of genuine cause and effect. We are plainly in the presence of that which Elisabeth Leseur called 'a high and fruitful form of action, the more secure that it is secret'. On the other hand, the prayer may seem to have no specified aim; and this is especially true of its more developed forms. As spiritual writers say, its energies may simply be 'given to God'. Thus it may do a work which remains for ever unknown to the praying soul; contributing to the good of the whole universe of spirits, the conquest of evil, the promotion of the Kingdom, the increased energy of holiness. Such general and sacrificial prayer has always formed part of the interior life of the saints, and is an enduring strand in the corporate work of the Church. . . . genuine prayer in all its degrees, from the most naive to the most transcendental, opens up human personality to the all-penetrating Divine activity . . . it places our souls at the disposal of immanent Spirit. In other words, it promotes abandonment to God.

EVELYN UNDERHILL

from Contemplative Nuns Speak

IT was not I who chose. I was certainly incapable of doing so. Nevertheless I cannot doubt that I have been called. For the past twenty-two years it has pleased the Lord to let me hear that call. But why me? The reply is to be found in St. Paul: 'Blessed be that God, that Father of our Lord Jesus Christ, who has . . . chosen us out, in Christ, before the foundation of the world.' 'Each of us has received his own special grace, dealt out to him by Christ's gift . . . Some he has appointed to be apostles, others to be prophets, others to be evangelists, or pastors, or teachers . . . to building up the frame of Christ's body . . . until we all realize our common unity through faith in the Son of God, and fuller knowledge of him . . .' The mystery of our vocation is lost in this light. However, the words which have always put me back on my feet again in all my temptations – and they were acute some years ago – to abandon the religious life, are the Gospel words: 'That man will be saved, who endures to the last'.

TRAPPISTINE, aged 33, in religion 9 years

from Waiting on God

THE Key to a Christian conception of studies is the realisation that prayer consists of attention. It is the orientation of all the attention of which the soul is capable towards God. The quality of the attention counts for much in the quality of the prayer. Warmth of heart cannot make up for it.

It is the highest part of the attention only which makes contact with God, when prayer is intense and pure enough for such a contact to be established; but the whole attention is turned towards God.

Of course school exercises only develop a lower kind of attention. Nevertheless they are extremely effective in increasing the power of attention which will be available at the time of prayer, on condition that they are carried out with a view to this purpose and this purpose alone.

Although people seem to be unaware of it to-day, the development of the faculty of attention forms the real object and almost the sole interest of studies. Most school tasks have a certain intrinsic interest as well, but such an interest is secondary. All tasks which really call upon the power of attention are interesting for the same reason and to an almost equal degree.

School children and students who love God should never say: 'For my part I like mathematics'; 'I like French'; 'I like Greek.' They should learn to like all these subjects, because all of them develop that faculty of attention which, directed towards God, is the very substance of prayer.

If we have no aptitude or natural taste for geometry this does not mean that our faculty for attention will not be developed by wrestling with a problem or studying a theorem. On the contrary it is almost an advantage.

It does not even matter much whether we succeed in finding the solution or understanding the proof, although it is important to try really hard to do so. Never in any case whatever is a genuine effort of the attention wasted. It always has its effect on the spiritual plane and in consequence on the lower one of the intelligence, for all spiritual light lightens the mind.

If we concentrate our attention on trying to solve a problem of geometry, and if at the end of an hour we are no nearer to doing so than at the beginning, we have nevertheless been making progress each minute of that hour in another more mysterious dimension. Without our knowing or feeling it, this apparently barren effort has brought more light into the soul. The result will one day be discovered in prayer. Moreover it may very likely be felt besides in some department of the intelligence in no way connected with mathematics.

SIMONE WEIL

from The Swan in the Evening

HER new life sounds so rich and interesting that it is hard not to feel: 'I can hardly wait!' *But we have to earn these spiritualized and heightened modes of consciousness; we don't achieve them automatically*; and we must never forget the tremendous value and importance of our earth lives. We learn lessons here that can be learned nowhere else; and, after some trial and much error, I have realized that it is a great mistake to concentrate on 'hereafter' at the expense of here. We are all harnessed, or should be, to the needs of the age.

Our impediment, very difficult to shift, is that 'only religious people believe this sort of stuff'. I think that if it could be grasped that we don't become bodiless wraiths, ghosts, shades or spirits when we die, but develop and inhabit a body if you like of finer matter, a subtle body, an etheric body (these terms are interchangeable) – if this were grasped as true for all of us, whether or no we ever go to church, and true for all living things, sceptics might perhaps be less unwilling to suspend disbelief. Sensitives can see 'the dead' in their new bodies: I think it is possible that within the next (say) hundred years many more people will. Ordinary people like myself see and hear in flashes; and of course certain animals are much more finely equipped than humans with extended vision and hearing. These bodies are sometimes incredibly beautiful and self-luminous: not always: it depends. The sub-atomic worlds contain a myriad myriad forms, lovely, unlovely, strange, grotesque – and terrible.

I wish the Church would come out more positively and clearly on this important matter. After all, the Anglican Creed specifically declares belief in the resurrection of the body. In my rather lukewarm church-going teen-age days I found this article of faith so offensive to reason, feeling, and common sense that I used to press my lips firmly together while the passage was recited. Of course, it refers to the resurrection body, distinguished from the physical quite categorically by St. Paul. But nobody told me so. One was always left to infer that the only person who had ever risen from the dead was Jesus; and that the best we could hope for was that, 'through Jesus Christ', whatever that might mean, we might somehow achieve a feeble imitation of the same sort of transformation.

What humanity has said and done, all through the ages, in the name of *Credo quia impossibile est* never ceases to astound me; also what has been said and done, under the same banner, to poor humanity. Myself, I am by nature a person of little faith. Whenever I was told by well-wishers that all that was needed was one humble Act of Faith and lo! I should find myself safe and sound in the bosom of Mother Church, it seemed like being told that if only I would slip a pair of wings on I would find myself landing on the moon. So I am not unsympathetic to those who cry *Proof! Proof!* – though I always did understand, I think, that the mystical life can never be susceptible to the kind of proof which they require. Only direct experience can convince a doubter, once and for all: convince the doubter, that is, – not anybody else! Still, I have had the immense happiness of helping to convince several bereaved friends during these last years; or rather, I have been able to put them in the way of finding their own certainty. Others of course can't be approached; and on these one should never intrude.

Odd but true, you won't necessarily lead a more virtuous, more useful life because you believe that we 'go on'. You won't love the beauty of the world more, or appreciate the arts more deeply, or even love your fellow beings more and serve them better. You won't necessarily face death with greater equanimity. What I do think true is that you learn a greater sympathy with life in all its manifested forms of consciousness: for animals, birds, fish, trees, plants, as well as for human beings. Also, supposing that you were ever tempted to put an end to your own life you would refrain: not because it is a mortal sin that God will punish with damnation everlasting, as the cruel-minded old theologians used to teach, but because, generally speaking, it is a terrible *mistake*, a set-back that leads to bitter regret and self-reproach when those who have cut their own lives short wake up.

ROSAMOND LEHMANN

from The Land of Journey's Ending

IF we could blot out of our sight all the materiality with which man, even in our inmost vision of him, is forever in contact, we should see him floating in the bubble of his selfness, aloof, shut in by iridescent films of his own experience with the universe. What he thinks he sees, what he feels he knows: these give color and texture to the irised globe in which he moves, and, like a bubble, blows out and contracts with his own breath. I find this figure of the many-colored foam which the rain priest lifts through his cloud-blower in the Tewa rain-making, better suited to my use than the stiff phrase of the psychologists. When the yucca suds swirl in the ceremonial bowl, rise, under the rain priest's breath, heap on heap, shining half-globes that crowd and coalesce and break into one another, until something of its neighbor's wall has become a portion of every filmed inclosure. This is the figure of our sort of society, in which there are a million souls shut in the foam cloud, for whom the color and shape of the universe is the shell of their neighbour's thinking. Here and there great souls detach themselves and go sailing skyward in a lovely world of their own seeing, poets and prophets. But what happens in the pueblo is the gentle swelling of film into film, until the whole community lies at the centre of one great bubble of the Indian's universe, from which the personal factor seldom escapes into complete individuation!

MARY AUSTIN

To J. M. Murry

[Le Prieuré, Fontainebleau.
10 November 1922]

£5 note enclosed.
My darling Bogey

I had a letter from you today saying you had bought a pruning knife. I hope you succeed with the old trees. Here it is part of the 'work' to do a great many things, especially things which one does *not* like. I see the point of that. Its the same principle as facing people whom one shrinks from and so on. It is to develop a greater range in oneself. But what happens in practice is that no sooner do the people begin doing those things they don't like than the dislike changes. One feels it no longer. Its only that first step which is so terribly hard to take.

from *Katherine Mansfield: Selected Letters*

A Chorus

Over the surging tides and the mountain kingdoms,
Over the pastoral valleys and the meadows,
Over the cities with their factory darkness,
Over the lands where peace is still a power,
Over all these and all this planet carries
A power broods, invisible monarch, a stranger
To some, but by many trusted. Man's a believer
Until corrupted. This huge trusted power
Is spirit. He moves in the muscle of the world.
In continual creation. He burns the tides, he shines
From the matchless skies. He is the day's surrender.
Recognize him in the eye of the angry tiger,
In the sigh of a child stepping at last into sleep,
In whatever touches, graces and confesses,
In hopes fulfilled or forgotten, in promises

Kept, in the resignation of old men –
This spirit, this power, this holder together of space
Is about, is aware, is working in your breathing.
But most he is the need that shows in hunger
And in the tears shed in the lonely fastness.
And in sorrow after anger.

ELIZABETH JENNINGS

7

THIS LIFE IS THE GERM OF THE NEXT

Death is a clean bold word and has no second meaning

REBECCA RICHMOND

from A Very Easy Death

WHAT would have happened if Maman's doctor had detected the cancer as early as the first symptoms? No doubt it would have been treated with rays and Maman would have lived two or three years longer. But she would have known or at least suspected the nature of her disease, and she would have passed the end of her life in a state of dread. What we bitterly regretted was that the doctor's mistake had deceived us; otherwise Maman's happiness would have become our chief concern. The difficulties that prevented Jeanne and Poupette from having her in the summer would not have counted. I should have seen more of her: I should have invented things to please her.

And is one to be sorry that the doctors brought her back to life and operated, or not? She, who did not want to lose a single day, 'won' thirty: they brought her joys; but they also brought her anxiety and suffering. Since she did escape from the martyrdom that I sometimes thought was hanging over her, I cannot decide for her. For my sister, losing Maman the very day she saw her again would have been a shock from which she would scarcely have recovered. And as for me? Those four weeks have left me pictures, nightmares, sadness that I should never have known if Maman had died that Wednesday morning. But I cannot measure the disturbance that I should have felt since my sorrow broke out in a way that I had not foreseen. We did derive an undoubted good from this respite: it saved us, or almost saved us, from remorse. When someone you love dies you pay for the sin of outliving her with a thousand piercing regrets. Her death brings to light her unique quality; she grows as vast as the world that her absence annihilates for her and whose whole existence was caused by her being there; you feel that she should have had more room in your life – all the room, if need be. You snatch yourself away from this wildness: she was only one among many. But since you never do all you might for anyone – not even within the arguable limits that you have set yourself – you have plenty of room left for self-reproach. With regard to Maman we were above all guilty, these last years, of carelessness, omission and abstention. We felt that we atoned for this by the days that we gave up to her, by the peace that our being there gave her, and by the victories gained over fear and pain. Without our obstinate watchfulness she would have suffered far more.

For indeed, comparatively speaking, her death was an easy one. 'Don't leave me in the power of the brutes.' I thought of all those who have no one to make that appeal to: what agony it must be to feel oneself a defenceless thing, utterly at the mercy of indifferent doctors and overworked nurses. No hand on the fore-head when terror seizes them; no sedative as soon as pain begins to tear them; no lying prattle to fill the silence of the void. 'She aged forty years in twenty-four hours.' That phrase too had obsessed my mind. Even today – why? – there are horrible agon-izing deaths. And then in the public wards, when the last hour is coming near, they put a screen round the dying man's bed: he has seen this screen round other beds that were empty the next day: he knows. I pictured Maman, blinded for hours by the black sun that no one can look at directly: the horror of her staring eyes with their dilated pupils. She had a very easy death; an upper-class death.

SIMONE DE BEAUVOIR

from Mirror of an Eastern Moon

Nimrod's fire became cool and pleasant.
All its flames and its sparks were luminous roses.
All the roses died with a smile, and their petals
Turned into rose-oil . . . o breeze full of fragrance!
One drop fell on me.

Now, in long nights my heart is one with the roses,

And towards dawn the roses turn into fire,
Burning away the thorns and the straw of my hopes,
Until I learn to die with a smile like the roses,
Until I am
    nothing but your fragrant oil . . .
                                    ANNE MARIE SCHIMMEL

from The Swan in the Evening

THAT evening, talk sparkled and rippled round the table as if the unimaginable death which had drawn us together were – not forgotten or ignored, but somehow overcome; so that we could tease each other and be teased as usual. No, not as usual. Our laughter seemed to bubble up from some primordial spring of well-being; like an echo of the laughter of the gods. I am not sure when it was in the course of the evening that I became consciously aware that the room was ablaze with light: a white column of incandescent light was vibrating between floor and ceiling – visible, I suppose, only to my opened eyes; but it never occurred to me either to remark upon it or to doubt that it was there, objectively present. Behind the dazzling screen it interposed, the faces of my friends occasionally seemed to dematerialize. I watched one of them, and was surprised, as well as touched and amused, to see that the countenance, instead of being on the square and solid side, had become almost transparent, and seraphic-looking, set on a long graceful neck.

All things were pleasure to me and nothing could grieve me . . . Truly for twenty-four hours I knew the mystical meaning of those words: still know it, inasmuch as that glimpse remains, and always will remain, enough to live by, in sure and certain hope that the end is joy.

But by contrast, the light, or rather no light of common day when it returned was insupportable; and the worst was still to come.

I suppose I had imagined that after plumbing the depths of

suffering I was saved: that I had been set rocking, endlessly rocking, in an aerial cradle between two worlds. I had to learn, and re-learn, and learn again day after day, week after week, month after month, that I was truly left behind to crawl on as best I could, eternal exile, through the stone streets full of other people's daughters. Only indoors, in solitude, could I draw breath. That summer, a van with a loud speaker attached to it began to tour the Square in which I live; a voice shattered the air repeatedly, calling on people over twenty-one to come somewhere or other for their POLIO JABS. This commodity had just become available to Sally's age-group. . . . On the other hand, sometimes – and increasingly as the months of the first year went on – when I opened the door of my flat, a cloud of incomparable fragrance would greet me. What was it? – what could it be? At first I wondered if the old lady then living on the floor above me had begun to use some exquisitely perfumed bath essence whose echoes were somehow penetrating my rooms through the ventilating system. But the old lady went away, and still these exhalations pervaded all the air with an unearthly aromatic sweetness – spicy, yet delicate and fresh; compounded of lilies? clove carnations? frangipani? – and something indefinable as well. . . . It was not for me alone, this fragrance: I mean that it would, I think, have been quite perceptible to others; only, but for Patrick, I was so often alone in those days. However, I remember that Laurie Lee came in one evening, and after standing for a time in silence said three words only: 'Now I believe.' He had been one of the most passionately resentful of all those who loved and mourned her. I should add that he was acknowledging that the mystifying and pervasive scent I had mentioned to him was there, indubitably: I know nothing about his beliefs in the wider sense. As for myself, I don't know by whose agency this sign was given to me; much less how it was brought about. I only know that it was so; and therefore once I was sure of it, I murmured my thanks each time I came back into my empty flat. Months and months afterwards Sally referred to the phenomenon through two separate and independent psychic channels; but although these 'channels' have now become among my dearest friends, to whom I owe a debt of gratitude impossible to repay, I will not emphasize them further here. They will understand why this is not a 'psychic' book, but simply a personal record.

ROSAMOND LEHMANN

from Speculum of the Other Woman

DEATH really? But how does death come into this in(de)terminable procession? And, were it not for the tutor's orders, who would bother about death? It is not even sure that these 'children' have a word to designate it by, any more than a dream system to figure it in. And everything that happens/passes for them proclaims not an ending but the promise of a return, the next day. Were it not for the words of the philosophy teacher who talks to you about immortality, who would be preoccupied with such an issue, wholly absorbed in his dream that begins over and over again? Messenger of death, then. But which death? That of the beginning? Of 'matter'? Of the mother? Only recognizing life in (its) representation? In (its) specula(riza)tion? Its repetition, with terms that can be enumerated? All of which is, of course, impossible in relation to the indefiniteness of what had been before? Conception, 'for example,' which would find its 'proper' meaning only in the re-birth into truth. And truth, in order to escape any hint of verisimilitude, will be situated in a time that predates birth. An eternity beyond appearances, that closes (over) the inherence of re-production. Which demands *its double repetition* in the Being that is, always, in one way or another, *a trinity*. The One is the One only when mirrored *at least twice*. But this two obviously doesn't simply amount to a sum. Each specula(riza)tion modifies the properties of representation to the point at which it makes a complete *ring around* its attributes that thus become, inseparably, the constituents of the subject itself (as same). And the subject is claimed to have always existed in that perfection of self-identity from before birth.

A precedence battle is set up as to what comes next, after. Whatever came after is sent back earlier so as to mask its relationship to projection and the repercussions of the way it was determined, the re-mark of the definition of beginning. Origin thus suspends all of time in the feigned immutability of its genesis: its presence. No scission. No death. The two deaths and their two betweens and their den (of) death sink endlessly into the blindness of a certain divine speculation in which the question of the auto-copy of being is withheld. This is not the case for the tricks of the magicians, those demiurges who bastardize the divine projects by making them obvious, making them apparent in their very conception.

LUCE IRIGARAY

Night Sky

There came such clear opening of the night sky,
The deep glass of wonders, the dark mind
In unclouded gaze of the abyss
Opened like the expression of a face.
I looked into that clarity where all things are
End and beginning, and saw
My destiny there: 'So', I said, 'no other
'Was possible ever. This
'Is I. The pattern stands so for ever.'

What am I? Bound and bounded,
A pattern among the stars, a point in motion
Tracing my way. I am my way: it is I
I travel among the wonders.
Held in that gaze and known
In the eye of the abyss,
'Let it be so', I said,

And my heart laughed with joy
To know the death I must die.

KATHLEEN RAINE

To Maggie Lukens

Feb. 14th [1884]

Dear Maggie.

I am glad that my letter pleased you, & though always busy I at once answer your last because if by word or act one can help a fellow creature in the care or conduct of a soul that is one's first duty.

About the great Hereafter I can only give you my own feeling & belief, for we can *know* nothing, & must wait hopefully & patiently to learn the secret.

Death never seemed terrible to me, the fact I mean, though the ways of going & the sad blow of a sudden end are of course hard to bear & understand.

I feel that in this life we are learning to enjoy a higher, & fitting ourselves to take our place there. If we use well our talents, opportunities, trials & joys here when we pass on it is to the society of nobler souls, as in this world we find our level inevitably.

I think immortality is the passing of a soul thro many lives or experiences, & such as are *truly* lived, used & learned help on to the next, each growing richer higher, happier, carr[y]ing with it only the real memories of what has gone before. If in my present life I love one person truly, no matter who it is, I believe that we meet somewhere again, though where or how I dont know or care, for genuine love is immortal. So is real wisdom, virtue, heroism &c. & these noble attributes lift humble lives into the next experience, & prepare them to go on with greater power & happiness.

I seem to remember former states before this, & feel that in them I have learned some of the lessons that have never been mine here, & in my next step I hope to leave behind many of the trials that I have struggled to bear here & begin to find lightened as I go on.

This accounts for the genius & the great virtue some show here. They have done well in many phases of this great school & bring into our class the virtue or the gifts that make them great & good.

We dont remember the lesser things, they slip away as childish trifles, & we carry on only the real experiences. Some are born sad, some bad, some feeble, mentally & morally I mean, & all thier life here is an effort to get rid of this shadow of grief, sin, weakness in the life before. Others come as Shakespere, Milton Emerson &c. bringing thier lovely reward with them & pass on leaving us the better for thier lives.

This is my idea of immortality. An endless life of helpful change, with the instinct, the longing to rise, to learn, to love, to get nearer the source of all good, & go on from the lowest plane to the highest, rejoicing more & more as we climb into the clearer light, the purer air, the happier life which must exist, for, as Plato said 'The soul cannot imagine what does not exist because it is the shadow of God who knows & creates all things.'

I dont believe in spiritualism as commonly presented. I dont want to see or feel or hear dead friends except in my own sense of nearness, & as my love & memory paint them. I do believe that they remember us, are with us in a spiritual sense when we need them, & we feel thier presence with joy & comfort, not with fear or curiosity.

My mother is near me sometimes I am sure, for help comes of the sort she alone gave me, & May is about her baby I feel, for out of the innocent blue eyes sometimes come looks so like her mother's that I am startled, for I tended May as a child as I now tend Lulu. This slight tie is enough to hold us still tenderly together, though death drops a veil between us, & I look without doubt or fear toward the time when in some way we shall meet again.

from *The Selected Letters of Louisa May Alcott*

NOT to believe in the immortality of the soul, but to look upon the whole of life as destined to prepare for the moment of death; not to believe in God, but to love the universe, always, even in the throes of anguish, as a home – there lies the road toward faith by way of atheism . . .

SIMONE WEIL, from *Notebooks*

from Smile at Time

'BUT if one really believes in another, more alive life after this,' I rejoined, bent on sticking to what I believed to be true, 'there is no reason to pity you. I'm like various primitive tribes or the old Red Indians who thought death a cause for rejoicing and not sorrow; they wail when someone comes into the world – not when he leaves it.' 'I see,' he laughed; 'then I may expect you to envy me. Well?' he queried, as I remained silent. 'I was just thinking that this would seem a very queer form of conversation to most, wouldn't it? It would seem heartless to talk so much of death to a sick man?' 'But it was your conversation that I wanted and not anyone else's. I shouldn't have insisted on your coming here otherwise. I can get the usual stuff from anyone.' 'You won't get much from most English people,' I said impatiently. 'They are astonishingly dull along this line; quite incurious, almost asleep. I wish I'd lived in Germany in Goethe's time when everyone discussed such things, and he said that men were dead even in this life if they didn't believe in another, and metaphysics was the common coin; or I wish I had lived near Emerson and his friends.'

'Well, it's too late for that now, – but do go on. What, I wonder, started you thinking like this? You have never been ill, I imagine?'

'No, indeed. It was not illness, nor sadness, nor loss in my case; it was, just the *value* of life, the value of all the beauty and love I experienced that I felt must have an enduring existence. I believed almost as a child, and I believe still more now, in Blake's phrase, "the ruins of Time build mansions in eternity;" and that, as the ancient Egyptian said, "Long lost hearts burn in the oil of the lamp of the King; they are not extinguished." And more,' I continued, warming to the subject, 'I believe we are only at the beginning of things here; this life is the germ of the next which expands and bears fruit. People call themselves Christian, yet to how few is this a living thought! I've tried to understand all the different ways men and religion have of stating the same thing, and it's amazing how they all dovetail together, in all the races, in all periods.'

CONSTANCE SITWELL

The Dry Heart

The world where the dead live is a dry heart.
Every world is a heart, a rhythm spherical,
A rhythm of impossible intentions
That yet sings itself, imagining heard music.
The world where the dead live is a silent choir.
It does not hear itself, it sings itself not.
Its will has frozen into memory,
Black as still blood, without flow.
To the painless sorrow of death it throbs.
The world where the dead live is a heart alive
In a body once alive.
The dead move neither into heaven nor hell.
Their afterwards is their before.
The world where the dead live is a dry heart,
The same heart as always, even dry.

LAURA RIDING

from An Old Woman's Reflections

MY spell on this little bench is nearly finished. It's sad and low and lonely I am to be parting with it. Long as the day is, night comes, and alas, the night is coming for me, too.

I am parting with you, beautiful little place, sun of my life. Other people will have your pleasure in future, but I'll be far away from you in a kingdom I don't know. Big Peig, as the children call me, will be there no more, but maybe a better woman would. But she won't have as much pleasure as I had, because great as was my sorrow and heart-torment, God of Glory and His Blessed Mother helped me. I was often standing here studying the works of the Creator and tasting His royal sweetness in my heart. Everything He created was a consolation to me, even unto the grief itself, it would make me think deeper. I thought there was nothing in the things of this life but poverty – this place full today and empty tomorrow – hadn't I got it to be seen, clearly. The people I knew in my youth, it was often they had the stone in the gauntlet for each other. They were strong, courageous, strong-worded, but they all fell, they were cleared out of the world. It was the same do the people who were there before them got, and may God have mercy on us, where is their work today? Other people to be in their place, without the slightest thought for them. I think everything is folly except for loving God!

I am now at tight grips with the years, and many a thing I saw. Everything I was interested in I didn't let it astray. Someone else will have pastime out of my work when I'm gone on the way of truth. A person here and a person there will say, maybe, 'Who was that Peig Sayers?' but poor Peig will be the length of their shout for them. This green bench where she used to do the studying will be a domicile for the birds of the wilderness, and the little house where she used to eat and drink, it's unlikely there'll be a trace of it there.

These thoughts appearing in my heart today are lonely. They are not pleasant for me but I can't help them. Here they are towards me in their thousands; they are like soldiers. As I scatter

them, they come together again. It's no good for me to be at
them. They have beaten me. My blessing and the blessing of
God be with Youth; and my advice to everyone is to borrow from
this life, because a spool is no faster turning than it. My life is
spent, as a candle, and my hope is up every day that I'll be called
into the eternal kingdom.

O God who is in Heaven, my trust and my hope is fully in
you! May you guide me on this long road I have not travelled
before! It's often during my life you helped me. Well I know
your holy help, because I was often held by sorrow, with no
escape. When the need was highest, it was then you would lay
your merciful eye on me, and a light like the shining of the sun
would come on my worried mind. The clouds of sorrow would be
gone without trace; in place there would be some spiritual joy
whose sweetness I cannot describe here.

But I have this much to say, that I had good neighbours. We
helped each other and lived in the shelter of each other.
Everything that was coming dark upon us, we would disclose it to
each other, and that would give us consolation of mind.
Friendship was the fastest root in our hearts.

It was like a little rose in the wilderness I grew up; without for
company only those gems that God of Glory created, eternal
praise to Him! Every early morning in the summer when the sun
would show its face up over the top of Eagle Mountain I was
often looking at it and at the same time making wonder of the
colours in the sky around us. I remember well that there used to
be little yellow, golden rays as slender roads coming to me from
the top of the mountain, and that the mountain used to be red
and a big belt of every colour, between white, yellow and black,
around the sky and every colour giving its own appearance on the
great, wet sea. I think, there was welcome in the heart of every
creature for the sparkling of the morning.

There are people and they think that this island is a lonely, airy
place. That is true for them, but the peace of the Lord is in it. I
am living in it for more than forty years, and I didn't see two of
the neighbours fighting in it yet. It was like honey for my poor

tormented heart to rise up on the shoulder of the mountain footing the turf or gathering the sods on each other. Very often I'd throw myself back in the green heather, resting. It wasn't for bone-laziness I'd do it, but for the beauty of the hills and the rumble of the waves that would be grieving down from me, in dark caves where the seals of the sea lived – those and the blue sky without a cloud travelling it, over me – it was those made me do it, because those were the pictures most pleasant to my heart, and it's those I was most used to.

A person would say, maybe, that it was a simple life we were living, but nobody would say that our life was comfortable. Our own hardships followed us. It's often we were in a way to go with fear and fright, because when winter came it wasn't its habit to come gentle and kind. The great sea was coming on top of us and the strong force of the wind helping it. We had but to send our prayer sincerely to God that nobody would be taken sick or ill. We had our own charge of that because there wasn't a priest or doctor near us without going across the little strait and the little strait was up to three miles in length. But God was in favour with us, eternal praise to Him! For with my memory nobody died without the priest in winter-time.

Farewell to the things of this life now, and especially to the pleasant, gay time I have spent here. I'm afraid I'll do no more work in future for the language of the superior men, but I have done a person's share, maybe. I would do as much more, and have the heart for it, but the time is spent.

Pray for me, friends and dear people, that God will give me help for the long road!

PEIG SAYERS

On Death

> Tell me thou safest end of all our woe,
> Why wretched mortals do avoid thee so:
> Thou gentle drier o'th'afflicted's tears,

Thou noble ender of the coward's fears;
Thou sweet repose to lovers' sad despair,
Thou calm t'ambition's rough tempestuous care.
If in regard of bliss thou wert a curse,
And than the joys of Paradise art worse;
Yet after man from his first station fell,
And God from Eden Adam did expel,
Thou wert no more an evil, but relief;
The balm and cure to ev'ry human grief:
Through thee, what man had forfeited before
He now enjoys, and ne'er can lose it more.
No subtle serpents in the grave betray,
Worms on the body there, not souls, do prey;
No vice there tempts, no terrors there affright,
No coz'ning sin affords a false delight:
No vain contentions do that peace annoy,
No fierce alarms break the lasting day.

Ah since from thee so many blessings flow,
Such real good as life can never know;
Come when thou wilt, in thy affrighting'st dress,
Thy shape shall never make thy welcome less.
Thou may'st to joy, but ne'er to fear give birth,
Thou best, as well as certain'st thing on earth.
Fly thee? May travellers then fly their rest,
And hungry infants fly the proffered breast.
No, those that faint and tremble at thy name,
Fly from their good on a mistaken fame.
Thus childish fear did Israel of old
From plenty and the Promised Land with-hold;
They fancied giants, and refused to go
When Canaan did with milk and honey flow.

                                        ANNE KILLIGREW

Study: The Death of a Rose

IT is a sensation that can never be forgotten, to sit in solitude, in semi-darkness, and to watch the slow, sweet, shadowful death of a Rose.

Oh, to see the perfection of the perfumed petals being changed ever so slightly, as though a thin flame had kissed each with hot breath, and where the wounds bled the colour is savagely intense . . . I have before me such a Rose, in a thin, clear glass, and behind it a little spray of scarlet leaves. Yesterday it was beautiful with a certain serene, tearful, virginal beauty; it was strong and wholesome, and the scent was fresh and invigorating.

To-day it is heavy and languid with the loves of a thousand strange Things, who, lured by the gold of my candlelight, came in the Purple Hours, and kissed it hotly on the mouth, and sucked it into their beautiful lips with tearing, passionate desire.

. . . So now it dies . . . And I listen . . . for under each petal fold there lies the ghost of a dead melody, as frail and as full of suggestion as a ray of light upon a shadowed pool. Oh, divine sweet Rose. Oh, exotic and elusive and deliciously vague Death.

From the tedious sobbing and gasping, and hoarse guttural screaming, and uncouth repulsive movements of the body of dying Man, I draw apart, and, smiling, I lean over you, and watch your dainty, delicate Death.

from *Poems of Katherine Mansfield*

from Teaching a Stone to Talk

THERE were flies buzzing over the dirt by the henhouse, moving in circles and buzzing, black dreams in chips off the one long dream, the dream of the regular world. But the silent fields were the real world, eternity's outpost in time, whose look I remembered but never like this, this God-blasted, paralyzed day. I felt myself tall and vertical, in a blue shirt, self-conscious, and wishing to die. I heard the flies again; I looked at the rooster who was frozen looking at me.

Then at last I heard whistling, human whistling far on the air, and I was not able to bear it. I looked around, heartbroken; only at the big yellow Charolais farm far up the road was there motion – a woman, I think, dressed in pink, and pushing a wheelbarrow easily over the grass. It must have been she who was whistling and heaping on top of the silence those hollow notes of song. But the slow sound of the music – the beautiful sound of the music ringing the air like a stone bell – was isolate and detached. The notes spread into the general air and became the weightier part of silence, silence's last straw. The distant woman and her wheelbarrow were flat and detached, like mechanized and pink-painted properties for a stage. I stood in pieces, afraid I was unable to move. Something had unhinged the world. The houses and roadsides and pastures were buckling under the silence. Then a Labrador, black, loped up the distant driveway, fluid and cartoonlike, toward the pink woman. I had to try to turn away. Holiness is a force, and like the others can be resisted. It was given, but I didn't want to see it, God or no God. It was as if God had said, 'I am here, but not as you have known me. This is the look of silence, and of loneliness unendurable; it too has always been mine, and now will be yours.' I was not ready for a life of sorrow, sorrow deriving from knowledge I could just as well stop at the gate.

I turned away, willful, and the whole show vanished. The realness of things disassembled. The whistling became ordinary, familiar; the air above the fields released its pressure and the fields lay hooded as before. I myself could act. Looking to the rooster I whistled to him myself, softly, and some hens appeared at the chicken house window, greeted the day, and fluttered down.

Several months later, walking past the farm on the way to a volleyball game, I remarked to a friend, by way of information, 'There are angels in those fields.' Angels! That silence so grave and so stricken, that choked and unbearable green! I have rarely been so surprised at something I've said. Angels! What are angels? I had never thought of angels, in any way at all.

From that time I began to think of angels. I considered that sights such as I had seen of the silence must have been shared by the people who said they saw angels. I began to review the thing I had seen that morning. My impression now of those fields is of thousands of spirits – spirits trapped, perhaps, by my refusal to call them more fully, or by the paralysis of my own spirit at that time – thousands of spirits, angels in fact, almost discernible to the eye, and whirling. If pressed I would say they were three or four feet from the ground. Only their motion was clear (clockwise, if you insist); that, and their beauty unspeakable.

There are angels in those fields, and, I presume, in all fields, and everywhere else. I would go to the lions for this conviction, to witness this fact. What all this means about perception, or language, or angels, or my own sanity, I have no idea.

ANNIE DILLARD

from The Spiritual Life

THE spiritual life, then, is not a peculiar or extreme form of piety. It is, on the contrary, that full and real life for which man is made; a life that is organic and social, essentially free, yet with its own necessities and laws. Just as physical life means, and depends on, constant correspondence with our physical environment, the atmosphere that surrounds and penetrates us, the energies of heat and light, whether we happen to notice it or not; so does spiritual life mean constant correspondence with our spiritual environment, whether we notice it or not. We get out of gear in either department, when this correspondence is arrested or disturbed; and if it stops altogether, we cease to live. For the most part, of course, the presence and action of the great spiritual universe surrounding us is no more noticed by us than the pressure of air on our bodies, or the action of light. Our field of attention is not wide enough for that; our spiritual senses are not sufficiently alert. Most people work so hard developing their correspondence with the visible world, that their power of corresponding with the invisible is left in a rudimentary state. But when, for one reason or another, we begin to wake up a little bit, to lift the nose from the ground and notice that spiritual light and that spiritual atmosphere as real constituents of our human world; then, the whole situation is changed. Our horizon is widened, our experience is enormously enriched, and at the same time our responsibilities are enlarged. For now we get an entirely new idea of what human beings are for, and what they can achieve: and as a result, first our notions about life, our scale of values, begins to change, and then we do.

Here the creative action of God on a human creature enters on a new phase; for the mysterious word creation does not mean a routine product, neatly finished off and put on a shelf. Mass-production is not creation. Thus we do not speak of the creation of a pot of jam; though we might speak of the creation of a salad, for there freedom and choice play a major part. No two salads are ever quite alike. Creation is the activity of an artist possessed by the vision of perfection; who, by means of the raw material with which he works, tries to give more and more perfect expression to his idea, his inspiration or his love. From this point of view, each human spirit is an unfinished product, on which the Creative Spirit is always at work.

The moment in which, in one way or another, we become aware of this creative action of God and are therefore able to respond or resist, is the moment in which our conscious spiritual life begins. In all the talk of human progress, it is strange how very seldom we hear anything about this, the most momentous step forward that a human being can make: for it is the step that takes us beyond self-interest, beyond succession, sets up a direct intercourse with the soul's Home and Father, and can introduce us into eternal life. Large parts of the New Testament are concerned with the making of that step. But the experimental knowledge of it is not on the one hand possessed by all Christians, nor on the other hand is it confined to Christianity.

There are many different ways in which the step can be taken. It may be, from the ordinary human point of view, almost imperceptible: because, though it really involves the very essence of man's being, his free and living will, it is not linked with a special or vivid experience. Bit by bit the inexorable pressure is applied, and bit by bit the soul responds; until a moment comes when it realises that the landscape has been transformed, and is seen in a new proportion and lit by a new light. So the modern French woman whose memoirs were published under the name of Lucie Christine was not conscious of any jolt or dislocation of her life, but only of a disclosure of its true meaning and direction, on the day when she seemed to see before her eyes the words 'God Only!' and received from them an overwhelming conviction of His Reality which enlightened her mind, attracted her heart and gave power to her will. Yet this was really the gentle, long prepared initiation of her conscious spiritual life.

But sometimes the step is a distinct and vivid experience. Then we get the strange facts of conversion: when through some object or event – perhaps quite small object or event – in the external world, another world and its overwhelming attraction and demand is realised. An old and limited state of consciousness is suddenly, even violently, broken up and another takes its place. It was the voice of a child saying 'Take, read!' which at last made St. Augustine cross the frontier on which he had been lingering, and turned a brilliant and selfish young professor into one of the giants of the Christian Church; and a voice which seemed to him to come from the Crucifix, which literally made the young St. Francis, unsettled and unsatisfied, another man than he was before. It was while St. Ignatius sat by a stream and watched the running water, and while the strange old cobbler Jacob Boehme was looking at a pewter dish, that there was shown to each of them the mystery of the Nature of God. It was the sudden sight of a picture at a crucial moment of her life which revealed to St. Catherine of Genoa the beauty of Holiness, and by contrast her own horribleness; and made her for the rest of her life the friend and servant of the unseen Love. All these were various glimpses of one living Perfection; and woke up the love and desire for that living perfection, latent in every human creature, which is the same thing as the love of God, and the substance of a spiritual life. A spring is touched, a Reality always there discloses itself in its awe-inspiring majesty and intimate nearness, and becomes the ruling fact of existence; continually presenting its standards, and demanding a costly response. And so we get such an astonishing scene, when we reflect upon it, as that of the young Francis of Assisi, little more than a boy, asking all night long the one question which so many apparently mature persons have never asked at all: 'My God and All, what are Thou and what am I?' and we realise with amazement what a human creature really is – a finite centre of consciousness, which is able to apprehend, and long for, infinity.

EVELYN UNDERHILL

A Dream

This is a strange twilit country, but full of peace.
Faintly I hear sorrow; she sighs, moving away.
She goes, and guilt goes with her; all is forgiven.
Grey wolds and a slow dark river spell release
In this place where it is never quite night or day,
More like the elysian fields than the fields of heaven;

And no one here but I and this silent child.
She needs to sleep, I will carry her through the dim
Levels of this long river's deliberate mazes.
Nothing of man's is here, and never a wild
Creature to crop the grass or tunnel the brim
Of the full stream, or look up in our two faces.

She spoke so strangely that once, but she speaks no more.

Leans her head down in my neck, and is light to bear.
I think she walked here over the twilit stream.
I must find the tree, the elm by the river-shore,
Loosen her little arms and leave her there,
Under the boughs of sleep and the leaves of dream.

RUTH PITTER

from The Mind of the Maker

BUT there is this difference: that for the satisfaction of its will to
life it depends utterly upon the sustained and perpetually
renewed will to creation of its maker. The work can live and grow
on the sole condition of the maker's untiring energy; to satisfy its
will to die, he has only to stop working. In him it lives and moves
and has its being, and it may say to him with literal truth, 'thou
art my life, if thou withdraw, I die'. If the unself-conscious creature could be moved to worship, its thanks and praise would be
due, not so much for any incidents of its structure, but primarily
for its being and its identity. It would not, if it were wise, petition
its maker to wrest its own nature out of truth on any pretext at all,
since (as we have seen) any violence of this kind serves only to
diminish its vitality and destroy its identity. Still less would it
desire him to subdue his own will or alter his purpose in the
writing, since any such deviation from the Idea will disintegrate
the work and send the fragments sliding the random way to
chaos. If it possessed will and consciousness, it could achieve life
and individual integrity only by co-operating with the Energy to
interpret the Idea in Power.

The human maker, working in unself-conscious matter,
receives no worship from his creatures, since their will is no part
of his material; he can only receive the response of their nature,
and he is alone in fault if that response is not forthcoming. If he
tortures his material, if the stone looks unhappy when he has
wrought it into a pattern alien to its own nature, if his writing is
an abuse of language, his music a succession of unmeaning

intervals, the helpless discomfort of his material universe is a reproach to him alone; similarly, if he respects and interprets the integrity of his material, the seemliness of the ordered work proclaims his praise, and his only, without will, but in a passive beauty of right structure. If he works with plants, with animals or with men, the co-operative will of the material takes part in the work in an ascending scale of conscious response and personal readiness to do him honour. But a perfect identity of conscious will between himself and the creature can never be attained; identity is in fact attained in inverse ratio to the consciousness of the creature. A perfect identity of the creature with its creator's will is possible only when the creature is unself-conscious: that is, when it is an externalisation of something that is wholly controlled by the maker's mind. But even this limited perfection is not attainable by the human artist, since he is himself a part of his own material. So far as his particular piece of work is concerned, he is Godlike – immanent and transcendent; but his work and himself both form part of the universe, and he cannot transcend the universe. All his efforts and desires reach out to that ideal creative archetype in whose unapproachable image he feels himself to be made, which can make a universe filled with free, conscious and co-operative wills; a part of his own personality and yet existing independently within the mind of the maker.

DOROTHY L. SAYERS

Two Voices

L'instant de la mort est . . . l'instant où pour une fraction infinitesimale du temps la vérité pure, nue, certaine, éternelle entre dans l'âme.   Simone Weil

You learn the feasts of love when they are past,
Discern a banquet through a fast.

Not the death-bed only, and the silence
Clouding over it, but moments lit with sun –
Parting over the gate before an audience
Of smiling flowers, or on Ludgate Hill
Where we were silent, only the traffic bellowed
For pain, hearing the sentence of farewell. . . .

This too is the hour of death.

And as a wounded man whose hurt is mortal
Feels at first but little pain, or none,
The heart goes free at first perhaps, but later
Returning to the scene, time and again
Wakes its own anguish, would not wish its ending,
Trying to grasp the meaning by the pain.

Parting is death, and death ends love.

If that were true, why does the injured creature
Fly homing constantly to that one scene?
I have seen a sparrow, her nest moved by the thatcher,
Flutter for hours at the spot where it should have been,
Deaf to the chirps, blind to the beaks of her nestlings
Only a couple of feet away; and so
The heart flies to the past, and cannot enter.
What does it hope to achieve? Perhaps to improve
Its own performance in the past, to alter
Some gawky fact to a more endurable shape?
Some gesture of love or powerful word spoken
Instead of the stammer of history? That's not all,
That's not the inescapable need that beckons.

I was blind to my love, but when
He went from me, I saw him then.

The need that draws us back to the moment of death

Is this, then: that we know we sometime, somehow
Must make it good. That was the flash of truth,
Infrequent star just for that instant visible:
If there was anguish, that was not the point,
And to have missed the point was inexcusable.

I have forgotten the insight with the pain.

Did you see God in parting from Him? Learn
To make the moment bless you; haunt the scene;
For if the parting-point was the point of vision,
Then only through that gate can we return.

ANNE RIDLER

Nangsa replied:

'Please listen to me again, friends!
The precious human body is difficult to attain.
If you do not practice Dharma there is a great danger
Of falling into the lower realms.
Life is as brief as lightning between clouds.
Even if you friends do not want to practice the Dharma,
I am going.
Our life is like a drop of water on the grass,
Which can evaporate from little heat.
Even if you friends do not want to practice the Dharma,
I am going.
Life is like a rainbow in the grass,
Even though it looks nice,
It has no real worth.
Even if you friends do not want to practice the Dharma,
I am going.
Our life is as long as that of a butcher's sheep,

We are doomed to death.
Even if you friends do not want to practice the Dharma,
I am going.
Life is like the setting sun,
It looks strong and beautiful,
But before you know it, it is gone.
Even if you friends do not want to practice the Dharma,
I am going.
Life is like an eagle flying,
Now it is here but soon it will disappear.
Even if you friends do not want to practice the Dharma,
I am going.
Life is like a waterfall cascading from a high mountain,
Even though it makes a big sound,
It lasts only a moment then you pass it and it is gone.
Even if you friends do not want to practice the Dharma,
I am going.
Life is like a beggar's food,
Even if they have a lot in the morning,
By evening it is gone.
Even if you friends do not want to practice the Dharma,
I am going.
Life is like people walking in the streets,
For a moment we see them and then in a moment they are
    gone.
Even if you friends do not want to practice the Dharma,
I am going.
Our life is like a light,
The wind blows it and it doesn't rest anywhere.
Even if you friends do not want to practice the Dharma,
I am going.
Life is like a beautiful face,
It is with us when we are young,
But when we get old it will become ugly.
Even if you friends do not want to practice the Dharma,
I am going.

If I can find a good guru to teach me about impermanence,
Even if you friends do not want to practice the Dharma,
I am going.'

NANGSA OBUM

from Mysticism

TO be a mystic is simply to participate here and now in that real
and eternal life; in the fullest, deepest sense which is possible to
man. It is to share, as a free and conscious agent – not a servant,
but as a son – in the joyous travail of the Universe: its mighty
onward sweep through pain and glory towards its home in God.
This gift of 'sonship,' this power of free co-operation in the
world-process, is man's greatest honour. The ordered sequence of
states, the organic development, whereby his consciousness is
detached from illusion and rises to the mystic freedom which
conditions, instead of being conditioned by, its normal world, is
the way he must tread if that sonship is to be attained. Only by
this deliberate fostering of his deeper self, this transmutation of
the elements of character, can he reach those levels of consciousness upon which he hears, and responds to, the measure 'whereto
the worlds keep time' on their great pilgrimage towards the
Father's heart. The mystic act of union, that joyous loss of the
transfigured self in God, which is the crown of man's conscious
ascent towards the Absolute, is the contribution of the individual
to this, the destiny of the Cosmos.

The mystic knows that destiny. It is laid bare to his lucid
vision, as plain to him as our puzzling world of form and colour
is to normal sight. He is the 'hidden child' of the eternal order, an
initiate of the secret plan. Hence, whilst 'all creation groaneth and
travaileth,' slowly moving under the spur of blind desire towards
that consummation in which alone it can have rest, he runs
eagerly along the pathway to reality. He is the pioneer of Life on
its age-long voyage to the One: and shows us, in his attainment,
the meaning and value of that life.

This meaning, this secret plan of Creation, flames out, had we eyes to see, from every department of existence. Its exultant declarations come to us in all great music; its wild magic is the life of all romance. Its law – the law of love – is the substance of the beautiful, the energizing cause of the heroic. It lights the altar of every creed. It runs like ichor in the arteries of the universe. All man's dreams and diagrams concerning a transcendent Perfection near him yet intangible, a transcendent vitality to which he can attain – whether he call these objects of desire, God, grace, being, spirit, beauty, 'pure idea' – are but translations of his deeper self's intuition of its destiny; clumsy fragmentary hints at the all-inclusive, living Absolute which that deeper self knows to be real. This supernal Thing, the adorable Substance of all that Is – the synthesis of Wisdom, Power, and Love – and man's apprehension of it, his slow remaking in its interests, his union with it at last; this is the theme of mysticism. That twofold extension of consciousness which allows him communion with its transcendent and immanent aspects is, in all its gradual processes, the Mystic Way. It is also the crown of human evolution; the fulfilment of life, the liberation of personality from the world of appearance, its entrance into the free, creative life of the Real.

Evelyn Underhill

Remembrance

Cold in the earth and the deep snow piled above thee!
Far, far removed, cold in the dreary grave:
Have I forgot, my only Love, to love thee,
Severed at last by Time's all-severing wave?

Now, when alone, do my thoughts no longer hover
Over the mountains on Angora's shore;
Resting their wings where heath and fern-leaves cover
That noble heart for ever, ever more?

Cold in the earth, and fifteen wild Decembers
From these brown hills have melted into spring –
Faithful indeed is the spirit that remembers
After such years of change and suffering!

Sweet Love of youth, forgive if I forget thee
While the World's tide is bearing me along:
Other desires and other Hopes beset me,
Hopes which obscure but cannot do thee wrong.

No later light has lightened up my heavens;
No second morn has ever shone for me;
All my life's bliss from thy dear life was given –
All my life's bliss is in the grave with thee.

But when the days of golden dreams had perished
And even Despair was powerless to destroy,
Then did I learn how existence could be cherished,
Strengthened and fed without the aid of joy.

Then did I check the tears of useless passion,
Weaned my young soul from yearning after thine;
Sternly denied its burning wish to hasten
Down to that tomb already more than mine!

And even yet, I dare not let it languish,
Dare not indulge in Memory's rapturous pain;
Once drinking deep of that divinest anguish,
How could I seek the empty world again?

EMILY BRONTË

from Twenty Minutes of Reality

As a child I was afraid of world without end, of life everlasting.
The thought of it used to clutch me at times with a crushing

sense of the inevitable, and make me long to run away. But where could one run? If never-ending life were true, then I was already caught fast in it, and it would never end. Perhaps it had never had a beginning. Life everlasting, eternity, forever and ever: these are tremendous words for even a grown person to face; and for a child – if he grasp their significance at all – they may be hardly short of appalling. The picture that Heaven presented to my mind was of myself, a desperate little atom, dancing in a streak of light around and around and around forever and ever. I do not know what could have suggested such an idea; I only know that I could not think of myself caught there in eternity like a chip in a whirlpool, or say 'round again, and round again, and round again' for more than a minute, without hypnotizing myself into a state of sheer terror. Of course, as I grew older I threw off this truly awful conception; yet shorn of its crudeness and looked at with grown-up eyes, there were moments when, much as I believed in, and desired, eternal life, that old feeling of 'round again, and round again' would swoop back upon me with all its unutterable weariness, and no state of bliss that I could imagine seemed to me proof forever against boredom. Nevertheless, I still had faith to believe that eternity and enjoyment of life could in some way be squared, though I did not see how it was to be done. I am glad that I had, for I came at last to a time when faith was justified by sight, and it is of that time that I wish to write here.

I do not really know how long the insight lasted. I have said, at a rough guess, twenty minutes. It may have been a little shorter time, it may have been a little longer. But at best it was very transitory.

It happened to me about two years ago, on the day when my bed was first pushed out of doors to the open gallery of the hospital. I was recovering from a surgical operation. I had undergone a certain amount of physical pain, and had suffered for a short time the most acute mental depression which it has ever been my misfortune to encounter. I suppose that this depression was due to physical causes, but at the time it seemed to me that somewhere down there under the anesthetic, in the black abyss of unconsciousness, I had discovered a terrible secret, and the secret was that there was no God; or if there was one, He was indifferent to all human suffering.

Though I had hardly reëstablished my normal state of faith, still the first acuteness of that depression had faded, and only a scar of fear was left when, several days later, my bed was first wheeled out to the porch. There other patients took their airing and received their visitors; busy internes and nurses came and went, and one could get a glimpse of the sky, with bare gray branches against it, and of the ground, with here and there a patch of melting snow.

It was an ordinary cloudy March day. I am glad to think that it was. I am glad to remember that there was nothing extraordinary about the weather, nor any unusualness of setting – no flush of spring or beauty of scenery – to induce what I saw. It was, on the contrary, almost a dingy day. The branches were bare and colorless, and the occasional half-melted piles of snow were a forlorn gray rather than white. Colorless little city sparrows flew and chirped in the trees, while human beings, in no way remarkable, passed along the porch.

There was, however, a wind blowing, and if any outside thing intensified the experience, it was the blowing of that wind. In every other respect it was an ordinary commonplace day. Yet here, in this everyday setting, and entirely unexpectedly (for I had never dreamed of such a thing), my eyes were opened, and for the first time in all my life I caught a glimpse of the ecstatic beauty of reality.

I cannot now recall whether the revelation came suddenly or gradually; I only remember finding myself in the very midst of those wonderful moments, beholding life for the first time in all its young intoxication of loveliness, in its unspeakable joy, beauty, and importance. I cannot say exactly what the mysterious change was. I saw no new thing, but I saw all the usual things in a miraculous new light – in what I believe is their true light. I saw for the first time how wildly beautiful and joyous, beyond any words of mine to describe, is the whole of life. Every human being moving across that porch, every sparrow that flew, every branch tossing in the wind, was caught in and was a part of the whole mad ecstasy of loveliness, of joy, of importance, of intoxication of life.

It was not that for a few keyed-up moments I *imagined* all existence as beautiful, but that my inner vision was cleared to the truth so that I *saw* the actual loveliness which is always there, but which we so rarely perceive; and I knew that every man, woman, bird, and tree, every living thing before me, was extravagantly beautiful, and extravagantly important. And, as I beheld, my heart melted out of me in a rapture of love and delight. A nurse was walking past; the wind caught a strand of her hair and blew it out in a momentary gleam of sunshine, and never in my life before had I seen how beautiful beyond all belief is a woman's hair. Nor had I ever guessed how marvelous it is for a human being to walk. As for the internes in their white suits, I had never realized before the whiteness of white linen; but much more than that, I had never so much as dreamed of the mad beauty of young manhood. A little sparrow chirped and flew to a nearby branch, and I honestly believe that only 'the morning stars singing together, and the sons of God shouting for joy' can in the least express the ecstasy of a bird's flight. I cannot express it, but I have seen it.

Once out of all the gray days of my life I have looked into the heart of reality; I have witnessed the truth; I have seen life as it really is – ravishingly, ecstatically, madly beautiful, and filled to overflowing with a wild joy, and a value unspeakable. For those glorified moments I was in love with every living thing before me – the trees in the wind, the little birds flying, the nurses, the internes, the people who came and went. There was nothing that was alive that was not a miracle. Just to be alive was in itself a miracle. My very soul flowed out of me in a great joy.

MARGARET PRESCOTT MONTAGUE

The Meaning of Death for a Philosopher

THUS the father's 'face' is never made known to the son, the excellence of his Good can never be fully demonstrated. He is not in fact in any *spot*, or at least any that can be represented, nor on any *plane* that can be conceived by man. Man always remains *beneath* the project God has for him. At least in this lower life, separated from the 'other' by that *impenetrable paraphragm*, death. Obviously, no mortal will gaze upon death as he experiences it at the very moment of dying. He will still not know whether or not 'the entrance to another existence' corresponds to the desire to appropriate the 'other side' of representation which constitutes his 'interiority' but remains outside the field of his perspective. Break-through into what *remains* God's secret; which ensures the repetition of the same (history). No upheavals, no revolutions in which what had always *been* would appear as the *flip side* of what might be, the *shadow*, masked as such, of what would be, or else a possible perspective on things, a potential interpretation of reality which, because withheld from evidence and always positioned *behind*, defies all comparison. By excluding the gaze of the other, or others, this extrapolated point of view organizes and projects the world into a paralyzed empire. Formalizations of laws laid down in perpetuity, logos of the Father. And He never questions that (Id) which causes (him) but lays univocal claim to all that is, in his absolute science. Which would give account of everything without any change, for all eternity. Embracing from the outset all enumerations of 'beings,' their proportions and relationships, all the abstract operations that can occur betwen them and the very development of those relationships. Which are essentially copulative. Their causes, ends, and results. And perhaps their modes as well?

LUCE IRIGARAY, from *Speculum of the Other Woman*

Death is a clean bold word and has no second meaning.
Death means an end. By sight, touch, temperature we know.
Do not insult this strong word with a weak evasion
And say, 'He has gone on' – 'He passed away' – 'He sleeps.'

Speak not of the body and its lively grace
As paltry things that never mattered after all,
Creative hands and giving hands, hands calloused and deformed
As being nothing now but broken tools.

If you believe the soul, denied the dear familiar flesh,
Finds other place to live, keep to your faith,
But grant the body it illumined your candid grief.

Or if you must believe that when the light went out
Of eyes you loved and they stared back and told you nothing,
For that was all that could be told forever,
Salute Death. He demands you shall attain
Your fullest strength of honesty and courage.
You shall not bear your sorrow's weight upon a crutch of words,
You will stand straight, nor say your lover, friend, your child
Has 'gone' as though he'd wandered off somewhere,
But speak with dignity and say, 'He died.'

REBECCA RICHMOND

from Letter of Ann Griffiths

DEAR sister, I see more need than ever to spend my remaining
days in giving myself up daily and continually, body and soul,
into the care of him who is able to keep that which is committed
to him against that day. Not to give myself once, but to live continually giving myself, right up to and in the very moment when
I put away this tabernacle. Dear sister, the thought of putting it
away is particularly sweet sometimes; I can say that this is what
cheers me more than anything else in these days, not death in

itself, but the great gain that is to be got through it. To be able to leave behind every inclination that goes against the will of God, to leave behind every ability to dishonour the law of God, with all weakness swallowed up by strength, to become fully conformed to the law which is already on one's heart and to enjoy God's likeness for ever. Dear sister, I am sometimes absorbed so far into these things that I completely fail to stand in the way of my duty with regard to temporal things, but I look for the time when I may find release and be with Christ, for that is much better, although it is very good here through a lattice, and the Lord sometimes reveals through a glass, darkly, as much of his glory as my weak faculties can bear.

The Mackerel

Charcoal bitter evening
on Chesil Beach
where two mackerel

Lie making a silver
scaled cross
on a mound of wet pebbles.

Just caught, their heads severed
with a scout's knife
they're being baptised

In the frothy hem of a high
spring tide;
their abandoned bodies

Start to bleed, blood, congealed
as red-currant jelly
bordering a salty platter.

Only their eyes defy death,
fixing a watery gaze,
from a mother-of-pearl bed,

On the bearded traitor
who crouches low
behind a striped windbreaker

Cajoling a driftwood fire
to flame to cook
the fish; when a crow flaps down

From the setting sun
and carries off
the silver mackerel high

To a distant honeycombed cliff,
leaving the fisherman
lighting a premature lamp.

HEATHER LAWTON

from The Swan in the Evening

NOT till close on half a century later, when I in my turn suffered the cruellest and seemingly most unnatural of all human bereavements, did I think of her again, and of her father, who must have joined her long ago; remembering them as they had been together, in the harness-room, the hayloft, the bit of garden, each the other's innocent delight; then torn apart, stamped upon, stamped out. . . . They then, I now: or so it seemed in the first days after Sally left the earth. Yet at the same time, on another mysterious level, it was as if they had drawn close and were showing themselves to me in a way I can only describe as 'living pictures'. I could not account for this. Perhaps it was one of the hallucinations I must expect, now that I had joined the age-long procession of broken-hearted mothers and fathers, like Mr. and Mrs. Moody, and the parents of Marjorie Fleming, and Mr. and Mrs. William Wordsworth and Mary and Percy Bysshe Shelley, Patrick Brontë *père*, Monsieur du Perrier, and William Shakespeare, and countless, countless others, illustrious, obscure, anonymous . . .

Now that I know that death considered as extinction is an illusory concept based on the ignorance, or prejudice, or the intellectual arrogance or snobbery, or the natural dread or not unnatural despair, or the built-in death-wish – the *goût de cendre* – of blind humanity; and that life goes on – relentlessly you might say, whether or no we fancy the idea, and certainly in accordance with cosmic laws which human reason is ill-equipped to understand; and certainly not in accordance with orthodox Church creeds and dogmas: now that I know this for certain, it does not seem to me sentimental-fanciful, but possible, that within the eternally created and creating thought-web upon which are stamped our inter-connected dreams and destinations, those whom we seek with single-minded love we do find, or find again. And so, whether or not Wilma and her father 'came back', compassionately, to reassure me, there may well have been meaning in my seeing him, not in his old carapace of bitter blackness, I identified him with that father in that poem of Kipling's:

> *Far far, oh very far behind*
> > *So far she cannot call to him*
> *Comes Tegumai, alone, to find*
> > *The daughter that was all to him.*

but quietly showing himself, or shown to me, with Wilma by his side.

The last thing I intend is to set up dogmas of my own against the confirmed atheist, or the apostle of humanism or rationalism or any other kind of ism.

> *Reason has moons; but moons not hers*
> > *Lie mirrored on her sea,*

Confounding her astronomers,
But oh! – delighting me.

If these lines of Ralph Hodgson, whose symbols and imagery have haunted me since I was in my early teens, speak to me of reality and embody my own predilections, I hope I shall not be suspected of worshipping the dark gods of intuition and of mocking the paler gods of intellect. What I am writing is purely a personal testament, based upon experience; scrupulously recorded, and, I trust, consistent.

ROSAMOND LEHMANN

from Wuthering Heights

AND the thing that irks me most is this shattered prison, after all. I'm tired of being enclosed here. I'm wearying to escape into that glorious world, and to be always there; not seeing it dimly through tears, and yearning for it through the walls of an aching heart, but really with it and in it . . . I shall be sorry for you. I shall be incomparably beyond and above you all.

EMILY BRONTË

'Only Father, the Guru, obeisance!
The heart of the Dakinis, I bow to you!
Please listen to my song, Lhau Darpo,
I am not rolang,
I am a delog.
I was dead but I came back to life,
So you can be happy.
There is nothing and no one who does not die,
But there are few who die and come back to life.
It is difficult to be a delog.

Death may come at any time.

I am like a snow mountain,
And you are a snow lion,
Do not be attached to me!
I am just like an ordinary snow mountain,
Unlike my husband who is a big one,
So I can be melted by the sun . . .
It is very dangerous.

You are a golden eagle,
Do not be attached to me,
I am just a small rocky hill,
I might get blown up by lightning.

You, a beautiful deer,
Do not be attached to me, I am like a grassy hill,
There are other, better meadows,
I am dangerously small when autumn comes.

You are a little golden fish,
Do not be attached to me,
I am like a small lake that may dry up in the sun,
There are big oceans that are safer.

You are a beautiful bird,
Do not be attached to me,
I am like a little garden that may dry up.
There are bigger gardens.

You, a beautiful golden bee,
Do not be attached to me,
I am just an ordinary flower.
There are big lotuses nearby.
I could be destroyed by hail.

My little son, do not be attached to me,
The delog Nangsa Obum.
The Rinang family is more secure,
I may die,

Listen to my words and keep them in your mind,
    Lhau Darpo!'

NANGSA OBUM

FURTHER READING

This list includes sources for all material included as well as other books of interest.

AKHMATOVA, Anna
  Selected Poems. Anna Akhmatova, trans. Richard McKane. Bloodaxe Books, 1989
ALCOTT, Louisa May
  The Selected Letters of Louisa May Alcott, ed. Joel Myerson and Daniel Shealy. Little, Brown, 1987
ALLCHIN, A.M. and de WAAL, Esther (eds)
  Threshold of Light: Prayers and Praises from the Celtic Tradition. Darton, Longman & Todd, 1986
ALLEN, Warner
  The Timeless Moment. Faber 1946
ALLIONE, Tsultrim
  Women of Wisdom. Arkana, 1986
D'ANGEVILLE, Henriette
  My Ascent of Mont Blanc, trans. Jennifer Barnes. HarperCollins, 1991
AUNG San Suu Kyi
  Freedom from Fear. Penguin, 1995

AUSTEN, Jane
Pride and Prejudice. Oxford University Press, 1965
AUSTIN, Mary
Experiences Facing Death. Bobbs Merrill Co., 1931
The Land of Journey's Ending (1924). University of Arizona Press, 1983
Love and the Soul Maker. 1914
A Woman of Genius. Appelton & Co., 1912
BARNSTONE, Aliki and BARNSTONE, Willis (eds)
A Book of Women Poets from Antiquity to Now. Schocken Books, 1980
BEAUVOIR, Simone de
A Very Easy Death. Penguin, 1976
BEER, Frances
Women and Mystical Experience in the Middle Ages. Boydell Press, 1992
BELL, Diane
Daughters of the Dreaming. McPhee Gribble, 1985
BESANT, Annie
Birth and Evolution of the Soul. Theosophical Publishing Society, 1903
ST BIRGITTA of SWEDEN
Doom of the Kings:: From the Revelations of Saint Birgitta of Sweden, trans. Patrick O. Moore. Clarino Press, 1982
BOULDING, Maria
The Coming of God. SPCK, 1984
A Touch of God. SPCK, 1982
BRO, Bernard
Contemplative Nuns Speak. Geoffrey Chapman, 1963
BRONTË, Emily
Wuthering Heights. Oxford University Press, 1847
BROWNING, Elizabeth Barrett
Sonnets from the Portuguese. Caradoc Press, 1906
BUTTLES, J.R.
Queens of Egypt. Constable, 1908
BYLES, Marie Beuzeville

By Cargo Boat and Mountain. Seeley Service, 1931

Journey into Burmese Silence. George Allen & Unwin, 1962

BYRNE, Lavinia

Women before God. SPCK, 1988

BYRNE, Lavinia (ed.)

The Hidden Journey. SPCK, 1993

The Hidden Tradition. SPCK, 1993

CARMAN, Bliss (ed.)

The Oxford Book of American Verse. Oxford University Press. 1927

CARMICHAEL, Alexander

Carmina Gadelica: Hymns and Incantations with Illustrative Notes on Words, Rites and Customs Dying and Obsolete, orally collected. Norman Macleod, 1900

CARSON, Rachel

The Sea around Us (1950). Signet Books, 1961

CATHER, Willa

The Professor's House. Knopf, 1925

ST CATHERINE of SIENA

Saint Catherine of Siena as seen in her Letters, ed. Vida D. Scudder. J.M. Dent, 1905

COLEMAN, T.W.

English Mystics of the Fourteenth Century. The Epworth Press, 1938

COSMAN, Carol, KEEFE, Joan and WEAVER, Kathleen (eds)

The Penguin Book of Women Poets. Penguin, 1979

COUZYN, Jeni (ed.)

The Bloodaxe Book of Contemporary Women Poets. Bloodaxe Books, 1985

COX, Janice Nunnally

Foremothers: Women of the Bible. Seabury Press, 1981

DAVID-NEEL, Alexandra

Initiations and Initiates in Tibet. Rider, 1970

DICKINSON, Emily

The Poems of Emily Dickinson. The Belknap Press of Harvard University Press, 1983

DILLARD, Annie
Teaching a Stone to Talk. HarperCollins, 1982
Three. HarperCollins, 1990
DUNCAN, Isadora
My Life. Gollancz, 1928
ELIOT, George
Adam Bede. Wm. Blackwood, 1859
ELLIS, Alice Thomas
The 27th Kingdom. Duckworth, 1982
FAINLIGHT, Gloria
To See the Matter Clearly. Macmillan, 1968.
FERNEA, Elizabeth Warnock and BEZIRGAN, Basima Qattan (eds)
Middle Eastern Muslim Women Speak. University of Texas Press, 1980
FLANNER, Hildegarde
At the Gentle Mercy of Plants. John Daniel, 1986
FREMANTLE, Anne (ed.)
The Protestant Mystics. Weidenfeld and Nicolson, 1964
GAGE (BARING), Anne
The One Work: A Journey Towards the Self. Vincent Stuart Publishers Ltd, 1961
GASKELL, Elizabeth
The Well of Pen-Morfa. Pandora, 1983
GHANANANDA, *Swami* and STEWART-WALLACE, Sir John (ed. advisors)
Women Saints East and West. Vedanta Press, 1979
GOUDGE, Elizabeth
The Dean's Watch. Hodder & Stoughton, 1960
The Joy of Snow. Hodder & Stoughton, 1974
A Vision of God, ed. Christine Rawlins. Spire, 1990
GOUDGE, Elizabeth (ed.)
A Book of Faith (1976). Spire, 1989
A Book of Peace (1967). Spire, 1989
A Diary of Prayer (1966). Spire, 1991
GREEN, Rayna (ed.)
That's What She Said: Contemporary Poetry and Fiction

by Native American Women. Indiana University Press, 1984

GRIFFIN, Susan
Woman and Nature: The Roaring inside Her. Women's Press, 1984

GRIFFITHS, Ann
Letters of Ann Griffiths: Farmer's Wife of Montgomeryshire, ed. A.M. Allchin. University of Wales Press, 1976

HADFIELD, John (ed.)
A Book of Love. E. Hulton and Co., 1958

HAMILTON, Jane
A Map of the World. Doubleday, 1994

HARRIS, Ann Sutherland and NOCHLIN, Linda
Women Artists 1550–1950. Museum Association of Los Angeles County Museum, 1976

HÉLOÏSE
The Letters of Abelard and Héloïse, ed. and trans. Betty Radice. Penguin, 1974

HILDEGARD of BINGEN
Hildegard of Bingen's Book of Divine Works, ed. Matthew Fox. Bear & Co., 1987

IRIGARAY, Luce
Elemental Passions. Athlone Press, 1992
Speculum of the Other Woman. Cornell University Press, 1985

JAEGHER, Paul de (ed.)
An Anthology of Mysticism. Burns, Oates & Washbourne, 1935

JENNINGS, Elizabeth
Moments of Grace. Carcanet, 1979

JEWSBURY, Geraldine
A Selection from the Letters of Geraldine Jewsbury to Jane Welsh Carlyle, ed. Mrs Alexander Ireland. Longman, Green & Co., 1892

JULIAN of NORWICH
Revelations of Divine Love, ed. Grace Warrack. Methuen, 1958

KAVANAGH, P.J. (ed.)
A Book of Consolations. HarperCollins, 1992

KELLER, Helen
  The Story of my Life. Doubleday, 1903
KING, Ursula
  Voices of Protest: Voices of Promise Exploring Spirituality for a New Age (Hibbert Lecture 1984). Hibbert Trust.
  Women and Spirituality. Macmillan, 1993
KINSLEY, David
  Hindu Goddesses. University of California Press, 1986
KROEBER, Theodora (ed.)
  The Inland Whale: Nine Stories retold from Californian Indian Legends. Gollancz, 1976
KÜBLER-ROSS, Elisabeth
  On Children and Death. Simon & Schuster, 1983
  On Death and Dying. Tavistock/Routledge, 1973
LAWICK-GOODALL, Jane van
  In the Shadow of Man. Collins, 1971
LEBRUN, *Madame* Vigée
  Memoirs of Madame Vigée Lebrun, trans. Lionel Strachey. Grant Richards, 1904
LE GUIN, Ursula K.
  Dancing at the Edge of the World. Gollancz, 1989
LEHMANN, Rosamond
  The Swan in the Evening: Fragments of an Inner Life. Collins, 1967
LEVERTOV, Denise
  Oblique Prayers. New Directions Publishing Corp., 1984
  Selected Poems. Bloodaxe, 1986
LEWIS, I.M.
  Ecstatic Religion. Routledge & Kegan Paul, 1989
LEWIS-SMITH, Anne
  Flesh and Flowers. Mitre Press, 1967
LIEDLOFF, Jean
  The Continuum Concept. Futura, 1977
LINDBERGH, Anne Morrow
  Gift from the Sea. Chatto, 1955
MANSFIELD, Katherine
  Katherine Mansfield: Selected Letters, ed. Vincent O'Sullivan.

Oxford University Press, 1990

Poems of Katherine Mansfield, ed. Vincent O'Sullivan. Oxford University Press, 1988

MATTHEWS, Caitlin

Sophia: Goddess of Wisdom. Aquarian Press/Thorsons, 1992

MECHTILD von MAGDEBURG

Flowing Light of the Divinity, trans. Christiane Mesch Galvani. Garland, 1991

The Flowing Light of the Godhead, trans. Lucy Menzies. Longmans Green, 1953

MOINE, Claudine

You Looked at Me: The Spiritual Testimony of Claudine Moine, trans. Gerard Carroll. James Clarke, 1989

MONTAGU, *Lady* Mary Wortley

The Letters and Works of Lady Mary Wortley Montagu. Swan Sonnenschein & Co., 1893

MONTAGUE, Margaret Prescott

Twenty Minutes of Reality. E.P. Dutton & Co., 1918

MOORE, Geoffrey (ed. and intro.)

American Literature. Faber, 1964

NURBAKHSH, *Dr* Javad

Sufi Women. Khaniqahi-Nimatullahi Publications, 1990

OLSEN, Tillie

Silences. Virago, 1980

OSBORNE, Dorothy

Letters from Dorothy Osborne to Sir William Temple 1652–54 (1888), ed. Edward Abbott Parry. Clarendon Press, 1928

PITTER, Ruth

The Bridge. Cresset Press, 1945

Collected Poems. Enitharmon, 1990

Still by Choice. Cresset, 1966

PORTER, Katherine Anne

Katherine Anne Porter: Conversations, ed. Joan Givner. University Press of Mississippi, 1987

PRITCHARD, R.E. (ed.)

Poetry by English Women. Carcanet, 1990

RAINE, Kathleen
The Hollow Hill: Collected Papers 1925–80. Hamish Hamilton, 1981

RAMANUJAN, A.K. (trans.)
Speaking of Siva. Penguin, 1973

RICH, Adrienne
The Fact of a Doorframe: Poems Selected and New, 1950–1984. W.W. Norton & Co. Inc., 1984

RIDING, Laura
Collected Poems. Cassell, 1938

RIDLER, Anne
A Matter of Life and Death. Faber, 1959
Collected Poems. Carcanet, 1994

SACKVILLE-WEST, Vita
The Eagle and the Dove. Michael Joseph, 1943

SAND, George
Journey within the Crystal (a translation by Pauline Pearson-Stamps of *Laura. Voyage dans le cristal*). Peter Lang, 1992

SARASHINA, *Lady*
As I Crossed a Bridge of Dreams, trans. Ivan Morris. Penguin, 1975

SAYERS, Dorothy L.
Creed or Chaos and Other Essays in Popular Theology. Metheun, 1947
The Mind of the Maker. Methuen, 1941

SAYERS, Peig
An Old Woman's Reflections, trans. Seamus Ennis. Oxford University Press, 1980
Peig: The Autobiography of Peig Sayers of the Great Blasket Island, trans. Bryan MacMahon. Syracuse University Press, 1974

SCHIMMEL, Anne Marie
Mirror of an Eastern Moon. East-West, 1978

SCHREINER, Olive
Dreams. Thomas Bird Mosher, 1917

SHERWOOD, Jane

The Country Beyond: The Doctrine of Re-Birth (1944). C.W. Daniel, 1991

SITWELL, Constance
Bright Morning. Jonathan Cape, 1942
Seek Paradise. Jonathan Cape, 1948
Smile at Time. Private publication, 1963

SMITH, Lillian
The Journey. Cresset Press, 1955

SMITH, Margaret
Rabi'a the Mystic and her Fellow Saints in Islam. Cambridge University Press, 1928
Studies in Early Mysticism in the Near and Middle East. Sheldon Press, 1931

SPENDER, Dale and TODD, Janet (eds)
Anthology of British Women Writers. Pandora, 1989

STARHAWK
The Spiral Dance: A Rebirth of the Ancient Religion of the Great Goddess. Harper & Row, 1979
Truth or Dare. Harper & Row, 1990

STARR, Kevin
Americans and the Californian Dream 1850–1915. Oxford University Press, 1973

STEEGMULLER, Francis and BRAY, Barbara (trans.)
Flaubert-Sand: The Correspondence. Harvill, 1993

STEVENSON, Anne
Selected Poems 1956–1986. Oxford University Press, 1987

ST TERESA of AVILA
The Interior Castle or the Mansions, trans. J. Dalton. HarperCollins, 1852
The Life of Saint Teresa by Herself. Penguin, 1957
The Way of Perfection, trans. the Benedictines of Stanbrook. Thomas Baker, 1919

ST TERESA of LISIEUX
Soeur Thérèse of Lisieux: The Little Flower of Jesus, ed. T.N. Taylor. Burns & Oates, 1912
The Story of a Soul. Burns & Oates, 1951

TREVELYAN, Katharine
Through mine own Eyes (originally *Fool in Love*). Gollancz, 1963

TROLLOPE, Frances
Domestic Manners of the Americans. Oxford University Press, 1984

TWEEDIE, Irina
The Chasm of Fire. Element 1979

UNDERHILL, Evelyn
Collected Papers. Longmans and Co., 1946
Heaven a Dance: An Evelyn Underhill Anthology, compiled by Brenda and Stuart Blanch. Triangle, 1992
Immanence. Dent, 1913
The Letters of Evelyn Underhill (1943), ed. and introd. Charles Williams. Darton, Longman & Todd, 1991
Mysticism. Methuen, 1911
The Spiritual Life. Hodder & Stoughton, 1937

VORSTER, W.S. (ed.)
Sexism and Feminism in Theological Perspective. University of South Africa Press, 1984

WAAL, Esther de
Seeking God: The Way of St Benedict. Collins, 1984

WALKER, Alice
The Color Purple. Women's Press, 1983

WARNER, Marina
Joan of Arc. Weidenfeld & Nicolson, 1981

WEIL, Simone
Notebooks. Routledge & Kegan Paul, 1976
Formative Writings 1929–1941, ed. Dorothy Tuck McFarland and Wilhelmina Van Ness. Routledge & Kegan Paul, 1987
Waiting on God. Fontana, 1971

WILDENHEIM, Marguerite
Pottery, Form and Expression. Reinhold, 1959

WILKINS, Eithne
The Rose-Garden Game. Victor Gollancz, 1969

WILLEMER, Marianne

Divan by Goethe, Book of Zuleika. Odes to East and West Winds, trans. Alexander Rogers. G. Bell & Sons, 1890

WILSON, Katharina M. (ed.)

Medieval Women Writers. Manchester University Press, 1984

WOLLSTONECRAFT, Mary

Letters written during a Short Residence in Sweden, Norway and Denmark 1796. Penguin, 1987

WOODS, Richard (ed.)

Understanding Mysticism. Athlone Press, 1981

WOOLF, Virginia

Moments of Being. Chatto & Windus for Sussex University Press, 1976

A Writer's Diary. Hogarth Press, 1953

To the Lighthouse. Hogarth Press, 1927

WORDSWORTH, Dorothy

Grasmere Journals. Clarendon Press, 1991

YOUNGHUSBAND, *Sir* Francis

Modern Mystics. John Murray, 1935

COPYRIGHT
ACKNOWLEDGEMENTS

Taken from *Selected Poems* by Anna Akhmatova, trans. by Richard McKane. Bloodaxe Books. 1989.

Paula Gunn Allen for permission to publish 'San Ysidro Cabazon'.

Henriette d'Angeville *My Ascent of Mont Blanc*, trans. Jennifer Barnes, HarperCollins Publishers Ltd. 1991.

Copyright © Aung San Suu Kyi 1991. Reprinted with the permission of the author from her collection *Freedom from Fear and Other Writings*. (Pub. Viking/Penguin, 1991; revised edn. Penguin 1995). Other extracts from speech read at the NGO Forum on Women held in Beijing, August 31st 1995.

Mary Austin *The Land of Journey's Ending*. Reprinted with permission of The University of Arizona Press. 1983.

Anne Baring (Gage) *The One Work* for excerpt p. 59. Vincent Stuart Publishers. 1961. Published with permission of the author.

Extracts from the Authorized Version of the Bible (The King James Bible), the rights in which are vested in the Crown, are reproduced by permission of the Crown's Patentee, Cambridge University Press.

From *The Professor's House* by Willa Cather. Copyright © 1925 by Willa Cather and renewed 1953 by Edith Lewis and the City Bank Farmers Trust Co. Reprinted by permission of Alfred Knopf Inc.

Reprinted by permission of the publishers and the Trustees of Amherst College from *The Poems of Emily Dickinson*, Thomas H. Johnson, ed., Cambridge, Mass.: The Belknap Press of Harvard

C. Strong. By permission of Insel Verlag, Frankfurt am Main.

Reprinted from Luce Irigaray *Speculum of the Other Woman*. Translated by Gillian C. Gill. Copyright © 1985 by Cornell University Press. Used by permission of the publisher. Extract from *Elemental Passions* reprinted with permission of The Athlone Press.

Elizabeth Jennings 'Spell of the Elements' and 'A Chorus' from *Moments of Grace* (Carcanet). Reprinted with permission from David Higham Associates.

Helen Keller *The Story of My Life*. Reprinted with permission of Bantam Doubleday.

Reprinted with the permission of Simon & Schuster from *On Children and Death* by Elisabeth Kübler-Ross, M.D. Copyright © 1983 by Elisabeth Kübler-Ross.

Heather Lawton poems published by permission of the author.

Ursula Le Guin from *Dancing at the Edge of the World* by permission of Victor Gollancz.

Rosamond Lehmann extracts from *The Swan in the Evening*. Permission to publish: The Society of Authors as the literary representative of the Estate of Rosamond Lehmann.

Denise Levertov 'That Passeth All Understanding' from *Oblique Prayers* (New Directions, 1984) and 'Living' from *Selected Poems* (Bloodaxe Books). Reprinted with permission from Laurence Pollinger Ltd. US rights reprinted by permission of New Directions Publishing Corp.

Anne Lewis-Smith 'October Love' from *Flesh and Flowers*. Reproduced by kind permission of the author.

The Estate of Anne Morrow Lindbergh for extract from *Gift from the Sea*. Chatto and Windus. 1955. US rights. Copyright © 1955 by Anne Morrow Lindbergh. Reprinted by permission of Pantheon Books, a division of Random House, Inc.

Copyright © 1973 Agatha Christie Mallowan 'Dartmoor' and 'Remembrance'. By permission of Hughes Massie Ltd.

Katherine Mansfield extracts from two letters. Permission to publish from The Society of Authors as the literary representative of the Estate of Katherine Mansfield.

Letters of Abelard and Héloïse trans. Betty Radice (Penguin Classics, 1974). Copyright © Betty Radice 1974.

Dorothy L. Sayers extracts from *Creed or Chaos* and *The Mind of the Maker* published by Mowbray, reprinted with permission of David Higham Associates.

Copyright © Oxford University Press 1962. Reprinted from *An Old Woman's Reflections* by Peig Sayers, translated by Seamus Ennis (1962), by permission of Oxford University Press. Extract from *Peig: The Autobiography of Peig Sayers of the Great Blasket Island*, translated by Bryan MacMahon, pp. 176–78. Reprinted with permission of Syracuse University Press, Syracuse, NY. 1974.

Anne Marie Schimmel. Poems from *Mirror of an Eastern Moon*. Used with permission from East-West Publications.

Jane Sherwood extract from *The Country Beyond*. C.W. Daniel. 1991.

Constance Sitwell extracts from *Bright Morning*, Jonathan Cape. 1942. Permission to publish by Jonathan Cape.

Excerpt from *Truth or Dare* by Starhawk. Copyright © 1987 by Miriam Simos. Reprinted by permission of HarperCollins Publishers, Inc.

Copyright © Anne Stevenson. 1987. Reprinted from Anne Stevenson's *Selected Poems 1956–1986* (1987) by permission of Oxford University Press.

Giles Swayne. Copyright © 1995 for translations of poems by Louise Labé and Pernette du Guillet.

Irene Tweedie extracts from *The Chasm of Fire*. Copyright © and permission from Element Books.

Evelyn Underhill's 'Immanence' from anthology *Immanence*, by permission of the publishers. *Collected Papers, The Spiritual Life, Mysticism* (Methuen 1912).

Alice Walker extract from *The Color Purple*, first published in Great Britain by the Women's Press, Ltd, 1983, 34 Great Sutton Street, London, EC1V ODX. Copyright © David Higham Associates.

Eithne Wilkins. Extract from *The Rose-Garden Game*, published with the permission of Victor Gollancz.

BIOGRAPHICAL NOTES

Anna Akhmatova (1889–1966) (pseud. of Anna Andreeyevna Gorenko)
Born in Odessa, Ukraine, she studied in Kiev before moving to St Petersburg. In 1910 she married Nicholas Gumilev and with him started the Neoclassicist Acmeist movement which demanded poetry with a clarity of meaning free of Symbolist metaphysics. After the publication of *Anno Domini* in 1922 she was officially silenced until 1940 when she published *The Willow*. In the late 1930s she wrote *Requiem*, a poetic cycle on the Stalin Purges. In 1946 her verse was again banned, but she was 'rehabilitated' again in the 1950s.

Louisa May Alcott (1832–88)
She was born in Philadelphia and educated by her father whose school and vegetarian community failed, leaving them in great poverty. She sewed and taught, becoming the sole earner for the family. In 1862 she worked as an army nurse; she supported black rights and women's suffrage and published over 300 items, including *Little Women*.

Paula Gunn Allen (1939–)
Born in New Mexico she is a mixture of Laguna, Sioux and

Lebanese. She is a poet, writer and critic and has taught at the University of New Mexico and Berkeley. She is also a feminist and political activist being anti-war and anti-nuclear. She believes that in native traditions the beautiful and useful are usually synonymous.

St Angela of Foligno (1248–1309)
She led a chaotic life married to an Umbrian nobleman until reforming and becoming a Franciscan tertiary with a band of men and women gathered round her. She was a mystic who underwent terrible trials for two years. The words she uttered in ecstasy were written down by Friar Arnold.

Henriette d'Angeville (1794–1871)
Although not the first woman to climb Mont Blanc, she was the first woman who 'remembered her impressions'.

Anonymous author of The Golden Fountain
The author was an English society woman of French Huguenot descent who whilst enjoying a cosmopolitan social life and travelling with her husband, also liked being on her own. She was passionate about love and had a voracious appetite for the truth, eventually developing 'a terrible necessity for God'. She wanted to share her religious experiences without confiding in anyone, so wrote her books anonymously.

Aung San Suu Kyi (1945–)
She is the daughter of Burma's hero Aung San. In 1988 she returned to Burma to look after her dying mother. She became leader of the National League for Democracy, and her party won a convincing victory in the elections, but she was put under house arrest by the military junta, the SLORC. She was awarded the Nobel Peace Prize in 1991 and was released from house arrest in the summer of 1995.

Jane Austen (1775–1817)
She was the daughter of a rector and came from a well-connected family in the south of England. She was very well read, never married, but lived surrounded by family and friends.

Mary Austin (1868–1934)
She spent her Methodist childhood in Illinois, arriving in southern California in 1888 with her mother and brothers. She grew into a natural contemplative who hungered for mystical experience. She wrote knowledgeably on Native American culture in *The Land of Sunshine* and *The Overland Monthly*. She was known as an 'artist of place'; the desert restored her sense of mystery. She went to Italy in 1908, thinking she was going to die, but was restored to full health and threw herself into studying Roman Catholicism, but did not convert. After the First World War, California held no further attraction for her and she moved to Santa Fe.

Avvaiyār (?BC)
She was an orphan who lived several centuries BC. She wrote in Tamil (the oldest living language in the world). She was famous for her beauty, but devoted herself to religion and literature, refusing marriage. She prayed to become an ugly old woman and disguised as one, went round imparting wisdom.

Simone de Beauvoir (1908–86)
She was born in Paris, where she took a degree in philosophy at the Sorbonne in 1929, coming second only to Sartre. She taught in various *lycées* and after the Second World War emerged as one of the leading existentialists.

Aphra Behn (1640–89)
She went to Surinam as a young woman and became involved in a slave uprising there. In 1670 she became the first professional woman writer. She wrote sixteen plays. She is buried in Westminster Abbey.

Annie Besant (1847–1933)
She was born in London. In 1874 she became vice-president of the National Secular Society. She was an ardent proponent of birth control and socialism. Later, she became a theosophist, having met Madame Blavatsky and eventually became the leader of the Theosophical Society. In 1889, she went to India where she became involved in the independence movement. In 1911 she proclaimed Krishnamurti (b. 1895) to be the coming 'World Teacher'.

St Birgitta of Sweden (1303–73)
She is the patron saint of Sweden. She married a rich nobleman and moved to court; after her husband's death she founded a monastery in which in temporal matters the abbess was supreme, but in spiritual ones, the monks. She went to Rome in 1349. She never returned to Sweden, but spent the rest of her life on pilgrimages.

Maria Boulding (1929–)
Entered Stanbrook Abbey aged 18.

Anne Bradstreet (1612–1672)
Born in Northampton, England. She was possibly the first woman poet in the English language. She had access to a library and read widely. She married, aged sixteen, and left England to help found the Massachusetts Bay Colony. Her first book was published in London in 1650.

Emily Brontë (1818–48)
Emily Brontë was the fourth daughter. She had an unconventional education, which left her time to roam the moors around Howarth where she developed a passion for the landscape. It was accepted by the family that she should stay at home. In 1837 she became a governess in Halifax and then went to school in Brussels with her sister Charlotte for nine months and in 1845 embarked on a joint publication of poems. She became obsessed by her brother Branwell and after catching a cold at his funeral,

she died in December 1848. The intensity of feeling in her work and an almost mystical desire for union with nature reveal a deep longing for freedom. This passionate and imaginative writer is best known for *Wuthering Heights*.

Elizabeth Barrett Browning (1806–61)

Born in Co. Durham. She was a long-term invalid having seriously injured her back in a riding accident in 1821. Her first poems were published when she was 19 and further volumes appeared in 1838 and 1844. She met Robert Browning in 1845 and eloped with him in 1846, settling in Florence. Her best-known work is *Sonnets from the Portuguese* (1850), 'Portuguese' being RB's pet name for her. In later years she developed an interest in spiritualism and in Italian politics.

Marie Beuzeville Byles (1900–79)

An Australian woman who was a climber and lawyer. In Sydney she met a Burmese woman and decided that she very much wanted to go to Burma to learn meditation. There she went to different meditation centres and convents, learning Vipassana meditation. She wrote on political subjects and was a campaigner for women's rights. She founded an ashram for adherents of Buddhism.

Rachel Carson (1907–64)

She read biology at Pennsylvania College for Women and carried out graduate work at The Johns Hopkins University and at the Marine Biological Laboratory, Woods Hole. She then taught at the University of Maryland and at Johns Hopkins. She was the marine biologist and subsequently editor-in-chief of the United States Fish and Wildlife Service and a pioneer in the conservationist movement in the 1960s.

Willa Cather (1876–1947)

She was born in Virginia, but her formative years were spent in Nebraska where she went to the local high school and university

(1891–95). She was an unconventional student wearing her hair short and calling herself William. She became a journalist and taught Latin and English at high school. In 1912 she left journalism to become a full-time writer. She was very interested in the American Southwest. She wrote about independent women, preferring the company of women. She won the Pulitzer Prize in 1922 for *One of Ours*.

St Catherine of Siena (?1347–80)

Catherine Benincasa was the youngest of many children of a Sienese dyer. In 1367 she became a sister of the third order in the Dominicans, living at home and spending much of her time praying. She gathered a band of followers who accompanied her on journeys. She became involved in public affairs. She persuaded Pope Gregory XI to leave Avignon and return to Rome. His successor, Urban VI, was opposed by a rival pope. This began the 'great schism' into which she threw herself on behalf of Urban. However, her political activities have probably been exaggerated, and her greatness lies in her personal faith and holiness and in her great concern for the salvation of all mankind. She dictated her work as she never learnt to write.

Margaret Cavendish, Duchess of Newcastle (?1624–74)

She was at court as maid of honour to Queen Henrietta Maria whom she accompanied in exile to Paris. She published *Poems and Fancies* in 1653 believing that she could get away with more errors in poetry than prose. She wrote stories, plays and letters, but was probably better known as an eccentric.

Agatha Christie (1890–1976)

Born in Devon, she was educated at home until she was 16, being encouraged to both read and write a great deal. In 1906 she went to Paris to study singing and then moved to Cairo where she began to write seriously. In 1914 she became a VAD in Torquay, marrying Col. Archibald Christie the same year. She divorced him in 1927 and in 1930 she married the archaeologist Max Mallowan.

An Collins (17th century)
Very little is known about her, except that she was chronically ill.

Alexandra David-Neel (1868–1969)
Born in France she determined on a life of discovery and adventure; she became a student of philosophy and oriental languages, travelling widely in Europe and spending over 20 years in Tibet where she was taught by Buddhists and mystics.

Rebecca Harding Davis (?1831–1910)
She was the eldest of five children; her father was a successful businessman and she was sent to a female seminary for three years. She had a great 'hunger to know' and read avidly. In her first novel, *Life in the Iron Mills* (1861) she identifies strongly with the victims. It was published to great acclaim, but it is not known how she learnt so much about the mills. She married L. Clarke Davis, who had admired her books, in 1863 and the couple lived with his sister in Philadelphia. She had several children. Her writing addresses the issue of slavery. She pre-dates Zola, with whom she is compared.

Srī Sārāda Devī (1853–1920)
She was known as the Holy Mother. She was consort and first disciple of Sri Ramakrishna. She taught that all religions are paths to God. She had mystic visions. Betrothed to Sri Ramakrishna; when he died she went on a pilgrimage. She was simple and unostentatious.

Emily Dickinson (1830–86)
She was born in Amherst, Massachusetts. She had an autocratic father and apart from three sorties rarely left home. She saw only her family and close friends and always wore white. She was very intense and wrote her poems on odd scraps of paper. She died from Bright's disease and although had asked for her manuscripts to be destroyed, her sister felt unable to burn them.

Annie Dillard (1945–)
Born in Pittsburgh. She has written essays, poetry, memoirs
and literary criticism in carefully wrought language with keen
observations and original metaphysical insights. She won the
Pulitzer Prize in 1974 after the publication of *Pilgrim at Tinker
Creek*.

Isadora Duncan (1877–1927)
Born in San Francisco, she travelled widely in Europe performing
her own choreography, and founded schools in Berlin, Salzburg
and Vienna. She was a pioneer of modern dance, basing her work
on Greek-derived notions of beauty and harmony, but using
everyday movements such as running and walking. Her unconventional views on marriage and women's liberation gave rise to
scandal. She was killed in a car accident in Nice.

George Eliot (1819–80)
Mary Ann (Marian) Evans was born in Warwickshire. She went
to school in Nuneaton where she was influenced by Rev. John
Edmund Jones, an evangelical preacher. In 1836 her mother died
and she became her father's housekeeper, educating herself in
her spare time. In 1841 she moved to Coventry, and then
London. She nearly married Herbert Spencer, but he found her
too 'morbidly intellectual'. She began to live with George Henry
Lewes in 1854 who encouraged her to turn from philosophy to
fiction. He died in 1878 and she married J.W. Cross shortly
before she died. She is buried beside Lewes in Highgate.

Elizabeth I, Queen of England (1533–1603)
The daughter of King Henry VIII and Anne Boleyn, Elizabeth
was highly educated, spoke four languages and translated from
Latin.

Alice Thomas Ellis (1932–)
She writes novels, short stories, columns. She also writes as Anna
Haycraft.

Ruth Fainlight (1931–)
She was born in New York City; her father was born in London
and her mother in a small town on the eastern borders of the
Austro-Hungarian empire. She has lived mostly in Britain and
has published many books. Her poetry enables her to make contact with her spirit and the spirits that inhabit her, and gives her
insight into the incoherent aspects of herself. She thinks of
poems as dances and considers poetry and dance to be the most
primitive and enduring expressions of the sense and joy of being
alive.

Paula Fairlie (1940–)
She was born in Germany, but came to England as a child. She
studied at London University before going to Florence to study
Renaissance Studies. She became a Catholic in 1965 and later
became a nun, first in Italy, then in England.

Furugh Farrukhzad (1935–67)
Born in Tehran in 1935, she was educated exclusively at girls'
public schools and never received a high-school diploma. She
was married at 16 and divorced before she was 20. In Tehran she
was acclaimed as a great woman poet. A visit to Europe in 1956
had great effect on her. She worked on films and had a tremendous energy. She was killed in a car accident in February 1967.
Her poetry is a testament and mirror to her own life. She is
known as the founder of 'feminine culture' in Persian poetry.

Anne Finch, Countess of Winchilsea (1661–1720)
She became maid of honour to Mary of Modena, married Col.
Heneage Finch (who later became Earl of Winchilsea) and led a
quiet country life, publishing her poems anonymously.

Hildegarde Flanner (1899–1987)
Born in Indianapolis, she lived mostly in California. She wrote
essays and several volumes of poems. She was the sister of novelist Janet Flanner. 'I'm devoted to plants and have given a great

deal of my life to them, but I'm not a botanist. I am at the mercy of plants' she wrote.

Anne Gage (1931–)
She was educated in England and America and read history at Oxford. She is a searcher for the truth behind appearances, not as an abstract dogma, but as a living reality. She has visited many of the great religious centres in Asia. She now writes under the name of Anne Baring.

Gemma Galgani (1878–1903)
Born near Lucca she had visions from an early age and got the stigmata aged 21. The rest of her life was mystical, but she suffered the agonies of the passion. Her last illness was very severe. She often prayed aloud and some of her words were noted down.

Elizabeth Gaskell (1810–65)
The daughter and wife of Unitarian clergymen. She lived in Manchester and wrote about poor and deprived women.

Mary Gillies (19th century)
A cottar who lived at Moor of Aird, Benbecula, Outer Hebrides.

Elizabeth Goudge (1900–84)
She was born in Wells, England. Her father worked in theological colleges at Salisbury, Wells, Ely and Oxford and these places formed the backgrounds to her subsequent novels. She understood human frailty and the inner struggle for faith, but she believed in the inherent goodness of human nature and the beauty of childhood.

Dora Greenwell (1821–82)
Born in Co. Durham. She was strongly evangelical and wrote about religion and social issues.

Ann Griffiths (1776–1805)
Writer of Welsh hymns. She was the eldest daughter of a
Montgomeryshire farmer. A sermon led her to give up her formerly frivolous life. She joined the Methodists in 1797. In 1804
she married Thomas Griffiths and died the following year in
childbirth. Her hymns were published posthumously.

Pernette du Guillet (1520–45)
She lived in Lyons. Her poetry was published in 1544 and 1545;
she wrote 60 *épigrammes*. She was a friend of Louise Labé.

Jane Hamilton (1957–)
She lives, works and writes in an orchard farmhouse in
Wisconsin. Her novel, published in England as *The Frogs are
Still Singing*, won the PEN/Hemingway Foundation Award for
best first novel.

Joy Harjo (1951–)
A Creek, originally from Oklahoma. She has lived in Arizona and
New Mexico and is a film maker, artist and poet involved in
community services.

Hatshepsut (c. 1540–1481 BC)
Queen of Egypt of the XVIIIth dynasty, the daughter of
Thutmose I. She had a miraculous birth which is shown in great
detail, together with her early life, in the Queen's Temple. She
was presented to Amen and Horus who poured water over her
head saying, 'Thou art pure as thy double'. She travelled to various sanctuaries throughout the land with her father, symbolically
taking possession of her kingdom. She married Thutmose II, on
whose accession in 1516 BC she became the real ruler. On his
death in 1503 BC she acted as ruler for his son, Thutmose III,
and had herself crowned as Pharoah. She was represented with
male pharaonic attributes including a beard.

Héloïse (c. 1100/1101–63/64)

She came of unknown parentage but was educated by the nuns at Argenteuil. She was the pupil of Abelard with whom she had a passionate love affair. They had a son. She argued against Abelard's proposal of a secret marriage, on the grounds that marriage was no more than legalisation of the weakness of the flesh, taking a classical rather than Christian viewpoint, although they did eventually marry secretly. She became a nun after the tragic end of their love affair, and became abbess of the Convent of the Paraclete which Abelard had founded. She was acclaimed for her learning and administrative prowess.

Mary Herbert, Countess of Pembroke (1561–1621)

The sister of Sir Philip Sidney, she was the 'Urania' of Spenser's *Colin Clout* and suggested the publication of her brother's *Arcadia* which she revised and added to. She collaborated with Philip in metrical psalms; the translation of the psalms was her major achievement. She was patron to many and an epitaph on her by Ben Jonson was published in 1623.

Hildegard of Bingen (1098–1179)

She was placed in a Benedictine monastery by her parents when aged seven and had a very strong relationship with her tutor, the abbess Jutta. She went on to establish her own wholly female convent. She travelled and preached extensively. She was much respected and wrote many letters criticising those in authority: at one point, the whole order was excommunicated, because she buried a man who had been excommunicated and refused to give him up. She described her visions in very down-to-earth and practical terms. She was a successful administrator, preacher, scientist, musician and prophet.

Frances Howarth (1949–)

A writer who lives in London.

Julia Ward Howe (1819–1910)
An author and reformer, she was born in New York City. As a child she wrote poems and romances. In 1843 she married and travelled in Europe for a year. She returned to live in Massachusetts and met all the Boston intellectuals of the day. Her Boston house was the centre of anti-slavery activity. She wrote 'Battle-Hymn of the Republic' in a tent near Washington DC. From 1870 on she threw herself into movements and causes mostly to do with women. She was a great organiser and gave many lectures with a sense of humour.

Ricarda Huch (1864–1947)
She was born in Brunswick and graduated from the University of Zurich. In Germany she is regarded as the most important woman writer of the early twentieth century. She wrote poetry, novels and literary criticism. She finally settled in Munich.

Luce Irigaray (1939–)
A French feminist and psychoanalyst, she is a follower of the reinterpretation of Freud by Lacan and Derrida, and concerned with the repression of the female libido.

Elizabeth Jennings (1926–)
Born in Lincolnshire, England, she has lived for most of her life in Oxford, where she went to school and to university. She has been a Roman Catholic all her life, and after winning the Somerset Maugham award spent three months abroad, mostly in Rome which influenced her greatly. Her first volume of poetry, *Poems*, was published in 1953. She writes of herself that she distrusts the kind of self-examination that leads you to expose what you think you know about yourself, as she believes it makes you self-conscious and turns you too obviously inward towards the darkness which she does not believe should be the true concern of this life.

Geraldine Jewsbury (1812–80)
Novelist, essayist and letter-writer, she was born in Derbyshire,

England, and became very friendly with Jane Welsh Carlyle to whom she wrote intense letters.

Julian of Norwich (c. 1343–c. 1416)

Very little is known about her. She might have lived at home until her thirties or joined a religious community. She eventually chose to become a solitary and lived in a cell attached to the Church of St Julian of Norwich. She was a serene and self-contained character who was revered as a spiritual counsellor. She gives excellent descriptions of her physical, mental and spiritual condition on the occasion of her visions. Her femaleness is revealed in what she calls the motherhood of God: Jesus is the Mother as well as the Son, feeding and nurturing us.

Helen Keller (1880–1968)

Author and lecturer. She was born in Alabama and became both deaf and blind as a baby. Anne Sullivan, whom she called 'Teacher', became her tutor, taught her 'finger spelling' and other skills. In 1900 she went to Radcliffe, graduating cum laude in 1904. She learnt many languages. She stayed with Anne Sullivan till she died in 1936. Her radical political views had put an end to her lecturing by 1923.

Anne Killigrew (1660–85)

She was maid of honour to Mary of Modena. She published Poems in 1685. She was overtly virtuous.

Rachel Korn (1898–)

She was born in Galicia. She first wrote in Polish, but in 1919 began to write in Yiddish. When the Nazis invaded Poland she escaped to Sweden and Russia. Since the war she has lived in Montreal.

Theodora Kroeber (1897–1979)

She was born in Colorado. She was an anthropologist and author who wrote much about Native Americans.

Elisabeth Kübler-Ross (1926–)
Born in Zurich, she went to America in 1958 and was naturalised in 1961. She received the Teilhard prize in 1981. She writes mostly about death and dying. She is a founder member of the American Holistic Medical Association.

Louise Labé (1526–66)
She lived in Lyons, the daughter of a ropemaker, and was known in her lifetime as La Belle Cordière. Her complete works – a philosophical discourse, three elegies and 24 sonnets – were published in 1555 and 1556.

Lālleswāri or Lāl Diddi of Kashmir (14th century)
Born into a Kashmiri pandit family. She was a mystic poet, loved by the people. She was a proponent of Saivism, i.e. the belief that the essence of the human soul is one with God. She left her marriage and became the disciple of a well-known Saivite saint. She roamed the country, singing and dancing in divine ecstasy. She emphasised the impermanence of things.

Heather Lawton (1954–)
A poet who lives two fields away from the Dorset, occasionally crumbling, coastal path.

Madame Vigée Lebrun (1756–1842)
Born in Paris, she was the daughter of an obscure portrait painter. In 1776 she married Jean Baptiste Pierre Lebrun, a picture dealer, critic and gambler. She published her memoirs in 1835 and was a prolific painter.

Ursula Le Guin (1929–)
Born at Berkeley, California. She studied at Radcliffe and Columbia and became a prolific writer both for adults and children.

Rosamond Lehmann (1901–90)
She was born in Buckinghamshire. She was privately educated

and won a scholarship to Girton, Cambridge. Her first novel *Dusty Answer* (1927) was a big success. Her novels are controversial, posing awkward questions. Her daughter's death from polio in 1958, led her to believe in spiritual contact after death. She became president of the College of Psychic Studies.

Denise Levertov (1923–)

She was born in Essex and educated at home by her father, a Russian-Jewish immigrant who became an Anglican priest, and her Welsh mother, who was much travelled. She moved to America in 1948. From the age of 10, she felt that she was an 'artist-person' with a destiny. She grew up in a household full of books, and both she and her sister were given a great deal of freedom. She felt she didn't quite fit in anywhere, but developed a passion for England. Although shy, she grew up with great confidence in herself and in her abilities.

Anne Lewis-Smith (1925–)

A writer and poet who lives in Wales.

Jean Liedloff (20th century)

A writer and explorer, she left the sophisticated literary life of New York to live for over two years with the Yequana Indians in the Venezuelan jungle.

Anne Morrow Lindbergh (1906–)

The daughter of US ambassador to Mexico, Dwight Whitney, she was born in New Jersey. She flew on early experimental flights. She married Charles Lindbergh. Their baby was kidnapped and killed leading to much unwelcome publicity which they escaped by flying.

Ann Macdonald (19th century)

A crofter's daughter from Lochaber.

Mahādēviyakka (12th century)
She was born in Udutadi. At 10, she was initiated into Siva worship in a temple where the form of Siva was 'the Lord White as Jasmine'. She dedicated herself to Siva despite many human lovers pressing their suit. Recognised by her fellow saints as being the most poetic of them, she used secular love poetry to express herself. She died 'into oneness with Siva', barely into her twenties.

Katherine Mansfield (1888–1923)
Born in Wellington, New Zealand, she first sailed to England in 1903. She returned to New Zealand in 1906, but travelled back to London two years later. Her first stories were published in 1907. In 1909 she married George Bowden whom whom she left the same day. She met John Middleton Murry in 1911 and they became lovers a year later and married in 1918. She suffered from TB, and in 1922 she entered the Gurdjieff Institute for the Harmonious Development of Man at Fontainebleau.

Mechtild of Magdeburg (1210–97)
A nun from Saxony who wrote a visionary treatise called *The Flowing Light of the Godhead*. The text was outspoken and she was harassed by the authorities, finally taking refuge in Helfta, a Cistercian convent renowned as a centre for women's learning. Her imagery is predominately erotic – the divine union is seen as consummation between two lovers. She borrowed from courtly poetry, but replaced its inequality with unqualified mutuality. She lived austerely, idealistically and communally, helping the poor.

Alice Meynell (1847–1922)
She was born in London, and spent her childhood in Europe. She converted to Catholicism. An essayist and poet, she published several volumes of her own verse. She married Wilfred Meynell in 1877 with whom she launched the journal *Merry England* (1883–95). She contributed many essays to this journal as well as to *The Colour of Life* (1896) and *Hearts of Controversy* (1917).

Claudine Moine (1618–?)
She wrote to an Ursuline convent in Langres, France. She was eventually offered hospitality there but went on to Paris, arriving in April 1642. Unable to find domestic work, she became a poorly paid dressmaker. She presented herself to the Jesuits, attached to the Church of St Louis and took on Father Jarry as her director of conscience. She started confessing regularly to Father Jarry and embarked on her astonishing spiritual journey, being 'touched by God' in October 1642. What she wrote is as much an historical document as a spiritual testimony. She died after 1655.

Lady Mary Wortley Montagu (1689–1762)
She eloped with Edward Wortley in 1712 and in 1716 accompanied him to Constantinople, where she wrote *The Turkish Embassy Letters*. When she returned to England she wrote satire. In 1736 she became infatuated with a young Italian and planned to live with him, but this failed. She lived abroad, alone, for many years, writing and reading and becoming increasingly disillusioned with England.

Margaret Prescott Montague (1878–1955)
She was born in West Virginia. Her brother was an Episcopalian minister. She was a novelist, short-story writer and poet who suffered from progressive blindness and deafness. She published *Leaves from a Secret Journal* under the pseudonym of Jane Steger.

Edith Nesbit (1858–1924)
Born in London and educated at an Ursuline convent in France. She started a successful writing career, having married an unsuccessful and unfaithful man. She wrote many famous children's books and was a socialist and a founder member of the Fabian Society.

Nangsa Obum (11th century)
She was born in Central Tibet, during a renaissance of Buddhism there. She thought much about meditation, devoting her life to practising the dharma. She married a prince, Dragpa Samdrub,

by whom she had a son. The baby was swiftly taken from her and given to a wet-nurse; as a result she died of a broken heart. She was given a large funeral. After meeting the Lord of Death in the underworld, she came back to life as a *delog* ('one who dies and returns to life'). She returned to her parents, but left them again to practice the dharma in the mountains from whence she flew, leaving her thigh print and footprint on rocks and mountains, as though the hard stone was as soft as butter.

Dorothy Osborne (1627–95)
From a Royalist family, she lived at Chicksands in Bedfordshire, England. She corresponded with Sir William Temple for many years before they married in 1655. They moved to Ireland. Her husband consulted her in all state and political matters. She is buried in Westminster Abbey.

Ruth Pitter (1897–1992)
She was born at Ilford, Essex. Both her parents were teachers in the East End of London. Poetry was a life-long passion, for which she sacrificed everything. She wrote to attain 'the ineffable communion with the earth itself', 'the silent music, the dance in stillness' which resides in all things. She received the Hawthornden Prize in 1937 and was the first woman to receive the Queen's Gold Medal for Poetry in 1955. She was awarded the CBE in 1979.

Katherine Anne Porter (1890–1980)
She was born in Texas. Educated in convents she married in 1906 and became a Catholic in 1910. She worked as a journalist and teacher in Mexico. She won both the Pulitzer Prize and the National Book Award for *The Collected Stories of Katherine Anne Porter* (1965).

Rabi'a the Mystic (of Basra [al-Adawiya]) (?–c. 801 AD)
Born into a poor family, both her parents died when she was young, and she was sold into slavery. One night after seeing her at

prayer, her master set her free. Subsequently she devoted herself to various acts of piety, lived homeless among the ruins, and then built herself a secluded cell before going on the pilgrimage to Mecca, and finally returning to the desert. She is counted among the great Sufi saints. Attar wrote of her in the *Conference of the Birds*.

Rabiah Balkhi (c. 1100–?)

She was a pioneer of mystic poetry in Persian and an outstanding Afghan poet. She was a princess born in the palace at Balkh, 'the Mother of Cities'. She was beautiful and gentle, but had an evil brother called Haris who became so jealous of her involvement with an athlete and slave called Baktash, that he had his sister killed. She wrote a poem in her blood as she lay dying; Baktash then killed Haris before killing himself. She is still honoured in Afghanistan.

Kathleen Raine (1908–)

She grew up between London and Northumberland. She studied at Cambridge, taking natural science rather than English Literature 'Because, for me, literature and poetry had nothing to do with "school", they were part of life.' She has published thirteen books of poems, many works of criticism and her acclaimed three-volume autobiography. She was brought up in a household full of poetry, Shakespeare and the Bible. She sought incessantly for transcendant truth and converted briefly to Roman Catholicism. She sees her life as a series of significant moments, and believes that we are all exiles from Paradise to which we should be trying to make our return journey.

Adrienne Rich (1929–)

A poet, born in Baltimore, she graduated from Radcliffe in 1951 and taught at many institutions, including Cornell. She married and had three sons. Her early writings show intellectual clarity and control. A feminist interested in the crisis of identity, she is known for her very personal and individualistic poetry.

Laura Riding (1901–91) (pseud. Barbara Rich and Madeleine Vara)
A poet, critic, novelist and polemicist, she was born in New York City. She studied at Cornell. Her first collection of verse *The Close Chaplet* was published in 1926. She is associated with Robert Graves with whom she collaborated on many projects.

Anne Ridler (1912–)
A poet and writer, she was educated Kings College, London; and became T.S. Eliot's secretary and editorial assistant. Her poetry is mostly distillations from ordinary experiences; her plays tend to a religious orientation.

Christina Rossetti (1830–94)
Sister of Dante Gabriel Rossetti, her first poetry was published when she was 12. She was very religious and a High Church Anglican. Her faith took precedence over a love affair which led to her never marrying. Her death in 1894 was preceded by a long illness. Her work includes *Annus domini* (1874), *Seek and Find* (1879) *Called to Be Saints* (1881), *Goblin Market and Other Poems* (1862) and shows the influence of the Pre-Raphaelite movement.

George Sand (1804–76)
The pseudonym of Amandine Aurore Kucile Dupin, she was born in Paris and as a child was free to roam the countryside at Nohant, 175 miles south of Paris. In 1822 she married Casimir Dudevant, and although initially happy she became restless and longed to travel. She began writing in 1829 and was published first as 'J' and then as 'G' Sand. She met Alfred de Musset and travelled with him to Italy. Their stormy relationship ended in 1835. She separated from her husband in 1836, and met Chopin, with whom she had an affair which ended in 1847. She was politically active in Paris during the upheavals of 1848. She met Flaubert in 1857, and spent the rest of her life at Nohant. She delighted in nature and had a passion for art, and developed this theme in *Laura: Voyage dans le cristal* – 'Happiness lies in

our understanding and appreciation for the world in which we live.'

Lady Sarashina (c. 1008–60)
Japanese diarist, born at the height of the Heian Period, she spent her early years in Heian Kyo (Kyoto), but moved at the age of 9 to an eastern province of Japan. She was deeply involved with her father Fujiwara Takasue, who was a minor nobleman. She lived on the fringe of court society. She was married with two children. Little else is known about her, but that she made frequent visits to outlying temples. Her book *As I Crossed a Bridge of Dreams* is a classic of Japanese literature.

Dorothy L. Sayers (1893–1957)
Born in Oxford, she was educated at Salisbury and Somerville, Oxford, where she got a first in Modern Languages in 1915. She went into advertising and, to supplement her income, wrote detective stories for which she became well known. She developed a reputation as a leading Christian apologist through her plays, radio broadcasts and essays. She became involved in 'missionary' social work. She translated Dante.

Peig Sayers (1873–1958)
Born in the parish of Dunquin at the western end of the Dingle peninsula in Co. Kerry, where there was a tradition that poetry passed from father to daughter, she married into a neighbouring island, the Great Blasket, where she spent most of her life. She met her husband the day she married him, but it turned out to be a love-match. She had a very hard life: many of her children died and the rest left, some for the USA. People on the Blaskets were very close to the earth. She was a wise woman who could change from gravity to gaiety fast. 'It's hard to be growing old, but I'll be talking after my death, my good gentleman,' she said (to W.R. Rodgers).

Anne Marie Schimmel (1922–)
Born in Germany. A translator, educator, historian, she taught

religion and became professor of Indo-Muslim studies at Harvard in 1970.

Olive Schreiner (1855–1920) (pseud. Ralph Iron)
Born in South Africa. Largely self-educated, she read widely, loved nature and enjoyed being solitary. She became a 'free-thinker'. She was unable to become a doctor because she had no formal education. She worked in England as a governess (1881–89). In 1883 she published *The Story of an African Farm*, which attacks Christianity. She again lived in South Africa from 1889, returning to England in 1913 where she became active in the peace movement. She later became a passionate campaigner for women's rights, pro-Boer loyalty and pacifism.

Jane Sherwood (?–1990)
Her husband, Andrew, was killed in the First World War. Unable to accept that he had not survived, she determined that he lived on a different plane, and tried many methods of contacting him. Finally through automatic writing, she contacted her husband and two other communicators. Her description of the pitfalls of psychic investigation is backed by an unshakeable Christian faith, a keen logical mind and sound common sense.

Lady Sakina Shiraz (early 19th century)
The daughter of Mirza Abdo'llah, she came from a family descended from the Prophet. Her pen name was 'Effat' (the Pure One). She is remembered as being one of the most outstanding women with gnostic understanding.

Constance Sitwell (1888–1974)
She was born in Ceylon and lived there until she was 8, and believed that her passionate love for flowers was born there. She kept diaries from the age of 12. In 1912 she visited her brother in India and was married in Bombay to a much older army officer whom she hardly knew, called Willie. She lived first in Ootacamund then Lahore. The Foreward for her first book

Flowers and Elephants (1928) was written by E.M. Forster. She believed that the life of the mind and spirit is more important than anything else, and the continuity of life, the meaning of reality and the certainty of joy and fulfilment after death underpin all her books. She was president of the College of Psychic Science.

Lillian Smith (1897–1966)

Born in Florida, she was an American novelist and student of race relations. Her family had slaves which she disapproved of and which led her to question her life. She was a precocious reader and musician and taught music in China. Her novel *Strange Fruit* (1944), about the love of a black girl for a white man, was highly controversial. Dorothy Dunbar Bromley described her face as having: 'the tranquility of spirit which comes from listening to the pines on the mountain top'.

Starhawk (1951–)

The pseudonym of Miriam Simos. She was born and raised Jewish in Minnesota, she now lives in California. A feminist, she writes much about Wicca (witchcraft and paganism). She has worked for the environment. She is the 'leader of the religion of the Great Goddess'.

Anne Stevenson (1933–)

Soon after her birth in England, her American parents took her back to America. However, she returned to England and remained living in Britain, between England, Scotland and Wales. She has published several books of poems. She believes in living simply: 'In these days of superfluous affluence, rewarded wickedness and sophisticated violence, my answer is to live simply, reducing my needs to the level of the beautiful and the necessary. From a position of having much and little, it is possible to live more richly than I ever imagined.'

St Teresa of Avila (1515–82)

A mystic, born at Avila in Spain. In 1535 she entered a Carmelite convent and became famous for her ascetic practices. She was taught by a Dominican priest that God can be found in all things, and began to write down her mystical experiences, without giving them much significance. In 1562, with the help of St John of the Cross, she re-established the ancient Carmelite rule by founding St Joseph's, the first convent for reformed or *disalced* (barefoot) Carmelites. During the remainder of her life she travelled round Spain, often in great hardship, and founded 17 convents. Her great mystical work is *The Interior Castle*; her *Life*, written at the request of her confessors, and covering the period to 1562, is a mixture of practicality and contemplation.

St Teresa of Lisieux (1873–97)

She was the youngest of nine children, five of whom became nuns. In 1888 she entered the Carmelite convent of Lisieux where she remained until her death from TB. She became widely known through her short spiritual autobiography *L'Histoire d'une âme*, which she had been instructed to write. She did not rise to a position of authority in the convent, but her 'ordinary' existence gave inspiration to many, and showed them that sainthood was attainable by anyone, however humble. She was canonised in 1925.

Katharine Trevelyan (1909–)

The niece of historian G.M. Trevelyan, she published her 'autobiography of a natural mystic' in 1962 under the English title *Fool in Love*.

Frances Trollope (1780–1863)

Novelist and travel writer, she was the daughter of a clergyman and the mother of novelist Anthony Trollope. Her husband, a barrister, had continual financial difficulties and she had to support him and their six children. In 1827 she went to America. She wrote *Domestic Manners of the Americans* (1832) which was very successful in England. She went on to publish more than 100 books.

Irina Tweedie (1907–)

Born in Russia in 1907 and educated in Vienna and Paris, she moved to England and was happily married to a naval officer until his premature death. She sought consolation through religion. In 1961, she found a Sufi master, Guruji, in India. He instructed her to keep a diary of her experiences with him, which she eventually published as *The Chasm of Fire*. The diary describes her 'liberation' through 'a slow grinding down of personality' – of necessity painful, 'for man cannot remake himself without suffering': 'I was beaten down in every sense till I had come to terms with that in me which I had been rejecting all my life.'

Evelyn Underhill (1875–1941)

She was born in Wolverhampton, England, educated privately and read history and botany at King's College for Women. She married Hubert Stuart Moore in 1907, and lived in Campden Hill Square, London. In 1911 she met Friedrich von Hügel who became an important influence. Her first serious book, *Mysticism* was published in 1911. She much enjoyed Italian paintings and through art was drawn to religion. She became interested in Catholicism, but in 1921 became a practising member of the Church of England. She worked with the poor in North Kensington. During the First World War she was in Naval Intelligence. She was the theological editor of the *Spectator*. From 1924, she began to go on retreats. She suffered much ill health, but is reputed to have had a 'face illuminated with a radiant smile'.

Alice Walker (1944–)

Novelist and poet born in Georgia. She studied at Spelman College, Atlanta, and Sarah Lawrence College and then worked as a teacher and a social worker in New York City Welfare Department and as a lecturer. She joined the civil rights movement. *The Color Purple* (1982) won the Pulitzer Prize.

Simone Weil (1909–43)
She was born in Paris. A philosophical writer and mystic, she taught philosophy but interspersed it with manual labour in order to experience working-class life. In 1936 she served in the Republican forces in the Spanish Civil War. She settled in Marseilles in 1941, where she developed a deep mystical feeling for the Catholic faith, and studied Greek and Hindu philosophy, but was reluctant to join an organised religion. In 1942 she escaped to the USA and then joined the Free French in London before dying from voluntary starvation in an attempt to identify with her compatriots in France. *Waiting for God*, a collection of letters she wrote to Father Perrin who befriended her in Marseilles, shows her scholarship as well as her intense struggle with her idea of God.

Marguerite Wildenhain (1896–)
Born in France of German/English parents, she was educated at the Bauhaus where she subsequently taught. She went to America in 1940 and settled in California as a potter. She opened her own school at Pond Farm and lectured and gave seminars throughout the USA.

Eithne Wilkins (1914–75)
She was born in New Zealand and came to England as a child. She went to Somerville College, Oxford, and became Reader in German Literature at Reading University. She published *Oranges and Lemons*, a collection of poems, and *The Rose-Garden Game*. She translated from both French and German, including works by Musil, Kafka, Goethe, Balzac and Kokoschka. She also wrote a series of astonishing, as yet unpublished, love letters from Paris in 1938.

Marianne Willemer (1784–1860)
As Marianne Jung, she played bit parts in the theatre. When she was 16 she was seen by Willemer, a banker, who paid her mother 200 gold sovereigns and took her home where he taught her polite

behaviour. He later married her. She met Goethe who was writing the *West-östlicher Divan*, a reworking of the Persian lyrics of Hafiz, and in his poetry Marianne and Suleika are as one. Much of this great love poem was written by Marianne, but published under Goethe's name, who swore her to secrecy. She appears never to have written anything else.

Mary Wollstonecraft (1759–97)
She resented the education her elder brother received and aimed to achieve independence for herself by working as an editorial assistant to the publisher Joseph Johnson in London, on a new radical magazine. She fell in love with an American and had a child. When he left her she attempted suicide. He sent her to Scandinavia.

Virginia Woolf (1882–1941)
She was born in London and was educated privately. In 1904 she set up house with her sister and two brothers in Bloomsbury. In 1912 she married Leonard Woolf with whom she set up the Hogarth Press in 1917. Her first novel *The Voyage Out* was published in 1915. She made a major contribution to the development of the novel. She suffered a series of nervous breakdowns leading to her suicide in 1941.

Dorothy Wordsworth (1771–1855)
She was born in Cumbria, England, the sister of the poet William Wordsworth, to whom she became a lifelong companion. Her detailed journals, which were often used by her brother as source books, are vivid documents of her thoughts and her response to local country life. *Alfoxden Journal* (1798) and *Grasmere Journals* (1800–03) show a keen sensibility towards, and observation of, nature. After a breakdown in 1829, from which she never really recovered, her poetry became an obsession. She copied and recopied her verse and recited it continuously, but always felt she was in William's shadow.

INDEX

THE VIRAGO BOOK OF WOMAN GARDENERS

Deborah Kellaway

'Kellaway's intelligent and tender book enlarges the sense of human possibility' – *Observer*

From diggers and weeders to artists and colourists, writers and dreamers to trend-setters, women have richly contributed to gardening and gardens. Here the editor has collected irresistible extracts from the 18th century to the present, to create a book that is replete with anecdotes and good advice from Colette, Margery Fish, Germaine Greer, Eleanour Sinclair Rohde, Vita Sackville-West, Rosemary Verey, Edith Wharton and Dorothy Wordsworth among others.

Now you can order superb titles directly from Virago

☐	Two: The Book of Twins and Doubles	Penelope Farmer (ed)	£20.00
☐	The Virago Book of Love Letters	Jill Dawson (ed)	£15.99
☐	The Virago Book of Women Gardeners	Deborah Kellaway (ed)	£7.99
☐	The Virago Book of Women Travellers	Mary Morris (ed)	£8.99
☐	The Virago Book of Fairy Tales	Angela Carter	£7.99
☐	The Virago Book of Fairy Tales II	Angela Carter	£7.99
☐	The Virago Book of Love and Loss	Georgina Hammick (ed)	£6.99

Please allow for postage and packing: **Free UK delivery.**
Europe; add 25% of retail price; Rest of World; 45% of retail price.

To order any of the above or any other Virago titles, please call our
credit card orderline or fill in this coupon and send/fax it to:

Virago, 250 Western Avenue, London, W3 6XZ, UK.
Fax 0181 324 5678   Telephone 0181 324 5516

☐ I enclose a UK bank cheque made payable to Virago for £ ....

☐ Please charge £ .... to my Access, Visa, Delta, Switch Card No.

☐☐☐☐☐☐☐☐☐☐☐☐☐☐☐☐☐☐☐

Expiry Date ☐☐☐☐   Switch Issue No. ☐☐

NAME (Block letters please) ....

ADDRESS ....

....

....

Postcode ....Telephone ....

Signature ....

Please allow 28 days for delivery within the UK. Offer subject to price and availability.

Please do not send any further mailings from companies carefully selected by Virago ☐